W9-CRA-913

NO SHORTCUTS

NO SHORTCUTS

ORGANIZING FOR POWER IN THE NEW GILDED AGE

JANE F. MCALEVEY

OXFORD
UNIVERSITY PRESS

OXFORD
UNIVERSITY PRESS

Oxford University Press is a department of the University of Oxford. It furthers
the University's objective of excellence in research, scholarship, and education
by publishing worldwide. Oxford is a registered trade mark of Oxford University
Press in the UK and certain other countries.

Published in the United States of America by Oxford University Press
198 Madison Avenue, New York, NY 10016, United States of America.

CIP data is on file at the Library of Congress
ISBN 978–0–19–062471–2

9

Printed by Sheridan Books, Inc., United States of America

1199's Advice To Rookie Organizers

Get close to the workers, stay close to the workers.

Tell workers it's their union and then behave that way.

Don't do for workers what they can do.

The union is not a fee for service, it is the collective experience of workers in struggle.

The Union's function is to assist workers in making a positive change in their lives.

Workers are made of clay, not glass.

Don't be afraid to ask workers to build their own union.

Don't be afraid to confront them when they don't.

Don't spend your time organizing workers who are already organizing themselves, go to the biggest-worst.

The working class builds cells for its own defense - identify them and recruit their leaders.

Anger is there before you are - channel it, don't defuse it.

Channelled anger builds a fighting organization.

Workers know the risks, don't lie to them.

Every worker is showtime - communicate excitement, energy, urgency and confidence.

There is enough oppression in workers lives not to be oppressed by organizers.

Organizers talk too much. Most of what you say is forgotten.

Communicate to workers that there is no salvation beyond their own power.

Workers united can beat the boss. You have to believe that and so do they.

Don't underestimate the workers.

We lose when we don't put workers into struggle

taken from 1199 Organizing Conference February 6-9, 1985   Columbus, Ohio

CONTENTS

———◅◉▻———

ACKNOWLEDGMENTS

WHEN WE MASTER SOMETHING NEW, books can help, but a good mentor is worth a thousand books. The acknowledgments in this book can best be viewed as an update and (super) friendly amendment to the acknowledgments pages in my first book, *Raising Expectations (and Raising Hell)*, (Verso Press, 2014). Any intelligence I display in this book is the cumulative wisdom of many decades of work in the field, where I had, literally, thousands of teachers. *Raising Expectations* was about union campaigns I participated in and mostly led. For this book, my new academic mentors told me firmly, despite my at times fierce protestations, that I had to use campaigns that I'd had nothing to do with for my empirical evidence. They were correct, of course.

I haven't changed my opinion one iota of the many people to whom I owe tremendous thanks for their patience with me, for sharing key life lessons with me, for the endless time and skill they've invested in my thinking and my work, and, often, for their love. But I will limit my acknowledgments here to the players who have specifically helped me get through five years of a Ph.D. program.

Mapping my academic pursuit chronologically, I must first thank two people more than any others, the ones who talked me into the doctoral program: Larry Fox and Frances Fox Piven (who are not related on the Fox side, though I quickly discovered that they shared the gene for wicked intelligence). I'd had zero plans to attend graduate school, and couldn't imagine why I should shift out of full-time organizing. But when warfare inside the trade union movement led to the destruction of years of good efforts and dashed hopes and dreams and possibilities for thousands of workers, I knew it was time to step outside the fray, in order to observe and better reflect on and understand what was happening, and what it meant for the future. At that very moment, coincidentally, I received an early-stage cancer diagnosis that would require a full year of nothing but medically focused pursuits. It was during my Sloan-Kettering year that Bob Ostertag talked me into writing down my reflections and offered to mentor me through a book. That project, with enthusiastic support from my Verso editor Andy Hsiao, became *Raising Expectations (and Raising Hell)*. Frances and Larry were early readers of the manuscript, and each came to the same conclusion: I should weather the political storm generated by my first book by going to graduate school for a few years. They've always given me good advice, and I thank each of them enormously for guiding me through complicated chapters of my life. Frances became in academia what Larry had been in my SEIU years, an incredible mentor.

Once I made the decision to go back to school, there was the vexing issue of how to afford life in New York City as a graduate student. My sister Catherine, who'd always held higher education as a top value, was thrilled with my decision, and along with her life partner, Debra Hall, generously offered to support my housing needs for my first two years in New York. If my book has a dedication, it's certainly to Catherine, who lost her own cancer fight during my third year in graduate school. I loved her wildly, and she was ecstatic about my getting a Ph.D. My brother Ben and his wife, Melissa, and her mother, Anne Barnes, also provided great logistical support that made some of my graduate school research easier, and more of it possible. My sister Bri has been a full-on cheerleader and supporter, as have my many other wonderful siblings and extended family. Beverly Feuer's endless stories of how her generation, the CIO generation, built their unions strong has served as a timeless inspiration to my research.

My cohort, the 2010 Sociology cohort, is an extremely talented, fun, smart, supportive, and incredible team—a model of true solidarity. Most are women; a few are men we consider honorary women; all of them guided me through the early coursework and big exams. I could not have gotten through those first two years without my cohort. Marnie Brady and Bronwyn Dubchuck-Land were regular and crucial readers at every stage of my book work. They were patient and flexible, constantly trying to teach me to use signposts in my academic writing and to persuade me to say the same thing three ways in the same chapter—a concept with which I still struggle. Erin Michaels, Dominique Nisperos, and Martha King pulled me successfully through two semesters of Statistics. (I chose not to attempt OLS regression in my final work, despite all they taught me!)

My committee, headed by Frances Fox Piven, and consisting of Dan Clawson, Bill Kornblum, and Jim Jasper, were terrific. They gave real meaning to the word *patience*. Each of them played a different and special role in helping me through this process. Please hold them harmless for any flaws, weak spots, bad ideas, or problems in this book, but do credit them for all the good. They were encouraging, they generously made time for me, and, like my cohort, they had to help me transition from being a field organizer to a later-in-life academic—at times a very challenging endeavor. I have enormous gratitude for my committee.

Along the way, I had a robust, informal committee reading and commenting on various pieces of my writing. A team of overworked union and community organizers and union researchers, my "reality checkers," whose lives are fully in the field, read either the entire dissertation or full first draft of the book and offered cogent comments: Ian Allison, Drew Astolphi, Seth Borgos, Sarah Buckley, Jonah Gindin, Becca Kirkpatrick, John Lacny, Katie Miles, and John Page. Their solidarity, enthusiasm, time, and dedication to making this book stronger has been remarkable.

A second team donated brainpower and excellent suggestions on various chapters of this book, including Catherine Banghart, Colin Barker, Mark Brenner, Kate Bronfenbrenner, Sarah de Clerk, Janice Fine, Bill Fletcher, Marshall Ganz, Sam Gindin, Jeff Goodwin, Doug Henwood, Patty Hoffman, Jane Holgate, John Krinsky, David Morris, Peter Olney, Deepak Pateriya, Steve Pitts, Adolph Reed, Maryanne Salm, George Schmidt, John Stamm, Madeline Talbot, and Anthony Thigpenn.

As with my Ph.D. committee, please spare these incredible people the blame for any failings on my part, but do recognize that they helped sharpen my thinking and writing.

Additionally, James Cook, my editor at Oxford University Press, along with two anonymous peer reviewers in the Oxford review process, challenged me and greatly improved *No Shortcuts*. Rather than getting frustrated by one of my biggest weaknesses, impatience, James Cook may have set a record for getting this book to press. He was great.

I am deeply appreciative to several people amid many who are quoted in and were part of the fieldwork and cases I studied. I thank every person who made time for an interview, and all for sharing their thoughts and ideas. But there are a special few who generously opened doors for me, who encouraged people to talk openly and honestly with me, who dug through their own archives and file boxes for me. These include Deborah Axt, Gene Bruskin, Jackson Potter, David Pickus, and Jonathan Rosenblum. Their work inspires and challenges me.

In my field research and casework, a few people played key enabling roles: Susy Stewart, Maureen Pinto and Thea Chalmers cared for my trusted steed, Jalapeño, keeping him happy, in good physical shape, and well loved during my long absences. Rati Kashyap, the more than able assistant in the Sociology Department at the City University of New York's Graduate Center, made every single academic thing work!

Beyond individuals, a few institutions deserve credit in various ways for significant contributions during, and just after, my graduate school years. The fifth chapter of this book, the chapter on the Smithfield Foods campaign, I wrote while serving as a writing fellow and Boren Cherktov resident at the Blue Mountain Center (BMC), in upstate New York. I returned to BMC one year later to work on the revisions to the first full draft of this book. Verso Books published *Raising Expectations (and Raising Hell)* during my second year of graduate school, putting some of my ideas on a national and international stage—and greatly contributing to a crowd of new comrades in my life, people I met because they read my Verso book! *The Nation* magazine made me a contributing writer. The journal *Politics & Society* made me focus much more clearly on what I was trying to say as I worked through revising and resubmitting a September 2015 article that contains some of the core arguments in this book. The City University of New York's Graduate Center made me a fellow and underwrote my academic expenses. The American Association of University Women (AAUW) chose me as an American Dissertation Fellow for my final, fifth year, contributing decisive financial support that enabled me to stop consulting and focus on nothing but writing in my final push. And Oxford University Press, of course, is why this book is in your hands. Resources do matter.

LIST OF FIGURES

—◦())◦—

LIST OF TABLES

————◦(((◦)))◦————

NO SHORTCUTS

I

Introduction

Curiously, the labor movement is conventionally ignored by scholars of social movements.

Joseph Luders, *The Civil Rights Movement and the Logic of Social Change*[1]
[162nd Footnote]

THERE'S AN INFORMAL GESTALT IN much of academia that unions are not social movements at all: that *union* equates to "undemocratic, top-down bureaucracy." Yet not all so-called social movement organizations (SMOs) fit their own definition of *social*; many function from the top down as much as any bad union. An SMO's membership, if it has one, can be and often is as irrelevant and disregarded as the rank and file in the worst union. Likewise, scholars assume that material gain is the primary concern of unions, missing that workplace fights are most importantly about one of the deepest of human emotional needs: dignity. The day in, day out degradation of peoples' self-worth is what can drive workers to form the solidarity needed to face today's union busters.

Earning my doctorate after long practical experience—as a young, radical student leader, then as a community organizer, a full-time educator at the Highlander Center, and, eventually, a union organizer and chief negotiator and an electoral campaign manager—I find it impossible to sort the process of progressive social change into two distinct piles or traditions. All of the unions I worked with were by any definition social movements, characterized by progressive goals that reached

I

well beyond the workplace; prefigurative decision-making; and robust participation by workers, their families, and their communities.

In this book, in the term *movement* I consciously merge agencies that have been studied separately: the people in unions, who are called workers, and many of the same people after they have punched the clock at the end of their shift and put on their SMO (or "interest group") volunteer hats—people who are then called individuals. Workers, too, are individuals. A divided approach to workplaces and communities prevents people and movements from winning more significant victories and building power. To the extent that a dichotomous approach persists in academia, it deprives scholars, students, and practitioners from better understanding two longstanding questions: Why have unions faltered? and What must be done?

My hypothesis is threefold. First, the reason that progressives have experienced a four-decade decline in the United States is because of a significant and long-term shift away from deep *organizing* and toward shallow *mobilizing*. Second, the split between "labor" and "social movement" has hampered what little organizing has been done. Together, these two trends help account for the failure of unions and progressive politics, the ongoing shrinking of the public sphere, and unabashed rule by the worst and greediest corporate interests.

Third, different approaches to change lead to different outcomes, often very different outcomes. I discuss three broad types of change processes: advocacy, mobilizing, and organizing—although my emphasis, if not my obsessive emphasis, is on the latter two. Each method produces a different kind of victory, and not all of these victories are equal; some are actually defeats. Only organizing can effectively challenge the gross inequality of power in the United States. Today, there is very little understanding of what factors lead to small, medium-, and high-impact victories, or why.

Power and Power Structure Analysis

In the United States, C. Wright Mills popularized the concept of power and power structures in his book *The Power Elite*,[2] published in 1956. In the sixty years since then, progressives have largely ignored and omitted discussions about power or power structures. Nothing produces deer-in-the-headlights moments for activists in the United States like the question "What's your theory of power?" The 1967 follow-up book to Mills's work, *Who Rules America*, by William Domhoff (and his present-day website bearing the same name), is still considered the best all-around go-to resource for local activists trying to understand how to do power-related research on their opponents. But Mills, Domhoff, and others who offer academic discussions of power largely attend to the power structures of the elites, of those who routinely exercise a great deal of power (national power in Mills's work, local power in Domhoff's). And the conversations about elite power can get very circular (they exercise it because they have it, they have it because they exercise it, were born into it, have friends with it . . .). Part of what made Frances Fox Piven and Richard Cloward's 1977 book, *Poor People's Movements*,[3] so refreshing—and smart—is that they inserted ordinary people into discussions about who can exercise power.

In discussing power, I am going to put brackets around this very big concept. My interest, borne out by the empirical cases that follow, is in understanding the power structures of ordinary people and how they themselves can come to better understand their own power. There's plenty of evidence on the front pages of *The New York Times* that Mills's elites still rule. The level of raw privilege that a Mark Zuckerberg or Bill Gates or Jamie Dimon presently possesses isn't much different from that which Bertrand Russell described in his 1938 book *Power* as "priestly" and "kingly."[4] That helps explain why multinational CEOs were included, and indistinguishable from, the Pope, kings, and presidents in the many photos taken at the December 2015 climate talks.[5] It doesn't seem all that difficult to understand how today's priestly-kingly-corporate class rules. But for people attempting to change this or that policy, especially if the change desired is meaningful (i.e., will change society), it is essential to first dissect and chart their targets' numerous ties and networks. Even understanding *whom* to target—who the primary and secondary people and institutions are that will determine whether the campaign will succeed (or society will change)—often requires a highly detailed power-structure analysis.

This step is often skipped or is done poorly, which is partly why groups so often fail. Domhoff's website, combined with a dozen other more recent similar websites—such as LittleSis, CorpWatch, and

Subsidy Tracker—can help groups in the United States sharpen their analysis of precisely who needs to be defeated, overcome, or persuaded to achieve success. Understanding who the correct targets are and the forms of power they exercise should be only one step in a power-structure analysis,[6] but often when that step *is* taken, it only plots the current power holders in relationship to one another. Good start, but keep going.

What is almost never attempted is the absolutely essential corollary: a parallel careful, methodical, systematic, detailed analysis of power structures among the ordinary people who are or could be brought into the fight. Unions that still execute supermajority strikes have an excellent approach to better understanding how to analyze these power structures: to pull off a huge strike and win (as did the Chicago teachers in the new millennium) requires a detailed analysis of exactly which workers are likely to stand together, decide to defy their employer's threats of termination, and walk out in a high-risk collective action. Which key individual worker can sway exactly whom else—by name—and why? How strong is the support he or she has among exactly how many coworkers, and how do the organizers know this to be true? The ability to correctly answer these and many other related questions—Who does each worker know outside work? Why? How? How well? How can the worker reach and influence them?—will be the lifeblood of successful strikes in the new millennium.

Liberals and most progressives don't do a full power-structure analysis because, consciously or not, they accept the kind of elite theory of power that Mills popularized. They assume elites will always rule. At best, they debate how to replace a very naughty elite with a "better" elite, one they "can work with," who wants workers to have enough money to shop the CEOs out of each crisis they create, who will give them a raise that they will spend on consuming goods they probably don't need. The search for these more friendly elites frames the imagination of liberals and progressives. An elite theory of power for well-intentioned liberals leads to the advocacy model; an elite theory of power for people further left than liberals—progressives—leads to the mobilizing model, because progressives set more substantive goals that require a display of potential power, or at least a threat of it.

People to the left of both liberals and progressives have a different theory of power: different because it assumes that the very idea of who holds power is itself contestable, and that elites can be pushed from priestly-kingly-corporate rule. Though almost extinct nationally, there are still powerful unions operating at the local and regional level. These unions' democratic, open negotiations—in which tens of thousands of workers unite to stop bad employers from doing horrible things and then create enough power to pull up to the negotiations table as equals and determine something better—provide evidence that ordinary people can exercise both absolute power (power *over*) and creative power (power *to*). A focus of this book is on why and how to analyze this still vast potential power of ordinary people.

Marshall Ganz simplified the concept of strategy by explaining it as "turning what you have into what you need to get what you want."[7] The word *you* is crucial—and variable. How do people come to understand the first part of this sentence, "what you have"? And *which* people get to understand? Only those who understand what they have can meaningfully plot the "what you need": create the steps that comprise the plan, plot and direct the course of action, and then get "what you want." And because "what you want" is generally in proportion to what you think you can get, demands rise or fall based on what people believe they might reasonably achieve. Who is the actual *you* in "what you want"? To better understand outcomes—winning or losing, a little or a lot—requires breaking down each subclause in Ganz's excellent definition of strategy.

First, Ganz rightly suggests that the specific "biographies" of those on "leadership teams" can directly affect strategy because "diverse teams" bring a range of "salient knowledge" and varied and relevant networks to the strategy war room. It follows, then, that the bigger the war room, the better. I expand who should be in the strategy war room from people with recognizable decision-making authority or a position or title—such as lead organizer, vice president, researcher, director, steward, and executive board member—to specific individuals who have no titles but who are the organic leaders on whom the masses rely: nurse, teacher, anesthesia tech, school bus driver, congregant, and voter. I urge a deeper dive into the specific backgrounds, networks, and salient knowledge of the masses involved, rather than only those of the leadership team—the rank and file matter just as much to outcomes, if not more, than the more formal leaders. Why? Large numbers of people transition from unthinking "masses" or "the grassroots" or "the workers" to serious and highly invested actors exercising agency when they come to see, to understand, and to value the power of their own salient knowledge and networks. The chief way to help ordinary people go from object to subject is to teach them about their potential power by involving them as central actors in the process of developing the power-structure analysis in their own campaigns—so they come to better understand their own power and that of their opponents.

When they see that three of their own ministers and two of their city council members and the head of the PTA for their children's schools serve on commissions and boards with their CEOs, they themselves can begin to imagine and plot strategy. People participate to the degree they understand—but they also understand to the degree they participate. It's dialectical. Power-structure analysis is the mechanism that enables ordinary people to understand their potential power and participate meaningfully in making strategy. When people understand the strategy because they helped make it, they will be invested for the long haul, sustained and propelled to achieve more meaningful wins.

Three key variables are crucial to analyzing the potential for success in the change process: power, strategy, and engagement. Three questions must be asked: Is there a clear and comprehensive power-structure analysis? Does the strategy adopted have any relationship to a power-structure analysis? How, if at all, are individuals being approached and engaged in the process, including the power analysis and strategy, not just the resulting collective action? Many small advances can be and are won without engaging ordinary people, where the key actors are instead paid lawyers, lobbyists, and public relations professionals, helped by some good smoke and mirrors. That is an advocacy model, and small advances are all it can produce—but I am getting ahead of myself.

Progressives, broadly defined, have enough resources to achieve a massive turnaround of the long reactionary political and economic trends in the United States, perhaps in all of the so-called Western industrialized countries. And substantial change can happen fast—in just a few years. (Note this, climate-change campaigners: Correct strategy and deep organizing can make things happen quickly.) One implication of my argument is that the people controlling the movement's resources—the individuals who are decision makers in national unions and in philanthropy—have been focused on the wrong strategies for decades, leading to an extraordinary series of setbacks. Many of the biggest victories of the past 100 years, those won in the heyday of the labor and civil rights movements, have been all but rolled back.

Yet some of the victories achieved by the people in these two movements were durable—and so have not been entirely lost—because they instituted major *structural* changes that were embedded in government policies at the national, state, and local levels; they achieved strong or relatively strong enforcement mechanisms; they achieved better funding and staffing for the enforcement agencies; and, most important, each victory became part of the everyday consciousness of most people. We know this because people who say they don't like unions will also say, "At least in this country it's illegal for children to work in factories," or "I told the boss I wouldn't handle anything so toxic without protection," or simply, "Thank God It's Friday." That is, they don't like unions, but they see child labor laws, workplace safety regulations, the eight-hour workday, and the weekend—all benefits won by workers engaged in collective action through their unions—as the reasonable and beneficial norm. Similarly, many white people in the United States might find #blacklivesmatter overly confrontational, but they take it for granted that black people can vote, and that whites-only primaries and officially segregated schools are wrong, racist, and a thing of the past. And, despite their own continued contributions to maintaining de facto structural racism, they would not accept an official return to the apartheid of Jim Crow laws.

That is why reversing the gains of the two most successful movements—labor and civil rights—has required a sustained, multidecade, multifront campaign by the corporate class. The global trade rules that corporate elites methodically put into place have been a key strategy. From the 1970s through the 1990s, they gutted the power of U.S. factory workers, the biggest organized labor force of that time, by putting them in direct competition with workers earning $1 a day in countries where rights are minimal and repression high. Then they started a drumbeat about unionized workers in the United States being overpaid, and rallied national opinion to that message. This is but one example of how people, in this case the corporate class, can change what academics call the opportunity structure to suit their long-term goals. Global and regional trade accords also give multinational corporations the right to buy land anywhere in almost any country, and new corporate landlords have forcibly evicted or cheaply bought off millions of people from self-sustaining plots of land, directly contributing to a huge rise in immigration into the United States and Europe.[8]

During the same decades, the corporate class pocketed the courts, one judicial appointment at a time. The resulting deeply conservative judiciary has relentlessly chipped away at the major laws sustaining the victories of labor and civil rights, overturning hard-fought, key provisions of affirmative action and voting-rights protections. Moreover, along with austerity and privatization, conservative courts have facilitated a vertically integrated for-profit prison system, resulting in the mass incarceration of African Americans, detention centers overflowing with Latinos, and massive profits for the putrid penal system's corporate shareholders.[9]

The corporate class also created their version of a popular front, seizing the cultural apparatus through such rulings as the Federal Communications Commission's Clinton-era decision to allow multinationals to outright own the means of communication. They also built up, through very generous funding, the powerful Christian right.

In the zigzag of forward progress from the 1930s to the early 1970s, followed by defeats from the mid-1970s to the present time, what changed? Why were the achievements won during the heyday of the pre-McCarthy labor movement and the civil rights movement so substantial compared with the progressive achievements of the past forty years? Scholars and practitioners alike have numerous answers to these questions, overwhelmingly structural in nature. But in most of their answers they consider the labor movement as a separate phenomenon with little relationship to the civil rights movement. Social scientists have approached the study of each as if they were different species, one a mammal and the other a fish, one earthbound and one aquatic. Yet these movements have shared several key features that argue for understanding them as more alike than distinct.

The main difference between these two most powerful movements half a century ago and today is that during the former period of their great successes they relied primarily on—and were led by—what Frances Fox Piven has eloquently termed ordinary people. They had a theory of power: It came from their own ability to sustain massive disruptions to the existing order. Today, as Theda Skocpol documents in *Diminished Democracy: From Membership to Management in American Civic Life*, attempts to generate movements are directed by professional, highly educated staff who rely on an elite, top-down theory of power that treats the masses as audiences of, rather than active participants in, their own liberation:

> Aiming to speak for—and influence—masses of citizens, droves of new national advocacy groups have set up shop, with the media amplifying debates among their professional spokespersons. The National Abortion Rights Action League debates the National Right to Life Committee; the Concord Coalition takes on the American Association for Retired Persons; and the Environmental Defense Fund counters business groups. Ordinary Americans attend to such debates fitfully, entertained or bemused. Then pollsters call at dinnertime to glean snippets of what everyone makes of it all.[10]

As the cases in this book—all situated in the new millennium—illustrate, the chief factor in whether or not organizational efforts grow organically into local and national movements capable of effecting major change is where and with whom the agency for change rests. It is not merely *if* ordinary people—so often referred to as "the grassroots"—are engaged, but *how, why,* and *where* they are engaged.

Advocacy, Mobilizing, and Organizing

Here is the major difference among the three approaches discussed in the book. Advocacy doesn't involve ordinary people in any real way; lawyers, pollsters, researchers, and communications firms are engaged to wage the battle. Though effective for forcing car companies to install seatbelts or banishing toys with components that infants might choke on, this strategy severely limits serious challenges to elite power. Advocacy fails to use the only concrete advantage ordinary people have over elites: large numbers. In workplace strikes, at the ballot box, or in nonviolent civil disobedience, strategically deployed masses have long been the unique weapon of ordinary people. The 1 percent have a vast armory of material resources and political special forces, but the 99 percent have an army.

Over the past forty years, a newer mechanism for change seekers has proliferated: the mobilizing approach. Mobilizing is a substantial improvement over advocacy, because it brings large numbers of people to the fight. However, too often they are the same people: dedicated activists who show up over and over at every meeting and rally for all good causes, but without the full mass of their coworkers or community behind them. This is because a professional staff directs, manipulates, and controls the mobilization; the staffers see themselves, not ordinary people, as the key agents of change. To them, it matters little who shows up, or, why, as long as a sufficient number of bodies appear—enough for a photo good enough to tweet and maybe generate earned media. The committed activists in the photo have had no part in developing a power analysis; they aren't informed about that or the resulting strategy, but they dutifully show up at protests that rarely matter to power holders.

The third approach, organizing, places the agency for success with a continually expanding base of ordinary people, a mass of people never previously involved, who don't consider themselves activists at all—that's the point of organizing. In the organizing approach, specific injustice and outrage are the immediate motivation, but the primary goal is to transfer power from the elite to the majority, from the 1 percent to the 99 percent. Individual campaigns matter in themselves, but they are primarily a mechanism for bringing new people into the change process and keeping them involved. The organizing approach relies on mass negotiations to win, rather than the closed-door deal making typical of both advocacy and mobilizing. Ordinary people help make the power analysis, design the strategy, and achieve the outcome. They are essential and they know it.

In unions and SMOs in the United States today, advocacy and, especially, mobilizing prevail. This is the main reason why modern movements have not replicated the kinds of gains achieved by the earlier labor and civil rights movements. Table 1.1 compares the three models by their distinct approach to power, strategy, and people. Hahrie Han has a somewhat similar chart in her excellent book *How Organizations Develop Activists.*[11] However, Han focuses on what I call self-selecting

TABLE 1.1 Options for Change

	Advocacy	Mobilizing	Organizing
Theory of Power	Elite. Advocacy groups tend to seek one-time wins or narrow policy changes, often through courts or back-room negotiations that do not permanently alter the relations of power.	Primarily elite. Staff or activists set goals with low to medium concession costs or, more typically, set an ambitious goal and declare a win, even when the "win" has no, or only weak, enforcement provisions. Back-room, secret deal making by paid professionals is common.	Mass, inclusive, and collective. Organizing groups transform the power structure to favor constituents and diminish the power of their opposition. Specific campaigns fit into a larger power-building strategy. They prioritize power analysis, involve ordinary people in it, and decipher the often hidden relationship between economic, social, and political power. Settlement typically comes from mass negotiations with large numbers involved.
Strategy	Litigation; heavy spending on polling, advertising, and other paid media.	Campaigns, run by professional staff, or volunteer activists with no base of actual, measureable supporters, that prioritize frames and messaging over base power. Staff-selected "authentic messengers" represent the constituency to the media and policy makers, but they have little or no real say in strategy or running the campaign.	Recruitment and involvement of specific, large numbers of people whose power is derived from their ability to withdraw labor or other cooperation from those who rely on them. Majority strikes, sustained and strategic nonviolent direct action, electoral majorities. Frames matter, but the numbers involved are sufficiently compelling to create a significant earned media strategy. Mobilizing is seen as a tactic, not a strategy.

(*continued*)

TABLE 1.1 (Continued)

	Advocacy	Mobilizing	Organizing
People Focus	None.	Grassroots activists. People already committed to the cause, who show up over and over. When they burn out, new, also previously committed activists are recruited. And so on. Social media are over relied on.	Organic leaders. The base is expanded through developing the skills of organic leaders who are key influencers of the constituency, and who can then, independent of staff, recruit new people never before involved. Individual, face-to-face interactions are key.

groups that do not make class a central issue. This book does focus on class, and on the clear and vital distinction between the strategy of developing activists, who are not always drawn from the working class, and that of developing organic leaders, who always are.

Structure-based vs. Self-selecting Groups

The labor and civil rights movements were located in the landscape of what I call structure-based organizing. The structures were, respectively, the workplace and the black church under Jim Crow. Both movements chose organizing as their primary strategy. Mobilizing and advocacy also played a role, but the lifeblood of these movements was mass participation by ordinary people, whose engagement was inspired by a cohesive community bound by a sense of place: the working community on the shop floor, in the labor movement, and the faith community in the church, in the fight for civil rights. The empirical research that follows and the voluminous literature examining the outcomes of the 1930s through 1960s are fair grounds for arguing that structure-based organizing still offers the best chance to rebuild a powerful progressive movement. Unorganized workplaces and houses of faith remain a target-rich environment, and there are plenty of them, enough to return the labor movement to the 35 percent density it had when inequality was falling, not rising.[12]

Since organizing's primary purpose is to change the power structure away from the 1 percent to more like the 90 percent, majorities are always the goal: the more people, the more power. But not just any people. And the word *majority* isn't a throwaway word on a flip chart, it is a specific objective that must be met. In structure-based organizing, in the workplace and in faith-based settings, it is easy to assess whether or not you have won over a majority of the participants in the given structure to a cause or an issue. A workplace or church will have, say, 500 workers or parishioners, and to reach a majority, or even a supermajority, the quantifiable nature of the bounded constituency allows you to assess your success in achieving your numbers. An organizer intending to build a movement to maximum power who is approaching a structured or bounded constituency must target and plan to reach each and every person, regardless of whether or not each and every person has any preexisting interest in the union or community organization. Beyond understanding concretely when a majority has been gained, the organizer can gauge the commitment levels of the majority by the nature, frequency, and riskiness of actions they are willing to take. The process of building a majority and testing its commitment level also allows a far more systematic method of assessing which ordinary people have preexisting leadership within the various structures, a method called *leadership identification*. These informal leaders, whom I will call organic leaders, seldom self-identify as leaders and rarely have any official titles, but they are identifiable by their natural influence with their peers. Knowing how to recognize them makes decisions about whom to prioritize for *leadership development* far more effective. Developing their leadership skill set is more fruitful than training random volunteers, because these organic leaders start with a base of followers. They are the key to scale.

This process differs considerably from the self-selecting that goes on in movement work, such as environmental and other single-issue fights, women's and other identity-based movements, and nonreligious community efforts. Self-selecting groups rely on the mobilizing approach, and many of these groups grew out of, or in response to, the New Left project of the 1960s.[13] In self-selecting work, most people show up at meetings because they have a preexisting interest in or a serious commitment to the cause. As Skocpol says, "[M]any of the key groups were not membership associations at all. They were small combinations of nimble, fresh thinking, and passionate advocates of new causes."[14] In self-selecting work, movement groups spend most of their time talking to people *already* on their side, whereas in structure-based work, because the goal is building majorities of a bounded constituency, organizers are constantly forced to engage people who may begin with little or no initial interest in being a part of any group. In fact, in the beginning of a unionization campaign, many workers see themselves as opposed to the very idea of forming a union, just as many parishioners may be opposed to a more collective-action orientation in their church when first approached about joining or helping to build a new faith-based group. Consequently, organizers and the organic leaders they first identify and then develop devote most of their time to winning over people who do not self-identify as being "with progressives." Structure-based organizing deliberately and methodically expands the base of people whom mobilizers can tap in their never-ending single-issue campaigns. Han's book reinforces my argument that self-selecting groups develop an activist-based approach, whereas structure-based groups develop a strong, more scalable grassroots base, because they focus on developing organic leaders who themselves can mobilize to reach majorities.

Unions as the Hardest Test of Social Movement Success

There are very significant factors, however, that differentiate union and faith-based efforts, despite each being structure-based. The best lessons emerge from success in the hardest tests. Real union fights are always high-threat and high-risk—as were the fights of the civil rights movement.[15] A crucial distinction is that most faith- and broad-based organizations are known as O of Os, that is, "organizations of organizations." The O of Os more often than not are religious entities—individual churches, synagogues, and mosques—and the initial recruitment happens between an organizer and the leader, who in this model is an official, generally full-time position holder, typically a person with a title that confers a more formal style of leadership: priest, minister, rabbi, imam. Once that more formal leader has been won over to the project of building a broad, faith-based organization, he or she gives the organizer full access to the congregation. Today's organizers of faith-based groups don't face conditions anything like today's union organizers; there is no well-funded effort to prevent them from engaging individual people of faith in their effort to win over a majority of the flock. On the contrary, faith-based organizers are generally welcomed with open arms.[16]

When the structure is the workplace, the official leader of that structure, the company's chief executive, declares war on the employees at the first hint of a unionization effort, using tactics that often include threatening to fire any worker who talks with the organizers.[17] Organizers, whether paid professionals or volunteers from another, already organized facility, are forbidden by law from entering an unorganized workplace. This alone is a radical difference from faith-based settings; it means union organizers have to be really good at the art of what is called the one-on-one conversation, often the first engagement between organizers and potential recruits.

There also isn't a do-or-die hard assessment of whether or not faith-based organizers have succeeded in winning a majority of congregants, since there are no government-supervised elections in each church to reveal the number of new organization members. Dues collection, through tithing, incentivizes faith-based organizers to push for as many new members as possible, but the legal structures around union organizing make winning a majority in a union election or a strike a matter of absolute necessity.

Timing and urgency also matter. Faith-based organizations do not have externally imposed deadlines; unionization efforts do. The byzantine legal structure that dictates the rules for union formation and union governance imposes multiple deadlines, like so many obstacles to be overcome, starting with the union membership card, which expires in twelve months if the required level of unionization has not been won in that period. If unionization is won, then the clock is reset: a first collective agreement or contract must then be achieved, again within twelve months. Collective agreements themselves expire, triggering another round of deadlines. Faith-based organizing has no such exigencies, and faith-based organizers and organizations often take several years to build to something like an initial majority or to take a first action.[18]

For all of these reasons, union organizers, much more than faith-based organizers, must hone their skills in identifying organic leaders, persuading constituents, and developing what union organizers call structure tests. Of course, since the McCarthy era, most unions haven't even attempted to organize unorganized workers, run strikes, or win high-participation contract-ratification votes.[19]

This book's purpose is to draw lessons for power building from the best examples of success under the most difficult conditions. This book is not about union organizing; it is about organizing. That unions are the focus is a hint to social scientists and the intelligentsia that the failure to study or understand unions as social movements has resulted in a lack of understanding of the most effective way to build power. In the new millennium, as in the past, meaningful union success requires building to majorities in the workplace, a setting that does represent the most difficult conditions. As Dan and Mary Ann Clawson said, mechanisms in union organizing "offer social movement scholars an underused resource: the opportunity for systematic study of widely practiced, and often highly risky, forms of collective action."[20]

It sometimes seems there is a forged, collective resistance to seeing the best of labor organizing today as being every bit as moral, legitimate, and strength producing as the sixty-year-old civil rights movement. Charles Payne illustrates this indirectly in the preface to the 2007 edition of his masterful book on organizing in the civil rights movement, while commenting on the many reviews of his book. "By far, the chapter in *Light of Freedom* which has been least commented upon by reviewers is chapter 12 with its discussion of various corruptions within the movement."[21] When the discussion is about the labor movement, the reverse is almost always true: The focus seems to be mostly on internal corruption and rarely on the movement's moral crusade for worker dignity in a viciously antiworker economy. Yet high-participation organizing under high-risk conditions, using high moral standards, has continued; the lessons abound.

New Labor's Response to the Crisis of the Union Movement

Unions in the United States are experiencing a profound crisis. In 1995, the biggest shake-up in the U.S. labor movement in more than fifty years took place when a new generation of unionists forced the first contested election in the history of the American Federation of Labor–Congress of Industrial Organizations (AFL-CIO). The victors, called the New Voices slate, promised revitalization through aggressive new organizing. Two decades and hundreds of millions of dollars later, union ranks had declined even more, from 10.3 percent to 6.7 percent in the private sector and from 14.9 percent to 11.3 percent overall.[22] The unions aligned with the elections' winning team were mostly service-workers' unions, and I will refer to them throughout this book as New Labor.[23] Why has New Labor failed to reverse the decline of union power?

U.S. unions are not monolithic. Most unions have not been trying to organize the unorganized; mostly, they've been managing their own decline.[24] In 1995, though, one set of unions declared they would reverse the tide of their ebbing membership. This book focuses on that set of unions. The grouping is slightly porous but contains a core that self-identify as unions trying to change and grow their ranks. I rely on several intersecting groups of unions to constitute the universe I investigate: a list generated by Kate Bronfenbrenner, one that she used in her enormous body of union research; the list on the winning side of the AFL-CIO victory in 1995; the unions that broke from the AFL-CIO in 2006, known as the Change-to-Win (CTW unions); and, very recently, the two main national teachers' unions, which have gone through significant leadership changes. Owing to the ferocious national attack on teachers, these two unions—historically go-it-aloners that eschewed close ties to the larger house of labor—have become active participants with other unions for the first time in decades.

Dominated since 1995 by unions in the service sector, these overlapping lists include the Service Employees International Union (SEIU); Hotel Employees and Restaurant Employees (HERE) and Union of Needle Trades Employees (UNITE), which merged to become UNITE-HERE; American Federation of State, County and Municipal Employees (AFSCME); United Food and Commercial Workers (UFCW); United Auto Workers (UAW); United Brotherhood of Carpenters (UBC); Laborers International Union of North America (LIUNA); the United Farm Workers (UFW); the American Federation of Teachers (AFT); and the National Education Association (NEA). Who is in and out of the overlapping list depends on the exact months and years of various complicated turf wars.

Although the external environment of all unions is extremely hostile, unions could be winning much more. The reasons for the ongoing decline of union membership lie mainly in how unions engage with their existing members and with unorganized workers. Despite its now decades-old rhetoric about organizing, New Labor mostly uses a mobilizing approach. Much labor history and analysis focus on external factors to explain union decline—the employer offensive, hostile courts, globalization, automation, and a changing employment structure—ignoring strategy and methods for engaging workers. This book focuses on something movement actors can actually and easily control: their own strategy.

A critical factor in the failure of the union revitalization effort after 1995 has been the strategic choice made by key leaders of New Labor to move away from workers and the workplace. Because of adverse labor laws and unfriendly court rulings, these leaders decided they could no longer win traditional union elections. They shifted their strategy to securing so-called card-check and neutrality deals and fair election procedure accords with employers. Such agreements are anchored in a core idea: getting the employers to stop fighting unionization. New Labor unions invented new mechanisms for what they deemed carrots and sticks. Carrots included rewarding corporations by helping them increase their government subsidies and decrease their taxes, and also promising to cede control of the workplace and instead focus narrowly on wages and material benefits. If these carrots failed, there was the stick: the union's ability to impose potential costs on the employer. This might be done through a "corporate campaign," including publicity offensives against the employer's brand and stockholder actions ("brand damage"); by lobbying to have various public subsidies that flow into the so-called private sector decreased or cut off; by adding lawyers to press for environmental and other reviews; or by delaying or preventing zoning changes. Many of these tactics rely on politics, and so unions also invested more money in politics—not politics as in voters-to-the-polls, but politics as in million-dollar check writing and backroom "gotcha" deals.

Corporate collaboration isn't new, but when the labor-run corporate campaigns first developed in the 1970s as a response to the degeneration of worker protections under U.S. labor law, they were designed to complement worker organizing. By the early years of the new millennium, they had all but replaced it.[25] The strategy of weakening employer opposition to union organization through corporate campaigns made employers—not workers or their communities—the primary focus of

New Labor's energy. Today, corporate campaigns continue to locate the fight in the economic arena by threatening to disrupt profit making, but not through workers withholding their labor. Instead, a new army of college-educated professional union staff bypass the strike and devise other tactics to attack the employer's bottom line. New Labor's overreliance on corporate campaigns has resulted in a war waged between labor professionals and business elites. Workers are no longer essential to their own liberation.

New Labor's leaders, many of whom self-identify and are seen as progressives outside the union sector itself, have rationalized "carrots" and accords reached with big business that have stripped workers and their communities of the tools to defend themselves against their employers.[26] Moreover, New Labor's adoption and fetishizing of corporate tactics stands in contrast to the organizing style at the root of many of labor's great victories, won during an even more hostile period of industrial relations than that of the past four decades: the 1930s, which saw the successful establishment of the unions of the Congress of Industrial Organization (CIO). A key aspect of the CIO organizers' craft was identifying organic worker leaders in the shop and anchoring campaigns in the "whole worker," understood to be a person embedded in a range of social relationships in the workplace and in the community.[27]

The loss of the strength gained through whole worker organizing was one serious consequence of the alliance of business unionism with McCarthyism, which drove most organizers skilled in the CIO-era method out of the labor movement. Today, like World War II veterans, many CIO veterans have died, leaving few to tell their war stories. On the heels of the McCarthy era, union leaders adopted an increasingly accommodationist strategy that for a few decades achieved material gains and union security, but at the price of surrendering the option to strike and, often, all other real rights on the shop floor. Once the production-crippling strike weapon was abandoned, union leaders no longer saw a need to build a strong worksite-based organization among a majority of workers—one powerful enough that a majority decides to walk off the job, united, together, with common goals. New Labor doubled down on strategies that involved fewer and fewer workers, reinforcing instead of challenging the mistakes of the generation of leaders they replaced. As a result, wage increases and improvements in working conditions have come to a halt. Workers as the primary leverage of their own salvation have been replaced by the corporate campaign, a method of tactical warfare that takes union action away from the shop floor and away from the rank and file.

The Search for Black Swans: Unions that Still Run Successful Majority Strikes

Workers can still win substantial victories by building and holding majority participation—a very different strategy from the one deployed by New Labor or any national groups today. Because the most powerful strikes—those that shut down or cripple production—rely not on staff but on an overwhelming majority of workers to engage in collective action, the use of labor's strongest weapon requires an approach to workers that facilitates majority participation in the union. The preponderance of cases I examine in this book involve successful majority strikes carried out since 2000. Drawing an analogy to the industrial-era factory of the past, but updating the shop floors and the workforces that occupy them, I focus on cases in the dominant industries of today's service economy: health care and education, both fields in which many workers with a wide range of skill and education constantly collaborate in the same buildings. Unlike those of the past, the workforces in my case studies are mostly comprised of women (many of them women of color), and in the work they do, emotional labor and technical skill are equally crucial to success.

The transition from a manufacturing to a service economy radically altered traditional worker-consumer relations. Are there strategy implications here for unions? Does the strike strategy of a female-dominated, service-oriented workforce look different from the old one? Does labor need to view the public differently in contemporary strike strategy? Does the relationship between these workers and their patients or students (and the patients' and students' families) demand a different relationship between the workers' unions and the community? Yes to all. Strikes are essential to restoring the power of the working class, not just for the better standards strikes can produce, but also because they reveal high-participation organizing. Unions still successfully engaging in massive strikes—not simply protests borrowing the name "strike"—are concrete proof of highly successful methods that can challenge the root of all inequality: the inequality of power in society. The corporate class has been driving a wedge between the public and unionized workers; now the public in our neoliberal service-heavy economy must become an extension of the workers in the fight against the employers. The stories in this book tell how to restore strikes to prominence again in the United States, and demonstrate that doing so successfully will depend on labor adopting a radically different relationship with workers and the consuming public—a relationship that can only be built by the workers themselves.

These case studies represent a small section of union and community organizing. They include some failures, but most demonstrate successes, successes won in a period of massive decline for both unions and civil society. My aim is not to produce a theory that explains successes and failures in toto, but rather to explain in depth the dynamics, strategies, and contexts in which particular victories were achieved. Understanding these successes is key to rethinking and revitalizing a powerful progressive movement in the U.S.[28]

The twelve post-2000 cases I analyze involve one classic SMO, two national unions, and two local unions, one of them a local of one of the nationals—an outlier with an approach very different from its parent. The unions span the so-called private and public sectors (the distinction is a strategic frame more than a reality); the cases involve trade jobs and service jobs, filled by workers harder to replace (teachers and nurses) and easier to replace (factory hands, teacher's aides, nurse's aides, cooks, and cleaners). One case involves a mostly male workforce of diverse backgrounds, slaughtering and preparing pork in a right-to-work Southern state. Others involve mostly female workforces, teaching and caring for the young and tending to the sick and infirm in at least partly unionized Northern states. Multiple cases originated *within* each of these organizations. In one of the national unions, the United Food and Commercial Workers Union (UFCW), three separate campaigns to unionize workers in the same factory spanning more than a decade resulted in two defeats and one big victory. In *all* of the cases, losing and winning a little or a lot can be correlated with one common factor: the beliefs and motivations, or purposefulness, of the leadership team.[29] Table 1.2 provides a summary of the cases.

TABLE 1.2 Cases in the New Millennium, 2000 to 2014*

Organization Type & Name	SMO: Make the Road New York	Union: SEIU Service Employees International Union	Union: UFCW United Food & Commercial Workers	Union: AFT American Federation of Teachers
Sector & Type of Profession or Employment	Poor, "precariat," and small worksites Most fights in community terrain	Private sector, service Nursing homes	Private sector, manufacturing Pork production	Public Sector, service Education
Location	New York City	*National* strategy: Washington state *Local* strategy: Rhode Island, Connecticut	Tar Heel, North Carolina	Chicago
Legal Framework	Outside labor law framework (mostly)	Union security	Right-to-work	Union security
Demographics	Latin American immigrants, documented and undocumented	Mostly female African Americans and documented immigrants	Mostly male African Americans, whites, and undocumented immigrants	Mostly female whites and African Americans, a few Latin Americans and Asians
Numbers of Workers	Varies: from very small groups to statewide impact	6,000	5,000	30,000
Type of Effort	Litigation, statewide legislative change, blocking enforcement actions	Employer accords with neutrality agreements, National Labor Relations Board (NLRB) elections, collective bargaining, and strikes	NLRB elections, employer accords, and strikes	From decline to renewal strategies, collective bargaining, and strikes

*The two losses came in 1994 and 1997.

Methodology

I employ mixed qualitative and quantitative methods. I conducted fifty-eight semi-structured interviews with rank and file workers, civil society leaders, members of local media organizations, current and former lead strategists in the campaigns, and long-time active as well as retired union leaders and organizers. I analyzed data sets from the Federal Mediation and Conciliation Services (FMCS) work-stoppage databases from the year 2000 to present. I did archival research on each case's strategic planning documents; analysis of the current collective bargaining agreements of each local union; read published newspaper stories and internal memos; and I conducted a line-by-line content analysis of the key Saul Alinsky texts as well as the organizing training manuals of numerous Alinskyist organizations and unions. I utilized participant observation for chapter three, first as a young organizer being apprenticed at 1199 New England and later as national deputy director for SEIU's Healthcare Division, where I participated in numerous discussions leading up to the launch of what became known nationally as the Nursing Home Industry Alliance, which the Washington State case represents. I was trained as a community organizer in one strand of the Alinsky tradition prior to my years as a labor organizer and contract negotiator

Relying on what John Gerring's[30] calls "crucial" cases, I interrogate the relationship between rank and file worker agency and success. Gerring describes "crucial cases" as "paradigmatic" and within each of the four chapters I deploy the crucial case method (the approach to nursing homes in Washington state versus Connecticut, the achievements of one worker center, Make the Road New York as against all other worker centers, the massive and defiant strike by Chicago's teachers in a period defined by surrender by most teacher's unions, the abuse of labor law by one employer in the Deep South).

The Chapters

Chapter Two dissects the relationship between power and strategy and goes deeper into comparing and contrasting what have become two distinct approaches to social change, the dominating mobilizing approach and the underused organizing approach. I propose a blended approach called whole worker organizing. This approach is informed by the stories in this book as well as my own experiences. It tightly integrates workplace and nonworkplace issues, action, and learning in a holistic strategy. It responds to and attempts to overcome the challenge posed by Ira Katznelson in *City Trenches*:

> American urban politics has been governed by boundaries and rules that stress ethnicity, race, and territoriality, rather than class, and that emphasize the distribution of goods and services, while excluding questions of production or workplace relations. *The centerpiece of these rules has been the radical separation in people's consciousness, speech, and activity of the politics of work from the politics of community.* [author emphasis][31]

Whole worker organizing, laid out in Chapter Two and depicted in some aspects in all the subsequent empirical chapters, demonstrates that where unions understand their members and unorganized workers to be class actors in their communities, and when the workers systematically bring their own preexisting community networks into their workplace fights, workers still win, and their wins produce a transformational change in consciousness.

Chapter Three takes two similarly situated union locals—members of the same national union, SEIU—and examines the wildly different strategies each deploys in private-sector nursing homes. One local represents the best expression of Andrew Stern, whom the national media for years called the leading figure of New Labor and whose imprint still dominates the Washington state local's present culture and strategies (and those of the national union). The national media has begun to reify David Rolf, Stern's protégé at the Washington local, as the new future of labor, despite his many public pronouncements that he thinks unions are a twentieth-century concept. The other local is an outlier of the national SEIU and represents the past militant traditions of the CIO. The local is commonly known as District 1199 New England, a local through which workers in more than 100 nursing homes have waged strikes in the new millennium. This chapter lays bare the differences among the advocacy, mobilizing, and organizing approaches in the workplace, and demonstrates the superiority of the latter.

Chapter Four analyzes the history of the Chicago Teachers Union (CTU) during the quarter century from 1988 to the union's recent strike in 2012, a strike that captivated the nation. I show the CTU's slow and steady decline from a once mighty union—even in 1988—into a fairly typical weak, unimaginative organization that had lost the faith of many of the best teachers. I then trace the evolution of the steps that those disillusioned teachers took to rebuild their union to beat one of the nation's most powerful mayors at that time, Rahm Emanuel, who set out to break the CTU in the context of a broader and bipartisan assault on public-sector unions. Chapter Four shows how quickly a union can go from decline to renewal and the profound difference between a union leadership that enables the rank and file to fight and a leadership that uses staff as dutiful administrators in a top-down union that constrains the will of its own members.

Chapter Five returns to the private sector: the case of a big factory much like the factories that dominated the twentieth century. Most academics have long assumed organizing the unorganized might be possible among low-wage service workers, but this chapter, like the others, demonstrates that motivation and strategy may have more to do with failure and success across *all* sectors of workers than previously thought. This is a case study of the world's largest pork production facility, a Smithfield Foods plant in rural North Carolina, the state with the lowest rate of unionization in the United States. The workers are mostly men, and racial and ethnic tensions among them are exploited so profoundly, it is hard to believe Jim Crow is not still alive legally as well as culturally.

The workers in this factory are twice defeated in their attempts at unionization. On the third try, they win—and win big, bringing massive change to plant operations and to their own lives. Their story suggests a path forward for other large manufacturing plants in the South, a path where workers unite their workplace and community relationships into a single struggle for decency and respect. Chapters Three, Four, and Five, all provide evidence that when a union strategically engages the broader community, new and strong leaders develop within and outside the factory walls.

They also show that Robert Michels's "iron law of oligarchy" isn't actually iron, and suggest that the motivation and/or ideology of key leadership is a crucial factor in whether or not a union turns oligarchic.

Additionally, all three chapters show that there are key structural features that can institutionalize governance models that help to thwart oligarchic tendencies in large organizations like unions.

Chapter Six explores a group that organizes the working class as a class, but is not itself a union. Make the Road New York is a social-movement organization that is also a worker center, but it locates the worker center inside an organization that has managed to come as close to a modern union as any nonunion group in the United States today. With over 155 full-time staff, the organization combines direct services, advocacy, and mobilizing into a tight blend, and it has enjoyed more success than most similarly situated groups. Interestingly, many of the group's specific legislative victories, as well as their workplace efforts, largely rely on the continued strength of New York City's unions. While their work is impressive, it raises a fundamental question of whether groups like this can continue producing wins if the unions they rely on—which exist as key players in only a handful of states—get weaker.

The concluding chapter sums up the lessons of the case studies and argues that to reverse today's inequality requires a robust embrace of unions—but of unions that are democratic, focused on bottom-up rather than top-down strategies, and place the primary agency for change in workers acting collectively at work and in the communities in which they reside. The losses of the past fifty years, decades when the corporate right seized firm control of the power structure, can be recouped, but only by readopting and modernizing the methods and strategies deployed by the old CIO and the civil rights movement.

2

The Power to Win is in the Community, Not the Boardroom

Part of the legacy of people like Ella Baker and Septima Clark is a faith that ordinary people who learn to believe in themselves are capable of extraordinary acts, or, better, of acts that seem extraordinary to us precisely because we have such an impoverished sense of the capabilities of ordinary people. If we are surprised at what these people accomplished, our surprise may be a commentary on the angle of vision from which we view them. That same angle of vision may make it difficult to see that of the gifts they brought to the making of the movement, courage may have been the least.

Charles Payne, *I've Got the Light of Freedom*[1]

THE UNITED STATES HAS UNDERGONE profound changes since the era of the CIO. Yet today, the unions whose strategies most closely resemble the old CIO's—the unions that still use the strike weapon—are also the unions whose members are negotiating—and gaining—contracts with life-altering improvements. Many of them are situated in the new service economy, which is dominated by women, often women of color. These workers understand that their jobs can't easily be shipped abroad or automated—*yet*. But even these unions—the nation's best—are missing a crucial piece of classic CIO strategy, and if they want to continue to use the strike weapon, they are going to need it. The CIO's organizing methods were deeply embedded in, and reliant on, an understanding of workers in relationship to the communities in which they lived. Rhetorically and tactically, unions today that follow the methods of the old CIO understand that the community is important, but they fail to see their members' organic ties to their communities *strategically*.

This chapter begins by showing why a more transformational model for working with the broader community is so important today, and ends with a theory and strategy for how this work can be done, called whole worker organizing. Sandwiched between the why and how of deep community engagement is a focused discussion about the difference between organizing and mobilizing, the evolution of the mobilizing model, and why each approach produces different levels of power. The schematic showing power in relationship to strategy is built on Joseph Luders's work on concession and disruption costs in his book *The Civil Rights Movement and the Logic of Social Change*.[2]

Today's service worker has a radically different relationship to the consuming public than last century's manufacturing worker had. People buying a car don't meet and confer with the workers whose hands create it; they don't walk up and down the assembly line insisting that a tweak this way or that might make a better ride. But parents picking their kids up from school often meet with the people who spend more waking hours with their kids than they do: the educators who are helping their children prepare intellectually and socially for adulthood. And parents participate in the educators' production process, attending meetings and volunteering in the classroom. Similarly, nurses and other health-care workers charged with repairing the victim of a car crash are in constant contact with the family, who are also allowed in the workplace, that is, the patient's hospital room. The case studies in the following chapters are filled with evidence that these mostly female, multiracial service workers are as capable of building powerful organizations as they are of building a child's mind or rebuilding a patient's body. In fact, they are among the only workers today engaging in production-shuttering strikes. Their organic ties to the broader community form the potential strategic wedge needed to leverage the kind of power American workers haven't had for decades.

In large swaths of the service economy, the point of production *is* the community. Working on community issues isn't social-movement unionism, it is simply unionism.

As for the large number of manufacturing workers still in the United States, often situated in the underregulated, nonunion South, this book offers case evidence that those who rely more on the CIO-era methodology—a bottom-up model in which workers have primary agency and are understood to be their own lever of liberation—can also win life-altering improvements. They can do it by *systematically structuring* their many strong connections—family, religious groups, sports teams, hunting clubs—into their campaigns. That a more organic relationship with the public exists for some workers, such as mission-driven service workers, doesn't mean that only they should tether their quality of life to that of the broader community. All workers, whether their shop floor is a call center or a factory, can tell the story of their overstressed work situation—ordinarily not seen by the consumer, but certainly understood by the rest of the working class. Solidarity among human beings can happen spontaneously, as in a flood or fire, or by design, through organizing.

Service workers tend to be less structurally powerful economically in the workplace than the mostly male workers of the CIO era, because it is easier to replace them and because when they do strike, not only the employer but also the consumer immediately feels the repercussions of their collective action. But they are *more* structurally powerful when it comes to engaging their community in a fight. For today's service workers to restore the strike, still the most effective lever available to the working class, the additional power source they need is not a corporate campaign or funds for bigger political donations, but rather a more systematic way to merge workplace and non-workplace issues. There is enormous value to this approach, starting with the political education it offers. Plenty of CEOs whose workplace policies hurt workers on the job also serve on local and regional boards, commissions, and task forces whose public policies hurt the same workers at home and in their neighborhoods—for example, by promoting development schemes that displace working-class renters and homeowners and the shopkeepers they rely on. Workers who understand how corporate power is wielded both in the workplace and outside it can strengthen themselves in both spheres and carry the fight into both, tapping their social and community networks, including key people with access and influence, such as religious leaders.

To rebuild a base powerful enough to seriously push back against the economic and political crises strangling most workers today, unions will have to practice the best organizing methods both inside *and* outside the workplace, simultaneously, in a seamless, unified approach. A bifurcated union and community alliance, which is what Richard Trumka promoted at the quadrennial convention of the AFL-CIO in 2013, will not be as effective, because the groups Trumka proposed to ally with and that most unions do engage are too weak themselves to make any real difference. Maintaining the bifurcation that has existed for the past forty years also denies agency to today's heavily female workforce. Women have long understood that issues such as child care, good housing, quality schools, clean drinking water, safe streets, and an end to mass incarceration and police violence are every bit as important as higher wages to the well-being of workers and their families. Understanding how to frame a more integrated approach that covers these needs requires further clarity about, and a little history of, the differences between mobilizing and organizing.

Many methods used in successful organizing today had their origins in the struggles of the CIO in the first half of the last century. Certainly, the most successful organizing described in this book draws heavily on methods first developed in the steel, auto, coal, and other heavy-industry sectors. The CIO from its founding in 1935 was grounded on the principle that all workers—skilled, semiskilled, and unskilled—who worked in the same industries and for the same employer should be brought together in one union.[3] In fact, it was founded in response to the refusal of the American Federation of Labor (AFL) to unify all workers regardless of skill level. After the early, enormous success of the CIO, the AFL eventually agreed to unionize workers the same way, though its chief motivation may have been expedience—inclusiveness adopted as a defense mechanism rather than a core principal.[4]

Modern Organizing Methods: The CIO's Legacy

Most CIO organizing was based on a mass collective action, high-participation model anchored in deep worker solidarities and cooperative engagement in class struggle. Strikes, the kind that could shut down production—strikes in which most if not all workers walk off the job in a high-risk collective action—were routine, and were evidence that workers *themselves* were the primary agents of their own liberation. "Left" organizers, those associated with various socialist and radical factions, flocked to the CIO because of the principal of inclusion, of uniting *all* workers across ethnicity, gender, race, skill level, and every other working-class division. The AFL had had a long, complicated history not just of excluding semi- and unskilled workers, and Black workers, but also of having taken positions against European and then Asian immigration, and very narrowly limiting the union struggle to wages and working conditions.[5]

The CIO's left organizers were intensely committed to recruiting and building power across the many "isms" and other divisions among the working class, and they had to develop special methods to do it. Jack O'Dell, an organizer for the CIO and later for the civil rights movement, recalls their success: "I grew up in Detroit, and when people asked you, 'What union are you in?' the guys didn't even say their union; they just said, 'the CIO.' Especially black workers, because the CIO would take on racism."[6]

Nelson Lichtenstein's *State of the Union: A Century of American Labor*,[7] Judith Stepan-Norris and Maurice Zeitlin's *Left Out: Reds and America's Industrial Unions*,[8] and Saul Alinsky's *John L. Lewis: An Unauthorized Biography*[9] all document that the left-wing organizers were the CIO's best. All of these authors record at length how the head of the CIO, John L. Lewis, though a fierce anti-Communist and anti-socialist, relied heavily if not primarily on organizers from the left to win the hardest organizing drives and the biggest strikes. Alinsky describes how Lewis hired these organizers as a pragmatic expedient, and was confident he could "control them." Today, people associate the name Reuther with the heyday of the United Auto Workers. As Alinsky himself points out, it wasn't the Reuther brothers—Walter, of great fame, or his brothers, Victor and Roy—who principally helped autoworkers form their union, though they played a part:

> When Lewis turned to help the auto workers, he saw that they were being organized and led by leftists. The leaders and organizers of the UAW group in General Motors were the left-wingers Wyndham Mortimer and Robert Travis. These two built the union inside the great General Motors empire. If Lewis wanted to take the auto workers into the CIO, he had to take in their left leadership.[10]

Earlier, Alinsky describes how the "inept" AFL had destroyed the hopes and dreams of the autoworkers in 1933 and 1934, which set the stage for Lewis and the new CIO to do what the AFL wouldn't and couldn't:

When the auto workers, filled with disgust, built bonfires with their AF of L membership cards, it was the left-wingers mainly who kept fighting against the disillusionment and cynicism that swept the workers. It was they who kept organizing and organizing and organizing and organizing.[11]

Later, Alinsky describes how Lewis failed in almost every organizing effort he attempted without the help of left organizers.[12] Stepan-Norris and Zeitlin reinforce the same point in great detail. It was organizers on the left who were the most committed to overcoming class divisions, and who, through uniting workers, were able to help them withstand and defeat the fiercest employer opposition. All three of these books document that employer opposition in those days included physical attacks against workers, and even the strategic use of murder, which ought to help put today's employer offensives in perspective.

Stepan-Norris and Zeitlin devote a chapter to Lewis's dealings with the left: He would hire organizers out of the Communist Party, then purge them once they'd won the campaign. The chapter is titled for Lewis's famous quip about this tactic: "Who gets the bird, the hunter or the dog?" The authors provide a small mountain of evidence that the unions led by these leftist factions were not only the most effective but also the most democratic. Their well-constructed analysis demonstrates that many of the elements that Robert Michels argued were essential to prevent the development of oligarchy in an organization—democratic constitutions, internal caucuses, alternative newsletters—actually existed in these leftist unions, unions that would later be obliterated by McCarthyism, not oligarchy.

One left-led union they discuss is also the subject of Howard Kimeldorf's *Reds or Rackets? The Making of Radical and Conservative Unions on the Waterfront*. Kimeldorf analyzes the stark differences between two mostly male dockworkers' unions, one on the East Coast and the other on the West Coast, that developed during the same period, the era of the CIO. On the East Coast, where workers and their leaders fought chiefly for money and other material gains, official corruption became legendary; bribes served to buy off the Eastern unions for decades. On the West Coast, where the unions fought for control of production, that is, for the right to negotiate rules governing safety, hours, and similar issues, bribes didn't work: Money wasn't what these workers were looking for. The West Coast's Wobbly-inclined base produced a leader, Harry Bridges, who was openly a socialist. Bridges and the West Coast workers routinely engaged in strikes; they had to; their demands were substantial and the employers weren't easy to beat. Kimeldorf concludes that the endless class struggle in which the West Coast workers engaged resulted in high-quality contracts that cemented a high level of participation, active membership, and a strong relationship between the rank and file and the union leaders. He demonstrates that this left-wing leadership showed superior skill in every aspect of running a union, and notes that members routinely reelected socialists to leadership positions, even though their own politics were not uniformly left-wing, but instead quite diverse.

What were the left's winning tactics? In a 1936 booklet, *Organizing Methods in the Steel Industry*, William Z. Foster writes, "Organizers do not know how to organize by instinct, but must be carefully taught."[13] He argues strongly for the importance of such training:

> The campaign can succeed only if thousands of workers can be organized to help directly in the enrollment of members. This work cannot be done by organizers alone. . . Very effective are small delegations of steel workers from one town or district to another and large mass delegations of workers from organized mills to unorganized mills.

Other methods of drawing in new members included music, and "social affairs such as smokers, boxing matches, card parties, dances, picnics, various sports, etc.," involving the workers *and their wives*.[14] The radicals in the CIO understood that workers were embedded in an array of important workplace and non-workplace networks, all of which could be best accessed—and, for organizing on a mass scale, *only* accessed—by the workers themselves. Foster describes the "list" and "chain" systems,[15] 1930s terms for methods of building a network of the most respected workers inside and outside the workplace who could then mobilize their own networks.

Unions that still run successful majority strikes today, or that run and win National Labor Relations Board (NLRB) elections in the private sector, offer our closest look at the methods deployed by the leftists in the early CIO. Because union staffers in a private-sector unionization effort are *barred* from entering the workplace, including its parking lots and cafeterias, they must master the old CIO craft of learning who the organic worker leaders are and persuading them to support the union. These organic leaders in turn can use their influence and are the best people to persuade their coworkers to join the struggle. The legal context of the private sector forces 100 percent worker agency: In these settings, the workers themselves are the only ones who can lead an "inside" campaign, which almost always must be waged in an extremely hostile climate.

To connect to rank-and-file dynamics in the workplace, union organizers use a mechanism called organic leader identification, in which they analyze the workers' preexisting social groups. This is done among the workers and in conversation with them, not apart from them. Workers themselves identify their organic leaders, who become the primary focus for full-time organizers. If these leaders are successfully recruited, they are taught the organizers' techniques, so that they can recruit their supporters on the shop floor, where outside organizers cannot go. Rarely, if ever, does a worker accurately announce himself or herself as a leader. Kristin Warner, a contemporary organizer in the CIO tradition, notes:

> [Organic leaders are] almost never the workers who most want to talk with us. More often than not, [they're] the workers who *don't* want to talk to us and remain in the background. They have a sense of their value and won't easily step forward, not unless and until there's a credible reason. That's part of the character that makes them organic leaders.[16]

These are the leaders needed for a serious struggle, such as a strike in which most workers must agree to walk off the job. In the CIO model—today as in the 1930s—strikes that cripple production are considered not only possible, but also the highest "structure test" of whether worker organization in a given facility is at its strongest.[17] It is the culmination of a series of tests that begin by measuring and assessing *individual* workers' power, and end by testing the power and collective organization of the workers worksite by worksite.

A structure test typically used early in the process will gauge how effectively and efficiently a worker identified as an organic leader can get a majority of her shift or unit to agree to a public, and therefore high-risk, action, such as signing a public petition demanding that the employer recognize the union. This will be followed by increasingly challenging tests, considered confidence-building actions, such as getting workers to pose for individual or group photos for a public poster, or join in a sticker day—only considered a success if a supermajority of workers come to work wearing a union sticker or button. These are all high-risk actions; they announce to the manager that the workers participating are pro-union.

Figure 2.1 below is an example of a "majority petition": a document publicly signed by a majority of workers in a large workplace and then printed as a three-by-five-*foot* poster to be marched by the workers themselves to the CEO. In this example, the workers are calling on management to settle their contract:

If the worker-leader given the assignment can turn this kind of action around in only one or two shifts, the organizer has correctly identified

FIGURE 2.1 An example of a structure test

an organic leader. On the other hand, if a prospective worker-leader, even one personally enthusiastic about the union, cannot get a majority of coworkers in his or her shift and unit to do anything quickly—let alone engage in high-risk actions—it is clear that the leadership identification was incorrect, and the organizer must start again, talking with all the workers to better assess which coworkers they most respect and will most willingly follow. The worker who fails at the test is likely a pro-union activist, not an organic leader, and leaders, not activists, win the campaign and have the capacity to build strong worksite structures. The process is not easy; even a true organic leader sometimes fails to get a majority of signatures, often because of either weak personal commitment to the union, or even active hostility toward it.

If an organic leader remains undecided, the recruiting organizer, because of the urgency that always exists in high-risk union fights where the employer's war is either imminent or already in motion, takes the next step: "framing the hard choice." The process begins with understanding an individual organic leader's self-interest and helping the leader come to his or her own understanding, through face-to-face discussions, that this self-interest can only be realized through collective—not individual—action; that is, through a union. Because these organic leaders are often considered good workers by management—for the same reasons that their fellow workers trust and rely on them—they are often favored in small ways; for example, by being given desirable shifts. But they cannot win big things like pensions, sick pay, or maternity leave on their own. The organizer therefore carefully polarizes the conversation so that the worker understands he or she faces a clear and stark choice: Take a risk in order to win the desired benefits, or be safe, do nothing, and get nothing.

For example: A group of workers has identified "Sally" as the most influential rank-and-file person on their shift and in their work area. The organizer has successfully gotten Sally, in a one-on-one conversation, to explain that she is overwhelmed and frustrated by how much her employer automatically takes from her paycheck each month to pick up the cost of an expensive family health-care plan. But she still hesitates when asked if she is willing to "join up with her coworkers to form a union by signing this membership card." Sally knows that signing the card is a big decision. In the United States, employers routinely fire workers for taking such actions, or punish them in other ways. A good organizer understands this, and at this point will say something like, "So, Sally, I want to be clear about what I am hearing. You are good with the boss continuing to charge you $440.00 per month, deducted from your paycheck, just to keep your kids healthy and you healthy enough to show up for work, for the rest of your life?"

The best organizers in the CIO tradition call the moment that follows "the long uncomfortable silence," because the organizer is trained to say *nothing* until the worker responds—and that can take several long minutes of dead silence between two people sitting face-to-face. The organizer respects that silence and waits it out, because the decision Sally is being asked to make is huge, and must be treated that way. Sally is not being lied to, she is not being promised anything, she is not being manipulated, and she is being advised that the employer will take swift and direct action against her and her coworkers. She is having a discussion about going on strike. This is worker agency. An axiom of organizers is that every good organizing conversation makes everyone at least a little uncomfortable. And it's a conversation that must be had. All other actions come from this one.

Majority petitions, majority photo posters, majority sticker days, majority T-shirt days all serve multiple purposes: They are public activities, socializing workers to take a risk together; they are solidarity- and confidence-building, showing workers the strength of their numbers; and they are part of an endless series of assessments of the strength of each organic leader. For big units, at the beginning of an organizing drive or lead-up to a contract-related strike, these goals might take weeks to achieve. Only true organic leaders can lead their coworkers in high-risk actions. Pro-union activists without organic leaders are not effective enough, and professional staff organizers certainly cannot do it; they aren't even allowed into the workplace. The organic leader is essential to the organizing model. It took hundreds of thousands of Sallys to lead us out of inequality once, and it will take hundreds of thousands to do it again.

Modern Mobilizing Methods: A Product of McCarthyism, Business Unionism, and Saul Alinsky

If the organizing model is so effective, why was it so widely abandoned? Many factors contributed to the decimation of the labor movement's best organizers and the end of high-participation unions. There were John Lewis's obsession with top-down power and his determination to rein in socialism—more important to him than reining in corporations. There was the self-inflicted wounds of Stalinism and increasing divisions in the American left. There was World War II's "peace treaty" between labor and capital, which instituted strike bans, decreasing opportunities for rank-and-file on-the-job problem solving, and centralized collective bargaining, disempowering rank and file–led negotiations. The Taft-Hartley Act of 1947 straitjacketed militants by banning solidarity strikes and forcing all unions and eventually all unionists to give an affidavit that they were not Communists or affiliated with the left. The finishing blow was dealt by Joe McCarthy and his Cold War witch hunts.[18] These developments destroyed the most revolutionary aspect of the earlier CIO: *the agency of workers themselves.* Driving leftists out of the unions, the ones who kept "organizing and organizing and organizing and organizing"[19] despite the stiffest odds, also drove out the methods of building strong worksite structures, the very kind that create high-participation organizing.

Marshall Ganz, in *Why David Sometimes Wins*,[20] says the purpose or motivation of leadership teams is central to outcomes. The early CIO did use some full-time left-wing organizers; this was the Depression era, and many were either donating their time or being paid considerably less than today's full-time professionals. More importantly, the old CIO's full-time organizers were *co-leaders* with rank-and-file organizers, the organic leaders among the workers. This point will be explored in more depth in Chapter Three, in an examination of 1199 New England, a local union that serves as a good contemporary example of the CIO organizing method and its results. This union, composed of mostly female health-care workers, routinely runs majority strikes (not without difficulty, but super majority strikes were never easy). In their model, as in the early CIO's, the role of the paid organizer is to identify the organic leaders, recruit them, and coach them how to most effectively lead their coworkers against the inevitable employer war. Organizers in 1199NE are understood to play a leadership role: They lead the organizing committee. The rank-and-file organizers lead the workers. Ganz's book documents a case involving farmworkers similar to the dockworkers' case described in Kimeldorf's *Reds or Rackets*. In Ganz's story, the *same* workforce is first defeated and later wins, but as in the case of the Western and Eastern dockworkers, it is the approach to strategy and to the workers themselves that is decisive, not how many resources are brought to each unionization effort. As in Kimeldorf's case, smarter demands—for more autonomy and control of the production process rather than for more money—lead to a smarter strategy, in which worker agency is primary to building the power needed to win.

Ganz's and Kimeldorf's in-depth studies reinforce a core argument in this book: What sociologists and academics have long labeled *structure* is actually human *agency*. Successful workplace organizers today who still run strikes regularly obsess about the two words *structure test*. But the structure these organizers are testing is simply worker agency: the power of the workers' own organization, built up and developed by individuals like Sally—organic leaders. In fact, all structure tests are agency tests. Global trade agreements are structure tests: they measure elite and corporate power. When a successful strike shuts down production and leads to a very strong contract for the striking workers, academics call that contract a "structure." But the real structure involved is the human power, or agency, that won the contract. Good organizers today, like those depicted in the following chapters, make sure the workers know that their ability to win a great contract is in direct proportion to their ability—and willingness—to fight the employer: a test of the agency of one against the agency of the other.

The left-wing organizers in the CIO who developed human structures powerful enough to defeat staggering inequalities, and who were committed to genuine worker agency, were replaced after World War II by a massive bureaucracy. Kim Moody and Nelson Lichtenstein document the expansion of professional union staff in the 1950s, an expansion that was later mimicked in social movements after the advent of the New Left at the end of the 1960s.[21] In her book *Diminished Democracy*,[22] Skocpol focuses on what she calls the "extraordinary reorganization of U.S. civic life after the 1960s, seeking to make sense of the abrupt shift from membership-based voluntary associations to managerially directed advocacy groups." That shift was precipitated by the abrupt and massive shifts in unions. During every period Skocpol methodically analyzes, U.S. unions represented the largest sector of what she calls "cross-class voluntary federations." The U.S. corporate class succeeded in taming unions by pushing for labor laws and regulations that encouraged or forced the replacement of workers and worker agency with a huge union bureaucracy, which they promised would promote the workers' interests better than could the workers themselves.

Skocpol's "abrupt shift" emerged in part because the corporate class realized they could institute the same weakening mechanisms to quiet the unruly left wing growing outside the unions. A vast new philanthropic focus in the 1970s shifted from naming buildings to professionalizing protest; social activism was legalized to death. Skocpol's exacting analysis of why democracy diminished when professionals replaced ordinary people can be applied in every respect to why democracy diminished in unions, though democracy *decimated* might be a more accurate way of putting it.

One underexplored aspect of this effort to rationalize and contain agency is the role played by the man considered the dean (or father) of modern community organizing, Saul Alinsky.

Saul Alinsky Changes and Compromises the Organizing Model[23]

Throughout the period that stretched from the CIO era to the Civil Rights movement and then into the forty years Skocpol describes, Saul Alinsky was codifying the idea of community organizing. Weeks before his unexpected death, Alinsky described his project to *Playboy* in a wide-ranging interview, published posthumously:[24]

> What I wanted to try to do was to apply the organizing skills I'd mastered in the CIO to the worst slums and ghettos, so that the most oppressed and exploited elements could take control of their own communities and their own destinies. Up until then, specific factories and industries had been organized for social change, but never whole communities.[25]

Alinsky, unfortunately, never truly mastered the CIO's organizing skills because he never did any workplace organizing himself; he was a mobilizer, outside the factories. In fact, Alinsky compromised the CIO organizing model in three significant ways that have weakened labor and nonlabor movements alike. First, he delinked the method he observed from the mission or motivation of the left-wing organizers— organizers who were committed not only to winning campaigns but also to *radically altering the power structure itself*. He then grafted some of the method to an elite theory of power, and in so doing, he laid the groundwork for what I call the mobilizing model. Second, he was the bifurcator-in-chief: He proposed that unskilled, easily replaced workers in "the community" could—independently of their natural allies, the semiskilled and skilled members of the working class—generate enough power outside of the economic arena to actually challenge the corporate class by themselves. Third, Alinsky, who idolized John Lewis, created an organizing model much more like Lewis's than like that of the left-wing organizers upon whom the CIO was originally built. Alinsky ensured Lewis-like control of the masses through a fiction, still upheld today, that full-time organizers are not leaders and that they answer to the thousands of grassroots people they recruit, whom they call leaders. This fiction has obscured the accountability of the organizers for decades. As I will show in this discussion, and throughout this book, Lewis-Alinsky core beliefs were recycled into the post-1995 New Labor leadership, creating a mobilizing model dressed up as an organizing model.

Saul Alinsky's name has been synonymous with organizing for more than half a century. Though he died in 1972, shortly after the publication of his most famous book, *Rules for Radicals*, his influence today is everywhere. Both major candidates for the Democratic presidency in 2008, Hillary Clinton and Barack Obama (and Clinton again in 2016), are linked to Alinsky's legacy. Clinton met with him and in 1969 wrote her undergraduate thesis on him—more than 100 pages examining what she calls the Alinsky model.[26] During Obama's first presidential campaign, he spoke often about his experience working with an Alinsky-influenced community organization in Chicago. Since Obama came to power (perhaps *because* he did), Alinsky has been an inspiration to Tea Partiers, a development that has confounded many community organizers who consider themselves original, true Alinsky believers. In any casual Internet search, after Wikipedia the top three Alinsky hits are radical-right websites, including Glenn Beck's, and these sites urge anyone serious about building power to read *Rules for Radicals*—a top seller in 2008 and 2009 among right-wing grassroots activists, whose leaders received gift copies from Dick Armey, among others.[27]

Despite a world of differences between them, Saul Alinsky and Karl Marx have this in common: There is what they wrote, and what they did, and what has been done by their followers. There are Alinskyites and Marxists who denounce fellow Alinskyites and Marxists, insisting that other factions misunderstand the founder's true message. In both camps, devotees point to the good work that has been done by members of the tradition, and critics point to the ways the tradition has led the left into problems. Talking about Alinsky can be just as tricky as talking about Marx.

The single biggest source of funding for four decades of community organizing, starting in the early 70's, was the Catholic Campaign for Human Development (CCHD). A long article by Lawrence Engel in *Theological Studies*[28] asserts, with copious evidence, that the CCHD was developed to support Alinsky's work. Engel's research describes the Catholic bishops' 1969 commitment to raise $50,000,000 to alleviate poverty through a national collection strategy church by church. In today's dollars, this commitment to fund Alinsky-based work would be just over $330 million.[29] Engel asks, "Why would Catholic bishops approve funds for the poor to organize for power, much of which went to the community organizing projects associated with Saul Alinsky?"[30] One answer to Engel's question is that the Catholic Church was sincere in hoping to alleviate poverty. Another comes from Alinsky himself:

> So in order to involve the Catholic priests in Back of the Yards, I didn't give them any stuff about Christian ethics, I just appealed to their self-interest. I'd say, 'Look, you're telling your people to stay out of the Communist-dominated unions and action groups, right?' He'd nod. So I'd go on: 'And what do they do? They say, "Yes, Father," and walk out of the church and join the CIO. Why? Because it's their bread and butter, because the C.I.O. is doing something about their problems while you are just sitting here on your tail in the sacristy.' That stirred 'em up, which is just what I wanted to do, and then I'd say, "Look, if you go on like that you're gonna alienate your parishioners, turn them from the church, maybe drive them into the arms of the Reds. Your only hope is to move first, to beat the Communists

at their own game, to show the people you're more interested in their living conditions than in the contents of your collection plate. And not only will you get them back again, by supporting their struggle, but when they win, they'll be more prosperous and your donations will go up and the welfare of the Church will be enhanced."[31]

Alinsky was replacing union dues with Catholic tithing, mediated by bishops instead of bosses. It's not hard to understand why Alinsky-based organizations have dominated the field since the 1970s. And it is important to understand their contributions, but also their limitations. To do that, it is important to understand Saul Alinsky.

Saul Alinsky was born in Chicago in 1909 to two working-class Russian Jews.[32] In 1926, he entered the University of Chicago, where George Herbert Mead, credited with originating the field of Symbolic Interactionism, and sociologist Robert Park were significant intellectual powers. According to Alinsky's biographer Sanford Horwitt, Alinsky took many of Park's classes.[33] Alinsky also spent a full decade doing academically directed participant observation, first with youth gangs and then with the Chicago mob. He published several scholarly articles in the 1930s and early 1940s that reveal his early thinking about power analysis, based on his observations of the power dynamics of both of these nontraditional types of organization.

In the late 1930s, bored with criminal justice work (he often referred to boredom as a kind of chief life motivator) and alarmed by the rise of fascism in Europe, Alinsky transitioned from his job in the Joliet Prison to "moonlighting with the CIO."[34] This gave him his first contact with the people he later said were the best organizers of his day: the "Reds." Working as a volunteer, he helped raise funds for striking mine workers and for the International Brigades heading off to fight in the Spanish Civil War.

Alinsky, unlike the left-wing organizers in the CIO, wanted to defend and protect capitalism; his ideas were very close to Alexis de Tocqueville's. Both Alinsky and Tocqueville were enchanted by the concept of freedom; both failed to recognize that the wage labor system, the place most individuals spend most hours, is anything but a zone of freedom. Alinsky quotes Tocqueville more often than anyone else in both *Reveille for Radicals* and *Rules for Radicals*. He spins Tocqueville's long digressions about the importance of creating a middle class into his own vernacular, calling Tocqueville's middle class the "have a little, want some more class." Both he and Tocqueville believed that it's essential to have such a class to ward off the influence of Jacobins and socialists.

Stability in our freedom-loving society, Alinsky said, would be achieved by having strong unions, the guarantors of a strong middle class. The unions Alinsky wanted were the kind John L. Lewis believed in; his 1949 book, *John L. Lewis: An Unauthorized Biography*,[35] is a 400-page love letter to the man and his work. The book opens with a full-page black-and-white photo of a regal-looking Lewis standing over Alinsky, his hand gesturing as he explains a concept, while Alinsky takes notes. Both men are wearing crisp suits; the room they inhabit is furnished with handsome lamps and oversize leather chairs. C. Wright Mills's "men of power" would have felt at home in that setting. The photo conveys Alinsky's sense of Lewis as magisterial, and so does his text: "To me, Lewis is an extraordinary individual and certainly one of the outstanding figures of our time."[36]

In 1941, Alinsky wrote in the *American Journal of Sociology*, "The point of view of the [Back of the Yards] Council on organized labor is quite clear. First it looks to the national organized labor movements to cope effectively with many of those major social forces which impinge upon the Back of the Yards community with disastrous results."[37] He might not have been wrong to imagine, back then, that his job, his added value, was to strategically engage faith-based groups to complement, not substitute for, the power of unions. In the abstract for this article he says, "In the industrial area adjacent to the Stock Yards of Chicago, a community council was formed which included the two basic institutions of the area—(1) organized religion and (2) organized labor—as well as all the other interest and action groups in that community." Today, however, labor's power is almost nil, national unions cannot cope effectively with big issues or, often, small ones, and faith-based community groups can no longer simply attend to local affairs. Without real CIO unions, like those Alinsky knew in Chicago, the church and labor alliance can't possibly match in 2016 what it accomplished in 1939.

In fact, Horwitt notes that even in the later 1940s and early 1950s, when Alinsky first ventured outside of Chicago to Kansas City and Los

Angeles, he couldn't create a community-only model that worked as well as Back of the Yards.[38] This caused him real concern at the time, because he was fundraising and couldn't show the model working. It wasn't working because a crucial part was missing: He didn't have the very smart—and left-wing—Packing House Workers Organizing Committee with him. *Conditions and context matter.*

Alinsky's most serious dogma—one that he fervently preached—was that no one should have dogma. No dogma, and only one ideology, an ideology he repeated in everything he wrote and in every speech he made. He sums it up on page 11 of *Rules for Radicals*: "In the end [this is] a conviction—a belief that if people have the power to act, in the long run they will, most of the time, reach the right decisions." Yet that power has resulted in genocide against Native Americans; centuries of slavery; today's mass incarceration of people of color; right-wing opposition to immigrant rights, taxes, and government; and the ongoing denial that unpaid homemaking is as hard as most wage work. None of this easily squares with Alinsky's simple "conviction" that those who have the power to act will almost always act wisely and well. Seth Borgos, a former ACORN staffer, says, "From a historical perspective, that stance about the ends of organizing is astonishing."[39]

This is one reason why Gary Delgado, founder of the Center for Third World Organizing, and his successor and protégé Rinku Sen have each written solid, constructive, nonsectarian critiques of Saul Alinsky.[40] Delgado locates his in the limitations of the politics of place and race in segregated America. Sen, in her book *Stir it Up*, argues that Alinsky's obsession with pragmatism and nondivisive issues resulted in decades of well-meant efforts that often undermined the very people who need good organizing the most—the poor, the working class, and people of color, whose issues could hardly be characterized as nondivisive. She points out that Alinskyist groups focused locally and on winnable fights have often reacted to the infusion of drugs into their communities by calling for more police and more prisons. Enter #blacklivesmatter. Similarly problematic, some Alinskyist groups working on education reform today have embraced charter schools, which undermine teachers' unions and siphon public tax dollars out of the publicly controlled school system.[41] In Chicago, the Industrial Areas Foundation (IAF) has yet to stand with the Chicago Teachers Union (CTU), teachers, and parents who are struggling to keep schools open in black communities, a situation examined in Chapter Four.

A further weakness in the Alinskyist model for community organizing is his discussion of and framework for organizers and leaders, an aspect of his legacy that has deeply penetrated and negatively impacted major union segments, including the Service Employees International Union (SEIU) and the Hotel and Restaurant Employees Union (UNITE-HERE).

In *Rules for Radicals*, Alinsky obscured the issue of organizer strategy. He declared that there are leaders and there are organizers, and that the two are different. The organizer is a behind-the-scenes individual who is not a leader, has nothing to do with decisions or decision-making, and must come from outside the community. (They also had to be men: Alinsky didn't believe women were tough enough, even during the era of the feminist movement.) The leader, on the other hand, must come from the base constituency and "make all the decisions." This is a good narrative, but disingenuous: The organizers in the Alinsky model make many key decisions.

A lot of good ink has been devoted to the problems with Alinsky's view of the "outside organizer,"[42] including in Bardacke's *Trampling Out the Vintage*. Denying that the organizer is a leader, with substantial influence on the organization, leaves the organizer's actions unchecked and not well understood, as Jerry Brown, the longtime leader of 1199 New England—still one of the most militant and successful local unions in the SEIU—observes:

> I never heard anyone use Alinsky in any way as a model for us. He was always talked about only in the context of community organizing, and how their organizers always had to be behind the curtain—their job wasn't to speak publicly, their job was to find and recruit. [The union that] came closest to this was HERE (the Hotel Employees and Restaurant Employees Union), because they always had rank-and-file officers who appeared to be the leaders. The rank-and-file officers were often wonderful union members who put a lot of work into the union, but they were very seldom the real, strategic leaders. I thought the 1199 model, with all its troubles with staff being members and sharing leadership, not just facilitating recruitment, it was

100 percent more honest to what was going on, and actually who was really leading. I just always felt that the way in which HERE actually led, and the way in which it appeared they led, were very different realities.[43]

Chapter Three describes 1199NE, which Jerry Brown founded and led from the early 1970s to 2005. The union is well known for routinizing all-out strikes every few years; for setting and maintaining the nation's highest wage, benefit, and workplace standards in nursing-home contracts; and for being the most powerful player in Connecticut politics. The role of the organizer in the 1199NE model is transparent, not hidden, and the role of the members is primary, not secondary—only the rank and file can strike against the employers. Majority strikes are one strong indicator that workers themselves are determining their fate, rather than leaving it to a professional staff.

The biggest flaw in Alinsky's organizer-leader theory—one that critiques of the theory have failed to address—is that it never asks the question that grounds the CIO method: Who is a leader? How do you identify the organic leaders in the base? In *Rules for Radicals*, the Alinsky text that most self-identified radicals have read, Alinsky doesn't even discuss the *concept* of leader identification. He does discuss it in the less often read *Reveille for Radicals*, which he wrote in 1946, before McCarthyism and other factors wrecked the CIO. In *Reveille*, Alinsky devotes an entire chapter to leader identification, "Native Leadership." He offers no methodology—Alinsky explained most of his theories with stories. Not surprisingly, his only stories in "Native Leadership" are about unions, like this one:

> Any labor organizer knows of the Little Joes. When a man is being solicited to join a union he will usually respond along these lines: "Everything you say sounds pretty good, Mister, but before I sign up, I want to know if Joe has signed up."[44]

"Joe" is the organic leader: the person on the shop floor who has followers. "Joe" is "Sally," found through organic leader identification and structure tests, the mechanisms used to help map the power of individual workers and their networks and relationships.

There is a direct and profound relationship between leadership identification theory and building *powerful* mass-scale movements. The
distinction and relationship between leadership identification and leadership development is crucial, and strategists and organizers will have to
understand this before ordinary people, the rank and file, can regain the
kind of power they need to tackle inequality. The omission of this central discussion from *Rules for Radicals* did serious damage to the development of the community organizing field during the very period when
the largest source of money available to practitioners was founded in the
name of supporting Alinsky-style efforts.

To say that individual workers and people have relative degrees of
power should not in any way be construed as saying all people aren't
equally important and deserving as human beings. Of course they are.
But in community organizing and some social movement groups the
obsession with leadership development and not leader identification
prevents all members of a movement from gaining the collective power
they need and deserve. Leadership development without previous leadership identification is a bicycle without wheels. It severely limits how
far that movement can go—the success it can and should achieve.

Self-identified radicals, those for whom *Rules for Radicals* has been
a de facto organizing manual, exist in and outside of the field of community organizing. Social-movement organizations (SMOs) are typically the self-selecting type that Han's book describes. They, along with
most community-based organizations and now, unfortunately, unions
as well, label as a leader just about anyone who enthusiastically shows
up at two successive meetings (even one sometimes), making the words
activist and *leader* interchangeable. It's an egalitarian impulse, as is the
aversion to power. The Occupy movement has muddied this discussion
even more with its talk of "leaderless movements" and "horizontalism."
But in any strategy for building power, all people are *not* the same.

Given the $50 million ($330 million today) that the CCHD began
granting in the early 1970s to the organizations and groups that carried
on Alinsky's work, it's not surprising that Alinsky-based thinking has
dominated the field coming out of the New Left period. In the 1970s,
some of those funds were channeled into what Mary Ann Clawson[45]
calls the redistributionist movements, groups like ACORN and Citizen

Action and other local community-organizing groups. She suggests that these redistributionist groups embraced Alinsky's false "organizer-leader" definition as a way to deflect criticism from those identity-based groups that noted that mostly white, middle-class men, coming out of the New Left, were still leading groups made up largely of poor women of color. The full-time staff of most of these groups said, "Leaders make the decisions, we just implement them"—a claim still made today by SEIU, UNITE-HERE, and many other unions. Clawson points out that SEIU and UNITE-HERE made a conscious decision to hire from outside their ranks starting in this same era, the 1970s, which was atypical. Randy Shaw's 2008 *Beyond the Fields* offers a comprehensive examination of the strong ties between the United Farm Workers and the leadership of New Labor, in particular these two unions. Many of the CCHD-funded groups serve as what Howard Kimeldorf called the social base for New Labor's organizer recruitment.[46]

Aside from the articles and books documenting the links between many of these groups and SEIU and UNITE-HERE, I found evidence for this in my own earlier fieldwork. For example, the United Auto Workers (UAW) maintains a strict policy even today of hiring only from their rank and file. Yet a number of today's key organizers in the New Labor–era UAW came directly from the CCHD groups. Phil Wheeler, the former leader of Region 9A of the UAW, which spans the northeastern United States, a union I worked closely with as part of the Stamford Organizing Project, made unionizing the professional field staff of most of the community-organizing groups in his region a top priority. When I asked why, the union responded, "So we can hire their organizers as our organizers, because they will be considered rank and file." Several of these former community organizers are now in top positions in the national union, having being elevated during the New Labor era.[47]

After 1995, following New Labor's ascent to positions of power in the national AFL-CIO, justified by the Alinsky assertion "Organizers take orders—leaders lead," professional staffing ballooned, with many new positions added—researchers, political campaigners, and communicators. People in these positions have at least as much real power as the organizers, if not more, further diminishing the importance and voice of the real "leaders."

New Labor Doubles Down on Mobilizing: Corporate Campaigns (and Collaboration) Replace Workers

Saul Alinsky is frequently credited with helping to develop the concept of what is now called the corporate campaign. (We will never know whether he would have accepted such a designation or not.) The uncredited authors of a 1993 paper discussing corporate campaigns, published in the *Labor Research Review*, note:

> In fact, for those of us in the 40-something bracket, the classic strategic labor campaign of our formative years was the United Farm Workers Grape Boycott of the 1960s ... it came from Saul Alinsky and his Chicago brand of community organizing.[48]

Ray Rogers, in an interview he posted on his website, Corporate Campaign, Inc., proclaims the JP Stevens fight from 1976 to 1980 the birth of corporate campaigns, and he, too, references Alinsky.[49] Julius Getman's book *Restoring the Power of Unions* quotes Rogers as saying, "No question Saul Alinsky played a role in my thinking and SDS...."[50] In conversation, Marshall Ganz,[51] who was deeply involved in the UFW and other boycotts, resoundingly rejected the idea that Alinsky was the inspiration for the grape boycott, giving credit instead to the Montgomery bus boycott. But there are many references in recent literature, including a full chapter in Bardacke's *Trampling Out the Vintage*,[52] to the link between Alinsky and the UFW. Add to this the fact that in 1947, Saul Alinsky hired an organizer named Fred Ross to build a new organization in California, the Community Service Organization (CSO); it was Ross who hired Cesar Chavez to be an organizer with the CSO. In the early 1960s, Chavez decided to start the UFW, and in a twist, he hired Ross as its organizing director. Ross was an active organizer before he met Alinsky, and he developed some traditions that were different from Alinsky's, most notably the house-meeting strategy. But Ross, Chavez, and Alinsky were *well within* what Doug McAdams calls ideologically coherent families.[53] There's no reason to doubt Ganz's account, but there's also no reason to deny that Alinsky's name is frequently linked to the UFW's grape boycott and to corporate campaigns. And the corporate campaign model directs and trains unions to see the employer from the employer's point of view rather than the worker's.

~~This is why workers, who were once central to labor actions, are now~~
peripheral. The corporate campaign, emulating Alinsky's tactical warfare, led by a small army of college-educated staff, has taken hold as the
dominant weapon against corporations. Peter Olney, longtime national
organizing director of the International Longshore and Warehouse Union
(ILWU) expresses how disproportionate the leverage concept has become:

> Just before the split at the AFL-CIO, the conversations [that New
> Labor was driving] were about how workers really got in the way
> of organizing. We [the national organizing directors] would actually
> sit in rooms, in annual meetings about the state of organizing, and
> the discussion would be that workers often got in the way of union
> growth deals.[54]

It would be difficult to find a clearer statement of how workers are
viewed by key staff and leaders in the New Labor model. There are
many flow charts and organograms in circulation that outline the corporate campaign's focus on the employer, including on the website of
Corporate Campaign, Inc. Figure 2.2, below, is a fair representation.

In this graphic,[55] the workers are "flat," that is, shown as one actor in
relationship to a dozen others; they are a single piece of the "available
leverage points" used to get the employer to agree to union demands.
This power analysis, widely accepted by New Labor, rationalizes the shift
in focus away from workers as the primary source of leverage against
employers to *all other actors as equally important sources of leverage*. In
New Labor's imagination, since workers represent only one of a dozen
possible leverage points, it makes sense to rely equally upon the other
eleven. Unfortunately, the workers' interests also get only a twelfth-part
consideration in whatever deal is made, and rarely, if ever, are the workers present at negotiations with employers or consulted about terms
before the deal is concluded.

Further, because there are so many other leverage points besides the
workers, the proportion of union staff devoted to workers has been
reduced, while the proportion that drives toward securing victory in
card-check and neutrality campaigns and election-procedure accords
has been dramatically increased.[56] Nelson Lichtenstein noted this in the
spring 2010 issue of *Dissent*, in an article titled "Why American Unions
Need Intellectuals":

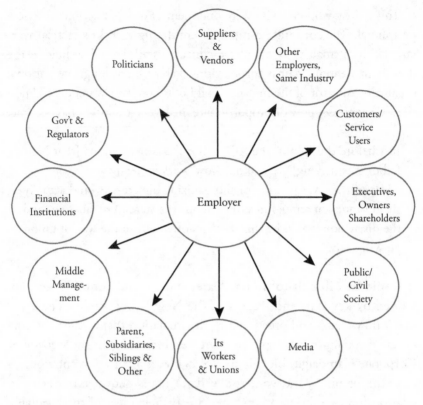

FIGURE 2.2 Typical Corporate Campaign Research Schematic
This Chart Produced by Andy Banks and Teresa Conrow, 2002

This new relationship between unions and intellectuals became apparent to me, as well as to columnist and Dissentnik Harold Meyerson, when we were invited to address the HERE research staff during separate weekend retreats in coastal California. I expected to talk to just a handful of number crunchers. During its heyday, when the UAW represented a million and a half workers, the research staff consisted of Nat Weinberg and three or four of his friends, old socialist comrades of the Reuther brothers. So I was surprised when more than seventy young and energetic researchers awaited my talk, brought together by a union with fewer than two hundred thousand members. There was even a former student of mine whose experience in Virginia's living wage campaign had turned her on to the labor movement. What could they possibly do to occupy their time and justify the expense of keeping all this ex-collegiate talent on the payroll?

Unfortunately, they had plenty of work. HERE's decision to create a cadre of corporate campaigners was based on the grimmest of circumstances. . . . The union used all those researchers to dream up new and creative ways to pressure hotels and casinos, first to get to a card-check certification and then to bargain for a satisfactory contract.

In this type of power analysis, now the dominant one, workers play the role of what is often called the authentic messenger. Some workers are needed—enough to be presented to the media and perhaps testify before legislative bodies—to dismiss or inoculate against an employer's claim that the fight is not about the workers but rather about the "union bosses." Workers are seen as a largely undifferentiated mass, and the chief criteria for engaging them is whether or not they initially favor a union. From among workers who do, staff select the most telegenic and likely to appeal to an elite audience such as the media, and use them as the public face of the campaign. They will then be called "leaders." Professional communicators write press and legislative statements for them and prepare them to present these well in public. In this model, union staff need not engage more than a minority of the workforce in the fight, since victory is pursued through one or more of the corporate campaign's other eleven points of leverage.

This sidelining of the majority of a workforce, engaging only those already predisposed to support the union—union *activists*—would be impossible in a CIO-style campaign, because the CIO approach is contingent on winning a majority of the workers in a workplace to the cause of the union: class struggle. Majorities are also practically necessary, because CIO-model unions run not symbolic but real strikes, in which a supermajority of workers participate.[57] And as in the case of 1199NE, the union expands its base by running and winning NLRB elections, a strategy that also requires a majority.

In the CIO approach to organizing a nonunion facility, beginning with the opening conversations among and with a newly formed organizing committee of identified organic leaders, one of the key subjects is the importance of being ready to strike to win the first contract. The conversation about strikes is directly linked to the ability of the workers to win *for themselves* the kinds of contract standards that are life-changing, such

TABLE 2.1 Two Models: Mobilizing vs. Organizing

Choice Point	New Labor/Mobilizing "For" = Low Participation	CIO/Organizing "By" = High Participation
Purpose of the Union	Material conditions only Pragmatic, business unionism	Material and nonmaterial conditions Belief system anchored in class struggle
Primary Leverage	No/few strikes, mostly "symbolic" ones No real strike fund	Production-disrupting, majority strikes Members build and maintain a strike fund
Goal (Power Analysis)	Power only calibrated to win growth deals Lower concession costs	Power is calibrated to raise quality-of-life standards at work and at home High concession costs
Worker Focus	Pro-union activists central Training of "authentic messengers" Workers "flat"; "Get Out the Vote" (GOTV) operation is staff-driven Minority of workers engaged	Organic worker leaders central Development of organic leaders into organizers Majority of workers engaged
Primary Actors	Union staff Consultants, including pollsters, political operatives, and legal and communications firms	Workers Organizers in a complementary role

Secondary Actors	Workers "The community," but disconnected from workers and reached via union staff or sub-contracted to other groups	Workers' own community, including faith leaders, and community organizations, activated and engaged via the workers in struggle; Researchers, lawyers, communicators
Types of Campaign	Corporate campaigns, driving a mostly national focus Amoral tactics: "anything to get the deal," including serious compromises Card check Election procedure agreements (EPAs) Bargain to organize (BTO)	NLRB elections, market-based, driving a mostly local & regional focus Principled tactics: ethical limits on tactics used *to get* a deal and, afterward, *in* the deal (if card check) Card check, EPAs, BTO
Collective Bargaining	Unimportant Strict limits on bargaining often tied to "agreement," few or no workers present Negotiators mostly lawyers or union representatives Narrow, material issues on the table Contract standards unimportant	Crucial Achieved through open, transparent bargaining, many workers present and involved Negotiators mostly organizers Contracts used as a tool for reaching self-governance; all issues on the table Contract standards crucial
Representation Model	Narrow, limited to contract terms Contract enforcement follows grievance and arbitration procedures (if allowed by accord; some prevent this)	Broad shop floor issue reach Direct action by workers Grievance and arbitration followed if direct action fails

as control of their hours and schedules, the right to a quick response to workplace health and safety issues, the right to increased staffing and decreased workload, and the right to meaningful paid sick leave and vacation time. Compared with these gains, a pay raise—too often the chief goal of the New Labor model—is a limited win.

In the cases discussed in this book, a set of common traits can be observed that correlate to the two distinct approaches—organizing and mobilizing. The campaigns that win workers the highest-impact success follow the classic CIO-era organizing model. The campaigns that gained lesser victories were fought using New Labor's mobilizing approach. Three core factors distinguish the two models: the purpose of the union, the power analysis defining the fight, and the union's governance method. The first, the purpose of the union, is the most important and frames the other two. Each of the three factors involves a set of strategic choices made by individual actors that determines which model they will adhere to. Table 2.1 above lays out and explains this process.

Very different purposes for forming a union produce very different approaches to power analysis and governance. If individual actors believe that the purpose of the union is to enable a majority of workers to engage in mass collective struggle—for the betterment of themselves, their families, and their class—then in the related choice point, the role of the workers in the union drive, workers will not be mere symbols of the struggle; they will be central actors in it. If, however, the purpose of the union is only to improve the material condition of workers by increasing the share of company profits they receive, the workers' role will be greatly diminished; they will function as symbolic actors, not central participants, much as they do in today's fast-food "wage" campaigns.

The conversation about gaining the strength needed to strike continues with governance, the third of the overall core factors that determine whether the approach is a low participation–mobilizing or high participation–organizing approach. In a union like 1199NE, governance methods are the same as unionization methods: high participation remains a constant goal. Bob Muehlenkamp, the organizing director of the old national 1199, explained this in a brief but brilliant speech, also published as an essay:

The theme here is organizing never stops. We can't afford to stop. That is why we must in our internal organizing work be as serious and as intense as we are during an NLRB organizing drive about building the union to fight the bosses.[58]

In 1199NE shops, the contract is not enforced primarily through the power of lawyers and arbitration, but on the shop floor, in direct actions led by organic worker-leaders, who ideally graduate from the organizing committee to the bargaining team to a delegate's or steward's post.

And to cement the idea of "three sides to two"—that is, that the union really *is* the workers and not a third party—a foundational principle of the union is that all workers are invited and encouraged to attend contract negotiations with employers. The collective bargaining table is the only place under U.S. law where workers *sit as legal equals* to their employer. As such, it's seen as crucial to the approach, as Bernie Minter notes in the unpublished manual he wrote for 1199:

> How to conduct negotiations becomes very important. If the real negotiations are going on behind the scenes, and the committee participation is a front, it will only further encourage three sides rather than two. Protecting the members from having to cope and deal with the problems the boss creates helps nobody. A maximum mobilization of the membership is our only real source of strength. To get this requires genuine participation. This in no way hampers the flexibility often needed for negotiations.

It's also a good test of whether or not a union is democratic. If the union is truly an organization of the workers, why wouldn't any worker be invited to at least observe his or her own contract negotiations? Three questions can determine whether or not the union is a third party in the renegotiation of a collective bargaining agreement: Does the process involve every worker? Are negotiations fully transparent? Can any worker attend?

In the New Labor mobilizing model, most collective bargaining is handled in top-down, staff-only negotiations with employers. If workers are present, there will typically be very few, say between five and ten, no matter how many thousands of workers are involved. Those chosen few are not expected, or even allowed, to speak during the negotiations. This process creates and solidifies the idea that the union is, in fact, a third party. In addition, most unions begin negotiations by signing a document with the employer that in fact they are not legally required to sign, known as the ground rules. These typically include a gag rule, stipulating that the already closed, already too small group of workers who sit, often with a hired lawyer, as representatives of the whole union are prohibited from discussing the details of the negotiations with any other workers throughout the entire negotiation process.

In negotiations for neutrality deals, whether those are for card-check or election-procedure agreements, it has become routine for union staff *alone* to prenegotiate certain conditions, including how "bargaining" will take place and sometimes even including actual contract terms. Alinsky was not known for his governance skills; he famously joked in the *Playboy* interview (and in documentaries) that none of his organizations were any good a few years after the initial campaign victory. New Labor has carried on this Alinskyist tradition too.

By contrast, as Chapter 3 illustrates, 1199 unions, even in negotiations with employers to win neutrality deals, bargain across the table, with no ground rules, and all workers are welcome to take part. Worker agency is a prerequisite for organizing and for building powerful structures.

Whole Worker Organizing: Restoring the CIO Approach for a New Economy

The working class does need more power to win. That is irrefutable. William Foster devotes an entire chapter of *Organizing Methods in the Steel Industry* to what he calls Special Organizational Work. The chapter is divided into four sections: "Unemployed—WPA"; "Fraternal Organizations"; "Churches"; and "Other Organizations." Under "Churches," Foster says, "In many instances, strongly favorable sentiment to the organization campaign will be found among the churches in the steel towns. This should be *carefully systematized* and utilized." Under "Fraternal Organizations": "There should be committees set up in the local organizations of these fraternal bodies in order to *systematically recruit their steel worker members* into the A.A. [Amalgamated Association of Iron, Steel, and Tin Workers]."[59] The CIO organizing

methods incorporated an appreciation of power inside and outside the
workplace. They used a *systematic* approach to recruiting support not
only from the shop floor but also from the broader community in which
the workers lived. Yet today, most good unions that *organize* inside the
shop *mobilize* outside it: deep inside, shallow outside. It's as if they can't
see the full extent of the battlefield or the vastness of their army.

A one-dimensional view of workers as workers rather than as whole
people limits good organizing and constrains good worker organizers
from more effectively building real power in and among the workers'
communities. Since the early 1970s—the period of focus for Skocpol's
Diminished Democracy, a period dominated by Alinsky's teachings—
community power, like workplace power, has decreased. Most groups
in the broader community now have little to no power. Yet even unions
that organize effectively at the local level have usually contracted their
"community support work" out to these relatively weak groups—
mobilizing rather than organizing. When the groups then fail to bring
serious power to back the workers in a tough private-sector fight, the
organizers who enlisted them conclude, incorrectly, "The community
stuff doesn't work." They miss that the problem with "the community stuff" is their own reliance on the weak approach of advocacy or
mobilizing, an approach they would never use for the fight inside the
workplace.

For the inside fight, these unions have a theory of power; they understand how to identify the most influential workers among the total
workforce; they pay attention to semantics; and they create structure
tests to assess precisely how much power they are building step by step.
Sadly, they check all this intelligence at the door when they step outside
the shop and shift their horizon line to the community, for which they
have no concomitant theory of power, no concomitant theory of leader
identification. If they see the community's potential contribution as
weak, it is because they don't apply the same standards to recruiting and
building it, with the workers themselves doing their own community
outreach among their own preexisting social networks. The very unions
that practice "two sides as two sides" inside the workplace practice "three
sides" out in the community. To restore worker power to 1930s levels
requires an organizing model inside and outside the shop, based on CIO
practice in the 1930s and 1940s but adapted to today's conditions.

CIO-model union organizers today frequently take the shortcut of engaging an already pro-union or progressive priest or minister, the equivalent of the staunchly pro-union worker activists inside the shop (who can't win), to stand with them at a press conference—a practice they know wouldn't be effective in the workplace. And just as the most enthusiastic worker activists are often not capable of leading their coworkers, so, too, the most committed activist religious leaders often can't lead *their* colleagues. To build power in the community, the good organizer must apply the same intelligence, skills, and techniques— beginning with painstakingly identifying organic community leaders— as he or she does to building power and organic leadership in the workplace. True organizing in the workplace plus true organizing in the community can and does win; organizing in the workplace plus mobilizing in the community does not.

To clarify the degree of power required, this book builds on a thesis developed by Joseph Luders in *The Civil Rights Movement and the Logic of Social Change*.[60] Luders's theory about costs structures related to protest outcomes is situated in the civil rights literature, not the labor literature, but interestingly, in order to construct his analysis about success in the civil rights movement he relies in part on *union* literature and the economic outcomes from strikes. This point, so salient, he makes not in his text but in his footnotes. The quote that opens this book is the 162nd footnote in Luders': "Curiously, the labor movement is conventionally ignored by scholars of social movements." Those words follow these:

> . . . I suggest that economic actors differ in their exposure to the disruption costs that movements generate in launching protest marches, sit-ins, boycotts, picketing, and so on. Some of these insights have been investigated by labor historians and economists seeking to explicate strike outcomes.[61]

Luders argues that the most successful organizing drives in the civil rights movement—a movement fighting for voting rights and individual civil liberties—were those that carried *high economic concession costs* for the racist regime, that is, those by which movement actors could inflict a high degree of economic pain. Luders created what he calls an economic opportunity structure to explain and predict outcomes of the power of people, that is, of agency. He argues that even though the movement's goals were civil and political rights, it took economic actors to move the entrenched political racists to shift their positions. His thesis is threefold:

> First, economic duress is a major proximate cause behind the decision of economic actors to make substantial concessions to movement demands; second, two general movement-imposed costs can be distinguished, and the uneven vulnerability among economic actors to these costs produces distinctive responses; and, third, economic sectors vary in their exposure to the costs movements generate.

The two movement-imposed costs are what he calls the concession cost, that is, how much it will cost a business to agree to the movement's demands, measured against the disruption cost, or the ability of the movement to create highly effective actions against the target.

Luders's concession and disruption costs are central to my overall analysis about power. I build on Luders's thesis, situated in the social movement theory literature, by unpacking it and showing that it can function as a tool for power analysis in workplace and nonworkplace settings. It makes sense that he drew on labor literature to arrive at his framework, because the same framework is routine in successful, high-stakes union negotiations. When I was a labor negotiator, we called Luders's concession costs the *cost of settlement*. And what he calls disruption costs we called the *ability to create a crisis* for the employer.[62] The two are always seen in relation to each other. I am using Luders's "concession costs" as a broader "power required" variable in this book's discussion of relative success (and relative defeat) in the new millennium. Success in any fight or any contestation waged by movement activists *across* sectors absolutely requires making an accurate assessment of Luders's concession costs *before* the fight begins. Movement actors can and must reasonably predict the concession costs in advance; otherwise, they enter the fight without knowing *which strategies to deploy*. As Luders says, different economic actors are unequally vulnerable and concession costs are not static—they are variable and contingent on the ability of actors to force disruption costs.

If, for example, the movement actors' demand is for single-payer health care, activists must understand what it will cost the health care industrial complex to concede that demand. Without that understanding they will not know the magnitude of the fight on their hands, and might adopt the wrong strategy, applying an insufficient mobilizing approach rather than an all-out organizing approach. An incorrect power analysis can lead people who want to end capitalism to think that small numbers of demonstrators occupying public spaces like parks and squares and tweeting about it will generate enough power to bring down Wall Street. Others might think that the good frames used for *or derived from* these occupations will marshal enough emotion to suddenly overwhelm lawmakers with the revelation that the system is unfair, and the lawmakers then will institute a set of fair regulations to govern corporate capital. Or if movement actors were to demand a more equitable funding of the public school system, but never grapple with what that would cost or where the money might come from, they might well apply strategies *insufficient to generate the disruptive power needed to force attention to their claim.*

Building on Luders's thesis about the relationship between disruption and concession costs in the civil rights movement,[63] I extend his logic into my overall argument about what kind of success is possible under the mobilizing approach versus what the organizing approach can achieve. In Table 2.2, Concession Costs = Power Required, I specify a set of conditions that will generate employer concession costs from low to high. The vertical axis is the cost of settlement—meaning, in real dollars, what the employer will have to pay out of the company's overall expense budget and profits to settle a contract with a given group of workers.[64] Importantly, this cost isn't just the absolute value of wages or benefits; it is the cost in relationship to the overall expense of running the business.

The horizontal axis is what I call ideological resistance. Drawing on my case analyses as well as my field experiences, I propose that there are two types of business leaders: the pragmatic, or practical, and the diabolically anti-union. There might be a partly pragmatic and partly diabolical resistance to unions where there are high-cost employees involved, but I have found no evidence of this. Chapter Three and some works in the literature do offer examples of large-scale employers straddling the two positions, but these are the employers with less at stake, dealing with lower-cost employees and facing lower-cost union demands. Such employers can be bought if the union pays or arranges to cover the concession cost, for example by securing higher government subsidies for the company, or lowering taxes for the employer (a typical strategy for New Labor era unions).

While ideological resistance is often correlated with, or assumed to be the cost of, doing business, it is not always so. In fact, the key to most high-impact, high-success union strategy for 100 years has been identifying the pragmatic-practical employer *within* the higher-cost workforce's field, because this is how unions with high-cost workers make significant breakthroughs. The entire concept of "pattern bargaining" is based on a union that follows the organizing model—such as the old United Auto Workers of the 1940s or today's 1199 New England. The workers must have the ability to strike, and they must have already "lined up the market," meaning strategically timed all their contracts in a given geography and/or industry to expire simultaneously. When these conditions are met, the union starts the bargaining process with the practical-pragmatic employer to "set the pattern high," assuring this employer that they have the power to win the same settlements with the next employer in the industry with whom they will sit across the table days later. Even in this scenario, striking— or the *credible threat* of a real strike based on recent real strikes—is *required to move employers at the high cost of settlement* level. Case studies in Chapter Three demonstrate that the reason 1199NE is able to win strong contracts—including defined-benefit pension plans enabling health service workers to retire when caring for patients has taken a physical toll, and even contracts winning neutrality deals for nonunion workers of the same employer (but without negative consequences for unorganized nursing home workers) is precisely because they run majority strikes often enough that the employers know their strike threat is real and credible.

Ideological resistance can also be relevant to the issue of shop floor rights versus material gains in contract settlements, since these carry different concession costs. Kimeldorf discusses the role this difference played in the strategies and outcomes of the West Coast and East Coast dockworkers. The West Coast workers, who wanted control of

TABLE 2.2 Power Required (Concession Costs)

		Concession Costs = Power Required to Win	
Cost of Settlement	High	Medium- to higher-wage workers and ***pragmatic, practical employer,*** willing to settle if union finds the money for costs, and union raises market to level; neutrality acceptable. Includes **some private-sector hospitals, some automakers, some Democratic mayors and governors, etc.**	Medium- to higher-wage workers and ***diabolically anti-union employer*** who hires top union-busting firms and under no circumstances stops fighting. Includes **most private-sector employers, many governors and elected officials in right-to-work and/or trifecta red states or regions.**
	Low	Low-wage workers, few to no demands, small workforce, no pensions, no real health care, union doing business for boss on subsidies and taxes, neutrality acceptable. Includes **janitors, fast food restaurants, car washes.**	Low-wage workers, small demands, such as a wage increase, regular hours or more hours, numbers of workers medium to large, employer hires union busters but **can be bought or will deal for right price.**
		Low	High
		Ideological Resistance	

production, had to strike to win. On the East Coast, because the union was only demanding more money, the boss was willing to settle without a strike. Some employers in the higher cost of settlement category might agree to increased wages and substantial benefits after a strike, but hold out on workers' rights over production decisions for ideological reasons, that is, belief in employer control of the shop floor.

In my own negotiations with hospital employers, there is evidence that the boss will even surrender on production issues when two conditions are present: the union can mount an effective strike, and the employer comes to understand that the workers might actually make better decisions than line managers, decisions that would positively impact the employer's bottom line. The Affordable Care Act offers a present-day example of this dynamic: New Medicaid and Medicare reimbursement rules tie higher reimbursement rates to better patient outcomes. Bedside nurses almost always have better ideas than management regarding what will heal the patient better and faster, so a pragmatic employer might even grant production decision-making to a high power–generating hospital workers' union.

On the other hand, janitors, for example, are low-wage workers and represent a tiny fraction of the overhead of the corporations whose buildings they clean. If the demand on the part of the union *is also low*, a mobilizing model with only a minority of workers and a handful of not very powerful community allies can "win." This is a typical Justice for Janitors campaign model, and too few people understand that it can't simply be exported to other sectors, especially not to higher-wage sectors where wage and benefit costs alone are literally 60 to 70 percent of the employer's overall expenses, for example teachers with public pensions or nursing home workers with classic defined-benefit pensions. In the mobilizing approach used in the far lower-cost Justice for Janitors model, essentially all the employer needs is the union's guarantee that it will negotiate a "trigger agreement," meaning that the small wage increase for the workers—fifty cents or one dollar per hour—won't take effect until the union succeeds at getting all cleaning contractors in the area to agree to the same terms. Such a settlement is very inexpensive to the corporation, taken as a ratio of cost to overall expenses (concession costs). It's considerably easier to shift even a conservative, anti-union corporate owner to the practical business decision to settle these low-cost workers' demands. I argue that little real power is built by this version of mobilizing. Although the union expands its membership and some janitors get a raise, it is not a life-altering change, and the process develops few real worker leaders, or none. Equally significant, such a fight rarely develops new organic community leaders—those involved are generally already involved, already pro-union priests and pro-union self-selecting activist types. They have not been recruited or trained systematically, and, so, this approach is not an organizing approach in the community, it is a mobilizing approach in and outside the workplace and isn't expanding the worker army.

With the exception of the Chicago Teachers Union, today even most organizing unions rarely systematize their brilliant approach with workers on the inside by using an equally brilliant approach to the workers' own organic community on the outside. The CTU learned from the British Columbia Federation of Teachers that to win a massive and illegal strike, it had to have staunch support—active support, tested and well prepared—from parents, students, and key community institutions. The Chicago teachers voted in a new leadership in 2010 that already met the first criteria for the organizing model; they believed the purpose of the union is to enable workers to radically change their lives in all aspects, that the union is a tool for class struggle. They knew that this condition could only be met if ordinary workers, not staff, were the primary agents of change. The teachers had built strong ties to key community- and neighborhood-based groups throughout Chicago. The leadership saw the relationship with parents, students, and the broader community as something more than an alliance: If they called a strike, parents would be key, either with decisive support, or potentially decisive hostility (in which case they'd be advancing the agenda of the mayor, not that of the teachers). They were right, and they had just enough of a direct rapport with parents directly through their students and indirectly through their many community allies to beat Mayor Rahm Emanuel and save their union by *rebuilding it through a strike*.

The most profound success of the Chicago teachers' strike was the building of powerful solidarities among teachers *and* between teachers and the whole of Chicago's working class. That their leader, Karen Lewis, an African-American high school teacher, would go on to poll consistently as the most popular person in the city to challenge the incumbent in the mayoral race would have been *utterly* unimaginable before the strike.

I propose a schematic different from the typical corporate-campaign example shown in Figure 2.2. Instead of making workers a one-twelfth peripheral consideration, as do some union strategists, in Figure 2.3 I put them at the very center of every campaign to challenge corporate power. If New Labor devoted the time and energy to understanding and engaging each and every relationship that workers organically possess in their community, rather than focusing on the boardroom

TABLE 2.3 Power Available (Disruption Costs)

		Disruption Costs = Power Group Can Generate	
Role of Workers Inside Workplace	**High = Organizing**	**Single-day or limited strike = High power** Majority worker support; organic leader model and either no secondary campaign (structurally powerful workers) or a comprehensive campaign with staff-led community-labor alliance on *workplace issues only.* **New Labor rarely uses this model; CIO-style unions use it often**	**Unlimited strike and high degree of community support = Maximum power** Majority worker support; organic leader model and workers leading community campaign on union-supported *non-workplace issues and workplace issues*; whole-worker organizing model. **CIO unions *can and do use* it, New Labor *could* choose to do so**
	Low = Mobilizing	**Symbolic strike=Low power** Minority of workers involved; activist model; corporate campaign (workers and their community are two of twelve units considered); **most commonly used by New Labor**	I have found no instances of this model. By definition, a majority of workers must be involved for community participation to also be high
		Low = Mobilizing	High = Organizing
		Role of Workers in Community	

of the employer, the kind and level of power of built would yield far greater success.

To blunt the employers' edge, rank-and-file workers need these strong ties; with them, they will be able to do the organizing and unionizing work themselves that today is mostly being done by paid staff—and do it far more effectively. When this model was followed in Chicago, the results were stunning.

Jake Rosenfeld, in his book *What Unions No Longer Do*,[65] published in 2014, argues that there are only two forces in U.S. society that have an equal (and high) rate of influence on how ordinary people vote: unions and religious institutions. He describes how well the right has applied this, making an intentional power move to build an evangelical base of voters, a base that grew steadily while leftists in good CIO-style organizing unions said, "I don't like religion, I do class, that's why I am not building relationships with *them*." That's an actual quote from this author's interview with an extremely successful organizer. Yet this is in direct contradiction to the belief system of good organizers, the kind that believe in worker agency. If a community or other tie matters to the workers, that should be enough for *good* union organizers. If faith matters to workers, I argue it has to matter to unions. Otherwise, the union remains a third party in the church—not of the membership, but apart from it. Reverend Nelson Johnson, a key player in a workers' victory discussed in Chapter Five, said that when union members who are also congregation members talk to faith leaders, and these engagements are personal conversations about the congregation member, labor wins many new and often powerful religious-leader converts to the cause of unions. This work is much more important than devoting time to tactical maneuvers with 1 percenter shareholders or businesses in the supply chain of a corporate target.

People in CIO-style labor unions who say they don't "do" religion should at least view working with religious leaders through their members as a viable defense tactic. As Rosenfeld points out, it is through religion that the right wing continues to expand into the labor base. As a result, this base has been voting against its own interests for Scott Walker and for Rick Snyder and for many other ultraconservative governors and state legislators, who cynically promise to cut taxes while gutting public pensions to "give the little people, the hardworking taxpayers in our state, a raise." The many statistics linking religion and voting are the most important numbers in Rosenfeld's book, because they don't tell us about the past, they tell us about the future. They hint loudly at the strategy described here; the effectiveness of that strategy is made very evident in the case studies described in this book.

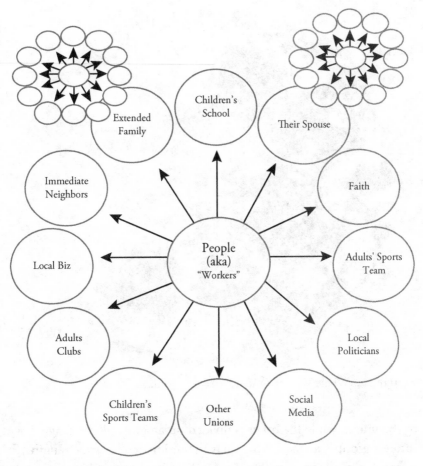

FIGURE 2.3 Whole Worker Charting: Social Networks

For the entire climate to change nationally as it changed in Chicago, good unions need to engage the broader community in the fight, so that the community, of which the workers are an organic part, transforms along with the workplace. That is an organizing model with a bottom-up strategy, capable of movement building rather than mere moment actualization. The large numbers of women in today's workforce—saddled with wage work and endless nonwage work—don't separate their lives in the way industrial-era, mostly male workers could, entering one life when they arrived at work and punched in, and another when they punched out. The pressing concerns that bear down on most workers today are not divided into two neat piles, only one of which need be of concern

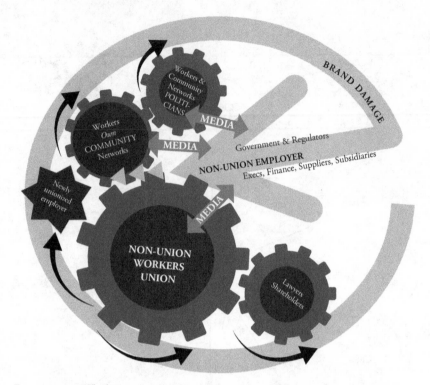

FIGURE 2.4 Whole Worker Comprehensive Organizing

to the union, while the other is divided up among a dozen single-issue interest groups, none of which has the union's collective strength. To effectively challenge neoliberal capitalism in the present moment, to successfully challenge the excessive corporate power that defines our era, unions must create a whole-worker organizing model that helps— rather than hinders—large numbers of Americans to see the connections between corporate domination of their work lives, their home lives, and their country's political structures. Figure 2.4 offers an illustration of how Chicago's teachers behaved after 2010, of how the workers at Smithfield won the third round of their fight, and what Connecticut looks like when the whole union brings the whole community into the fight.

3

Nursing Home Unions:
Class Snuggle vs. Class Struggle

The strike muscle is like any other muscle, you have to keep it in good shape or it will atrophy.
Jerry Brown, former president, Local Union District 1199 New England[1]

If workers are ready to go on strike in the United States, and we are ready to pay them to strike, it would be very costly. But paying workers in Indonesia or India or other places to go on strike against the same global employer isn't particularly expensive.
Andy Stern, former national president, SEIU[2]

THIS CHAPTER WILL ANALYZE TWO radically different approaches to forming and governing unions in *private-sector* nursing homes. To reflect how diverse big national unions can be, I have chosen two local unions that are part of the same national union, the Service Employees International Union (SEIU).

One model, represented by SEIU Local 775, exemplifies the strategies adopted by the national SEIU under Andrew Stern, president from 1996 through 2009. I argue that those strategies significantly diminish the role of workers in their own emancipation and have contributed to labor's ongoing decline.

The second model exemplifies the origins and traditions of another local—SEIU 1199 New England (1199NE), a union still steeped in the CIO-era influence of its founders—that has achieved the highest nursing-home standards in the nation. For the purposes of this chapter, I have turned to that particular local union and not to any other inside or outside SEIU, even those with "1199" in their official name.

I argue that 1199 New England's organizing model is similar today to what it was in 1968, when the New York–based national 1199 union began expanding into new regions across the U.S. (the national union no longer exists, sadly, as it merged mostly into SEIU in two waves, 1989 and 1998).

The workers in these two cases are similarly situated in the private sector, considered low-skilled and easy to replace, and are employed by some of the same national corporate owners in two blue states, Washington and Connecticut. (I agree with Barbara Ehrenreich that the term *low-skilled* is offensive and wrong: How could work with the sick and/or elderly be low-skilled?) In Washington, the union's strategy was to create a partnership with the employer that resulted in the unionizing of twenty-three nursing homes;[3] a small increase in pay; a constrained and limited set of worker protections; an absolute and "permanent" prohibition on the right to strike; and virtually no difference in benefits for union versus nonunion workers. In Connecticut, in a comparable period, the union conducted nearly sixty successful union elections, using militant trade-union methods, including strikes, and achieved strong contracts that substantially increased pay *and* benefits and greatly expanded on-the-job protections, resulting in the highest standards in the United States among nursing-home workers.

Each local union includes thousands of workers of other types— primarily from the public sector—and in the public sector *both* have achieved real material gains. But organizing and bargaining in the public sector is considerably easier than it is the private sector. And in the two states under discussion, public-sector unionization is a cruise ship vacation compared with the war-zone battleship tour of unionization in the private sector. Academics and movement strategists don't need books about how to win the easy fights, but rather books about how to win the difficult ones.

The different approach of each effort I describe was a far greater factor than any differences between the two states, and this accounts for the difference in outcomes. Because each local union in this chapter produces victories, in this chapter I focus on those outcomes that highlight the relative nature of victory and raise the question, What is built or developed from the two unions' "successes"? The evidence suggests that the strengths of the 1199NE model are capable of developing powerful member-led unions, the kind that can rebuild the labor movement in a hostile climate. The national union model, represented by the

Washington state local has succeeded better in the public sector than in the private because its model doesn't require class struggle, but rather an advocacy approach using behind-the-scenes political and financial transactions and deal making.

A union is never built by a single person. However, each of the local unions discussed in this chapter is associated with a union leader who is indelibly linked to the organization. And these two local union leaders personify two very different traditions in the labor movement past and present. Though his outward appearance is quite different, David Rolf, the president of Local 775, is in all other respects a clone of Andrew Stern, who ran SEIU as its president from 1996 to 2010. The speeches each make and quotes they gave in many published interviews would fool the best New Labor enthusiast in a blind test. Similarly, the founder and longtime president of District 1199 New England (1199NE), Jerry Brown, was long considered a close adherent of Leon Davis, former national president and founder of 1199 (when it was still a freestanding, national union). To understand the two locals today, it is important to understand more about Andy Stern and Leon Davis and the distinct traditions they represent, which still operate in local 775 and 1199NE.

Local 775, Origins and Approach to Private-Sector Nursing Homes

Andy Stern was the face of New Labor. He generated an endless stream of high-profile newspaper headlines, including a lengthy *New York Times* feature, "The New Boss"; a profile in *Fortune*, "The New Face of Labor (He's Like No Union Boss You've Ever Seen)"; a *Business Week* feature, "Can This Man Save Labor?"; and *The Wall Street Journal*'s "SEIU's Stern Tops White House Visitor List." Stern's rise to the leadership of the national SEIU began in 1972. In that year, he graduated from the University of Pennsylvania, where he initially studied business before switching majors, and got a job in the career he later chose, social work. As Stern recounts in a long interview, which he gave less than a year after his 2009 resignation, it all began this way:

> I had spent time trying to figure out how to change [American] foreign policy, or at least try to end the war in Vietnam. I had done

some work with welfare rights and other community organizations, and worker-client kind of relationships. So it was following more of a social activist trend. I don't come from a union family; unions were not discussed positively or negatively in my household. . . . When people would take over college administration buildings, I would supply the food. I was a much more practical, less ideological person.[4]

Stern suggested in this interview that the joke with which he opened many of his stump speeches over the years—that he went to a union meeting to get free pizza and wound up a steward—was slightly fictionalized version of the truth, played for a laugh. In fact, he said, "I was looking for a purpose, not pizza."[5] He would rise from steward in his union in Pennsylvania to local union president in 1977, and in 1983 to organizing director of the national union. For the next thirteen years, he functioned as a top confidant and lieutenant to then–SEIU president John Sweeney. And when Sweeney ran for president of the national AFL-CIO, leading the New Voices leadership ticket in 1995, Stern outmaneuvered the opposition to become president of SEIU. By defeating Sweeney's heir apparent, Stern demonstrated he was capable of overcoming the tradition of most unions, in which one president steps down and neatly hands the keys to his heir, Stern showed his ability to effectively manage convention politics, as in quadrennial union conventions. He'd had a chance to practice these convention tactics on the ground four years earlier, at SEIU's 1992 convention, where he first gained his reputation for running roughshod over the concept of union democracy. At the 1992 convention, Stern was a key national staffer, assigned as such to discipline and defeat a coalition of local union leaders who had arrived at the convention with demands for greater union democracy, including direct elections for national union officers, an end to dual payrolls (the national executive board members in SEIU received lavish pay as board members, and were also collecting full paychecks as union leaders in their own unions), and an even more basic demand: that they could bring these and other issues to the convention floor even though the executive board had earlier rejected them. Stern's top-down squelching of member debate and decision-making on that occasion would characterize his entire tenure at SEIU.[6]

Yet when Stern won the national presidency in 1996, most people inside the union were either excited or cautiously optimistic, because Stern was full of energy, was willing to review longstanding customs, and appeared open to real change. He was smart and charismatic, and he was raising all the important issues: We can't keep organizing just any worker who calls, it doesn't get us any power in any industry—how should we focus? We are shrinking faster in labor than we are growing—how can we recruit more members? The labor movement is in big trouble—what can we do to change the future? Many Stern critics can agree he was asking the right questions. But when he began to answer them, problems arose that went back to his 1992 actions: problems that, to borrow Skocpol's words, *diminished democracy* inside the union. At Stern's second convention as president, in 2000, the biggest push was to get a massive increase in per capita payments approved by the delegates. Per capita payments are the portion of union dues that local unions pay over to their national unions. Stern advanced one of the single biggest increases in per capita funds at that time that any labor leader could remember. The resolution won approval, and Stern essentially replicated the explosive growth in *nationally administered* resources and *national* staff that the UAW and others had achieved in the 1950s.

From the 2000 convention to 2012, the union's income from per capita payments almost tripled, from $101 million to just under $300 million.[7] Membership did increase in this period, by about 37 percent, but not enough to account for the huge increase in per capita revenue. Likewise, there were 416 union employees listed in the union's financial reports in 2000, and 863 in 2012. And these staff numbers do not include another significant layer of senior staff Stern brought on as full-time consultants, an addition that would increase the total substantially over 863. These consultants functioned as staff, but their salaries were often so large it was politically impossible to call them so; by calling them consultants, Stern could avoid reporting how many there were and how much they were paid, because consultants are handled differently in federal reporting. The union also began to spend lavishly on consultants who actually remained consultants, working out of their own firms, but in near total service to the union. There were and are hundreds of them.

SEIU had never previously been a big player in national politics, but the union's new resources allowed Stern to start lunching with governors and party leaders—and hand over million-dollar checks. With the shift to a massive national union staff and concurrent national budgets, Stern's profile and ambition began to grow.

The vast majority of these new funds were not spent on existing union members, but rather on launching a high-level and top-down program to "grow" the national membership. Servicing existing members—or paying them much attention of any kind—was not on the to-do list. Stern's top chief strategist for "growing" the membership was Tom Woodruff, one of his executive vice presidents, who also held the title of organizing director. Woodruff found dealing with existing members not only a distraction but also a drag on the strategy he and Stern were pushing with missionary zeal: working with corporations, so that those corporations would stop opposing unionization. Woodruff summed up a key aspect of this strategy: "The organizing model points us in the most narrow way . . . the better job you do with 15 percent of the market, the more the boss wants to wipe you out. We have to direct our energy outside."[8] That is, if SEIU insisted on being really good at representing the members when they had only a minority of employers in any particular industry, it would incentivize the employers against unions. The chief problem with their strategy is that most workers form unions precisely to get protections from their bad bosses. Stern and Woodruff weren't going to be sidetracked by this fact; instead, they focused on devising strategies, like the rest of the New Labor–era unions, to cut deals in corporate boardrooms, making actual workers' votes (and needs and opinions) less important to the "growth" process itself. The union leadership went from using CIO language about organizing to using Wall Street language about growth metrics. Semantics matter.

Two factors link Stern's ascent in SIEU to the evolution of the mobilizing model. First, he typifies the exact generation Skocpol analyzes in *Diminished Democracy*, the generation that emerged from college toward the end of the turbulent 1960s and that had been part of the New Left era:

Inspired by civil rights achievements, additional "rights" movements exploded in the sixties and seventies, promoting equality for women, recognition and dignity for homosexuals, the unionization of farm workers, and the mobilization of other nonwhite ethnic minorities.

Movements also arose to oppose U.S. involvement in the war in Vietnam, to champion a new environmentalism, and to further a variety of other public causes. At the forefront of these groundswells were younger Americans, especially from the growing ranks of college students and university graduates.[9]

Second, in his post-resignation interview, when Stern declared himself "less ideological and more practical," he was using the buzzwords of Saul Alinsky. The experience Stern refers to, his work with "welfare rights" and "community organizations," would have put him in direct contact with Alinsky's ideas, as these were the organizations that Alinsky and the Catholic Campaign for Human Development most deeply penetrated. And Stern at the time had switched from a major in business to the profession most influenced by Alinsky: social work. Seth Borgos, long associated with ACORN, progressive philanthropy (where he frequently collaborated with the Catholic Campaign for Human Development), and now the Center for Community Change, said in an interview:

> Alinsky's critique of the discipline [social work] was that it was insensible to power dynamics, dedicated to adjusting people to structural conditions rather than figuring out how to change the conditions. His obsession with power was a defining moment in the separation of community organizing from its social work origins, but the result is that Alinsky often seems far closer to Machiavelli than to a King, Reuther, or Marx.[10]

Stern himself was frequently accused of being hostile to the idea of democracy. So was Alinsky, and so is David Rolf.

Rolf's Rise as Stern's Protégé

David Rolf was and is a protégé of Andrew Stern; he may be the closest adherent to Sternism in the union today. He and Stern sound indistinguishable when they speak of their shared belief that unions are a twentieth-century concept (and you hardly ever hear either of them talk about actual workers). Harold Meyerson, writing in *The*

American Prospect in 2014,[11] links Stern and Rolf throughout his article:

> Rolf studied how Silicon Valley incubated start-ups. With Stern, he paid a call on former Intel CEO Andy Grove, that rare Silicon Valley guru who'd written critically about American business's abandonment of American workers. 'Grove told us he didn't know enough about the subject to offer specific advice,' Rolf says. 'But he did say to think about outcomes and treat everything else—laws, strategies, structures—as secondary. That made me understand the death of collective bargaining isn't something we should be sentimental about.

Later, in the same article, Meyerson reports of Rolf's critics, "Rolf and Stern's attraction to the culture of Silicon Valley, their belief that labor could profitably learn from the Valley's experience with start-ups, and their penchant for business school lingo have only further estranged their critics." *Profitably* may have been the perfect word choice, because both Stern and Rolf regularly use the term *growth* in place of the word *organizing*.

Between 1999 and 2000, the national SEIU hatched a plan to create what would become a breakthrough growth strategy, a plan to unionize public-sector homecare workers into a single union in the state of Washington. But to even attempt developing a statewide local, SEIU had to first create and pass a new state law, because in Washington, as in most of the nation in early 2001, homecare workers were treated as independent contractors. If successful, the creation of a *statewide homecare authority* would represent a *second* major breakthrough for SIEU in homecare worker unionization. The first breakthrough had been made in California, over an eleven-year period, 1987 to 1999. In 1992, after a five-year campaign to do it, the union passed a statewide law that gave *local authorities* at the county and municipal levels the right to form legal entities creating an employer of record, with which thousands of homecare employees could then negotiate over the terms and conditions of their work. This changed their employment status from that of independent contractors working for an individual to that of employees working for the local authorities who actually paid their salaries.[12]

As a result, between 1994 and 1997, 17,000 homecare workers had unionized in northern California as employees of three separate local authorities—Alameda, San Francisco, and Contra Costa counties, in that order.[13] Then, in 1999, SEIU succeeded in the largest single homecare victory: the unionization of 74,000 homecare workers in Los Angeles County. The person credited with the Los Angeles victory was David Rolf (though others previous to him actually did a lot of the leg work). The national SEIU decided it was too problematic to make him the top leader of that new Los Angeles local because, according to sources not willing to be officially cited by name, because he was a white man and the new union's workers were mostly African-American and Latino women. So it was partly to reward Rolf that SIEU's national president Andrew Stern suggested Rolf launch a new homecare effort in Washington state, where if he succeeded in forming a new union he could also get to become its head.

By November 6, 2001, in Washington, ballots were being counted on Initiative Measure 775, a referendum to create a *statewide* homecare authority.[14] The original plan was that after the ballot initiative passed, homecare workers would become members of Local 6, which began as a janitors' union and already included nonprofessional, private-sector health-care workers. Eventually, however, a new local union was created instead: Local 775, taking its name from the ballot initiative number.

What transpired between the original plan to put the newly unionized homecare workers into Local 6 and the formation of Local 775 is representative of how SEIU created, and destroyed, local unions during the Stern years. At the time the ballot initiative passed, there was no plan for the creation of yet another local in the state of Washington, which already had three SEIU locals: 1199NW (Northwest), which represented registered nurses in hospitals, clinics, and other health-care settings; 925, a local of mainly classified staff (so-called nonprofessionals) at the University of Washington, and later other types of workers; and Local 6, which began as a janitors' union and by 2001 also included non-nurse health-care staff.

When Rolf moved to Seattle to run the strategy for creating a statewide homecare authority, he became a staff member of Washington's SEIU Council—the lobbying arm SEIU establishes in each state that works across the local unions to coordinate politics and legislative affairs. Conveniently, shortly after Rolf's arrival in Washington, the longtime leader of Local 6, Marc Earls, announced his plan to retire, and Rolf quickly shifted to become a staff member at Local 6, which already had the appropriate jurisdiction for long-term care workers. Without wasting time, Rolf announced he was running for president and put together a slate: he invited a Local 6 indigenous leader, Sergio Salinas, to run with him, but in the number two spot, the position of secretary-treasurer. Salinas had been a union leader in his country of origin, El Salvador, where he was jailed for his union activism. He'd come to the United States as a refugee. He started working as a janitor in Seattle, became an organizer, and earned broad popular support among the rank-and-file base. Salinas was an organic leader.

One peculiarity of the SEIU model is that often the staff of a local union are also *members* of it, regardless of whether they come from the rank and file. Stern and Rolf's plan—that Rolf would become president of Local 6 when Marc Earls stepped down—became complicated when Salinas decided to rebel. It turned out that while Salinas had said yes to running with Rolf as his number two, Salinas had also quietly put together his own, alternative slate, on which he was running for president himself. He announced his candidacy when he filed his own election petition, complete with a full slate, on the final day on which candidates could gather signatures. In essence, he had outfoxed Stern and Rolf.

This created an urgent problem: the strong likelihood that the indigenous leadership slate would defeat Rolf's, successfully rebuffing what they perceived as something like a hostile corporate takeover. To fix it, Stern and the national legal team invoked the national union constitution. They called hearings and rearranged the structure of other locals in Washington, suddenly taking health-care jurisdiction away from Salinas and Local 6. (This rejiggering also moved jurisdiction for non-nurse hospital workers to the local that had historically consisted only of nurses, and mostly registered nurses, 1199NW.)[15] In the end, the long-term care jurisdiction for private-sector nursing home workers and public-sector homecare was consolidated into Local 775, in which Rolf didn't run the risk of losing an election. He was appointed the head of the union; a move that was possible because 775 was brand new.

To date, the Washington local has unionized twenty-three nursing homes under 775 contracts, and there has never been a strike run by any of them. Several nursing homes were given to Local 775 as part of the transfer and realignment of the nursing-home jurisdiction.

Despite being assigned private-sector nursing homes, Rolf kept his focus in the early years of 775 on the strategy with which he was familiar and successful: political deals and public-sector homecare workers. In keeping with his frequently expressed view that collective bargaining was dead and there was no need to be sentimental about it, he had no strategy for the rough-and-tumble world of private-sector organizing. As Steve Lopez discusses in *Reorganizing the Rust Belt*,[16] nursing-home operators had become first-rate union busters. Yet at the same time Lopez was writing this, the early 2000s, he was also describing in detail how another local SEIU union born from 1199, 1199P in Pennsylvania— along with a more militant western Pennsylvania union—was defeating the nursing-home operators in an all-out class struggle. Rolf didn't believe in class struggle, and so he didn't have a strategy for private-sector nursing homes—not until the national union devised a business plan to help the owners of the financially overleveraged nursing-home industry, that is.

The Stern-Rolf Growth Plan for Private-Sector Nursing Home Workers

The workers in the majority of 775's nursing homes were eventually unionized through a top-down and top-secret agreement as part of a national experiment: to partner with nursing-home employers in key states. In 2003, the national union staff, under Stern, decided to embark on an initiative with nursing-home operators aimed at increasing the pace of unionization in nursing homes. David Kieffer, the director of nursing-home operations for the national SEIU, began a series of discussions with CEOs of national nursing-home chains to explore whether the corporations were interested in the initiative.[17] No workers were invited to participate in any of these discussions, nor were they aware of the meetings.

Kieffer advanced the national union leaders' interest, which was growth via either card-check or an election-procedure agreement with employer neutrality. The employers wanted three things in return for SEIU's growth deals. First, the employers wanted the union to deliver increases in Medicaid spending at the state level, the largest source of their income (often called *rate reform* in policy circles). Second, they wanted tort reform, meaning less liability for nursing-home operators if, for example, accidents, deaths, or injuries occurred in their facilities. Finally, the employers wanted status quo management rights inside their nursing homes. In exchange, they would be willing to offer neutrality in unionization campaigns in some form and marginal improvements in the workers' pay, assuming the union could deliver the increases in Medicaid reimbursements to cover the cost. In addition, there was a caveat to the neutrality agreement: The employers would select which nursing homes could be unionized during the life of the accord. If workers at nursing homes not selected by the employer called 775 and wanted help forming a union, *the union would be bound to decline*. New Labor has a term for agreeing to create large geographic areas (an entire state, or perhaps a region of the U.S.) in which workers have no right to form a union, even if workers want one: *establishing no-fly zones*.

In Washington, Rolf embraced the deal immediately, although it would take another year or two before the final "Agreement to Advance the Future of Nursing Home Care in Washington" could be ironed out. Bigger states, such as California, were a priority for the employers (and therefore for Stern).[18] In 2005 the union and Rolf set to work implementing the agreement, and the deal was finalized between Local 775 and Washington state nursing-home employers in 2006.[19] That same year, not coincidentally, 775 lobbied hard for, and secured, sufficient increases in nursing-home funding to make it possible under the secret accord to unionize nursing homes, under what was called Phase I of the employer agreement. According to *The Seattle Times*, it was a $20 million transaction; the union had to secure $10 million in additional state Medicaid funding and then generate a federal match. "In exchange, SEIU local 775 got to organize 10 nursing homes, with management's blessing. The 750 new workers doubled the union's nursing-home membership."[20]

The same article states that in 2007, the union was to secure $120 million for an unnamed number of nursing homes, including funds that had nothing to do with patient care. "For instance, about a quarter of the new money in the alliance's proposal would reimburse for-profit nursing homes for the business and property taxes they pay." Paul Kumar, the former political and legislative director for SEIU's California health-care local under Sal Rosselli, and privy to the negotiations, explained the entire national accord as the "wounded-duck theory of organizing." By this he meant that the for-profit nursing-home industry had grossly overleveraged itself and that the national union's idea was to cut a deal to bail out a "scumbag" industry in exchange for dues payers.[21]

But the terms of the secret accord between the union and the employers placed severe limits on the rights of future union members. The union agreed to prohibit the workers from any form of negative messaging or negative campaigning during the life of the agreement. The grievance and arbitration clauses were constrained by language stating that any problem not brought to the grievance process within fifteen days would be null and void. Further, in some agreements, only suspension or termination could go to arbitration, which left management as final arbitrator on all other issues, just as in any nonunion nursing home. The no-strike clause in the contracts in these agreements excluded the two words modifying most no-strike clauses: *no lockout*. The final section of the 775 no-strike clause is highly unusual:

> Upon the termination of this Agreement, this Article 23 (No Strike Clause) shall remain in full force prohibiting workers from engaging in work stoppage over labor contract disputes and the parties shall engage in prompt, binding interest arbitration to resolve the dispute. The No Strike Clause shall survive the termination of this Agreement, and this language will automatically be included in all future contracts.[22]

Workers' wages in the Washington agreements are considerably lower than Seattle's newly won minimum wage of fifteen dollars an hour.[23] And the clauses on wages in the contracts are triggered up *or down* based on whether the union can deliver specified increases in Medicaid funding from the state. The final clause of a typical 775 nursing-home contract includes the following language:

> The Operator, Union, and/or Arbitrator shall not establish a collective bargaining relationship that would create an economic disadvantage

to Operator by requiring increases in worker pay, benefits, staffing levels and/or shift ratios that both were not adequately reimbursed by Medicaid revenues and prevented Operator's reasonable economic return on operation of the specific Operator-facility covered by this Agreement. *Operator will not be required to provide financial records to Union or arbitrators.* [Emphasis added]

Almost fifteen years after launching Washington's new long-term-care local, nursing-home workers have achieved little more than their non-union counterparts. The local union, however, gained several thousand dues payers.

1199 New England's Origins and Approach to Private-Sector Nursing Homes

Three widely respected books about the post-McCarthy labor movement, describing bottom-up grassroots organizing within unions—in which *dignity*, not wages, was the front-and-center issue, and the workers themselves were the primary lever of power—all focus in whole or in part on the same union: 1199. All three books celebrate the ingenuity of the working class and are routinely found on labor sociology syllabi: Rick Fantasia's *Cultures of Solidarity: Consciousness, Action, and Contemporary American Workers*,[24] Steven Lopez's *Reorganizing the Rust Belt: An Inside Study of the American Labor Movement*,[25] and Leon Fink and Brian Greenberg's *Upheaval in the Quiet Zone: A History of Hospital Workers' Union Local 1199*.[26] The very fact that 1199's story is ongoing, that this chapter picks up where these earlier authors left off, and that this union continues to enable workers to be the primary lever of power, including in militant actions and majority strikes, is evidence that Robert Michels was wrong: Oligarchy does *not* always win.

The two individuals chiefly responsible for creating 1199 were both members of the Communist Party: Leon Davis and Elliot Godoff. Both were Russian-born Jews, shipped as children to the United States to live with relatives in New York City, during the tumultuous period of the Russian Revolution. Both studied to be pharmacists. Davis dropped out of school to start working with the Trade Union Unity League, an arm of the Communist Party. Godoff completed school and began his career, but he, too, was quickly caught up in Communist Party activism. The two men separately navigated various attempts to form pharmacists' unions in New York City, bouncing and being bounced from one purge to the next. In 1957, they finally met.

Davis was already president of Local 1199 when he hired Godoff to do exactly what Godoff had long wanted to do: expand from organizing only pharmacists into general hospital organizing. William Z. Foster, head of the Communist Party during the years that Davis and Godoff were learning the organizer's craft, was churning out literature that called on followers to organize "every category of workers, not merely a thin stratum of skilled workers at the top."

Davis and Godoff were not enthusiastic writers of manuals. Davis was barely functional in written English, and in any case they believed that organizers, paid and volunteer, learn through struggle. But a long-time 1199 rank-and-file worker-leader, Bernie Minter, who organized Albert Einstein College of Medicine into the union in the late 1960s, did compile a fifty-one–page manual, typed up in the 1980s, that describes much of the same core technique as Foster's 1936 *Organizing Methods*, and includes some identical language.

Organizing Private-Sector Nursing Homes in 1199NE

When the exact arrangement that Local 775 had accepted for unionizing nursing-home workers was presented to the leaders at 1199 New England in 2004, "We told them to go fuck themselves," says current 1199NE president David Pickus, paraphrasing then president Jerry Brown. When I asked Brown in a recent interview what his objections were, he said, "The state is a huge player in nursing homes. It would be great if we could make demands for increased nursing-home funding with the industry, to cooperate with the employer—so long as we didn't have to give away the democratic principle of the workers running their own union. Our position was, we couldn't sell that which we didn't own, and we didn't own the workers' right to make their own decisions in the future. Kieffer and Rolf were selling something they didn't own. We refused to do that." Brown is now retired, but he was the longtime president of what used to be called District 1199 New England, a division of the old national union known as 1199. Brown apprenticed directly with and under Leon Davis, considered the founder of the national union.

Brown was a key leader of the contingent demanding greater union democracy at the national 1992 SEIU convention—the same convention where Stern earned his first anti-union democracy stripes. The reason for the 1992 convention's clash of ideology, or understanding of union purpose and function, went back to late 1989, when many of the local unions in the national 1199 voted to affiliate with SEIU, fulfilling (1199's leaders hoped) the vision of building a *national* health-care workers' union. Brown had attended many of the conventions held by 1199, the former national union, but SEIU was new to him, as it was to a slew of other leaders who had recently voted, local union by local union, to join up and affiliate with SEIU—bringing with them different ideas of the purpose of the union, the role of workers in their own liberation, and the level of democracy a union should have.

On March 20, 2001, while Rolf was planning the campaign to win the ballot initiative to create the homecare authority in Washington state, 1199NE was launching the largest nursing-home strike in U.S. history.[27] The workers, overwhelmingly women of color, voted to walk off the job even though they already had the highest wage and benefit standards of any nursing-home workers in the nation, including a substantial pension (a real one, not a 401(k)), an impressive self-funded health-care plan, a robust employer-paid training and upgrading fund, a two- or three-step grievance and arbitration procedure, and more workplace rights than almost any other nonmanagement employee in the United States enjoys today.[28] The strike was a strike for increased staffing. Jerry Brown said, "The strike muscle is like any other muscle, you have to keep it in good shape or it will atrophy."[29] Since the beginning of the new millennium, Connecticut's nursing-home workers have gone on strike every year except 2008 and 2011, for a cumulative total of more than 100 strikes. The action in 2001 was a large multiemployer strike; there have also been thirty-eight work stoppages since 2002. By constantly engaging in strikes and by practicing what is called open collective bargaining negotiations, 1199NE is constantly engaging in the hardest of structure tests—that is, tests that measure both union democracy and the participation levels of the rank and file.

In the same period—more than a decade—that Rolf has exercised jurisdiction over nursing homes in Washington, 1199NE in Connecticut has run almost sixty successful NLRB elections: some big, some small. Like the Washington union, Connecticut's leadership places a premium on securing multiemployer election procedure neutrality agreements. But unlike the Washington union's agreement, 1199NE's neutrality agreements are won by worker power and negotiated across the bargaining table, with workers in the room, in a collective-bargaining process transparent and open to all members of the union. Through this approach, they have been able to secure neutrality agreements such as one covering three unorganized nursing homes, an accord in which the workers surrendered nothing and are not bound by limitations in their contractual rights. In one such recent agreement, there are no binding contract provisions or clauses that are "automatically renewed," and the union is not required to lobby for money to pay the workers. The language, far from being secret, is actually printed in the contracts of the workers who fought to win them, and includes the following:

> The parties agree that the Employer will remain neutral and not conduct any campaign in any organizing drive conducted by New England Health Care Employees Union District 1199/SEIU in any unorganized center [for] long term care or assisted living owned or operated by the Employer or any of its related entities now or in the future in the State of Connecticut.

Fighting to expand their union to nonunion nursing homes, workers reached this agreement across the bargaining table in the final days of 2012. Under its terms, if the union can present union-authorization cards from 40 percent of workers from any of the three nonunion facilities, the employer must turn over a full employee list and release a letter to all employees declaring that during the union's campaign the employer will remain neutral and bargain in good faith. Any violation of the neutrality agreement goes to "expedited" arbitration, with the final decision resting with a preselected neutral arbitrator. The workers at the biggest nursing home covered by the agreement, St. Joseph's Manor, successfully won their election in July 2014. Despite the neutrality agreement, the organizers approached the campaign as seriously as they would have any organizing campaign—as *a struggle*. Rob Baril, the organizing director of the union and the lead on the campaign, explained the process:

> We blitzed the home's workers starting in February. We got a good idea of what the issues were and we began to do leader ID (identification) by work area. We talked about building to majority to fight

the boss, and filed for an election with 70 percent of the workers on a petition. We had volunteer member organizers with us in every committee meeting from the same employer. They would stand up and say, 'We won this for you, we expect you to now get strong, be prepared to fight and to strike because we expect you to win a common contract expiration with us, our standards are in jeopardy because you make $3 less than us and you don't have the pension, our future depends on you and you better be ready to stand up and fight.'[30]

When queried why this employer would give a neutrality agreement without asking the workers to surrender anything, David Pickus, the lead negotiator in the fight, explained,

We were negotiating with five other homes of theirs we already had under contract, so we said, 'If you don't give us these places, we are going to strike all five homes.' They knew from past experience we could cause a big problem because we had struck them successfully before.[31]

Even though the union had negotiated a neutrality agreement, Baril states, "the discussion with the workers was a traditional discussion. We didn't know if the employer would actually follow the neutrality agreement, so we talked about a fight, we talked about building a majority to be able to build to fight the boss, so that the workers understood that they would have to do the work to build the union."[32]

Using the word *strike* early in the organizing process, as Baril says they did above, is part of a strategy that pays very careful attention to semantics, which are absolutely key to successful organizing. As 1199's nursing-home case in this chapter shows, a key question in 1199 for generations has been "Are there two sides or three in a workplace fight?" Upon learning of a union drive, an employer will usually begin an anti-union campaign by declaring, "We don't need a third party in here"—by "third party" the boss means a union as a third party, with the boss being one party, and the workers being a second party. In good organizing and in the 1199NE approach, a key to victory (and to a successful strike vote and strike)—is that the workers see *themselves* as the union—in which case there are only two sides, a crushing answer to the employer's message.

Below are two examples from the opening of two separate new-millennium training workshops in a CIO-style organizing approach. Both are titled "Semantics," and they reveal the centrality of language and its meaning to the fight, and to the craft of organizing.[33]

Introduction

Everything an organizer does must have a purpose that is about moving the vision and the plan forward in their industry. Conversations are the primary vehicle for doing that.

EVERY CONVERSATION MUST INCLUDE THE FOLLOWING:

- Have a *purpose* = *70% DISCOVERY—worker speaks*
- *Shift* the worker = 30% UNION AS SOLUTION—organizer speaks
- Have an *ask*

Organizing conversations are **not about giving information**, giving updates, and leaving it up to the worker to decide what to do with that information. Good organizers **always have a conversation agenda**, which is about how to shift workers in their attitudes, beliefs, and commitment to both their coworkers and their campaign.

The second example is excerpted from a set of "semantics drills" developed by the local union with whom I worked in Nevada. We used fifteen examples of how to say something badly or the successful way; these were practiced for an hour daily in the organizing department:

Semantics Training

- Why do semantics matter (pose question to the group) 2-3 minute discussion
  - Point = People learn about their union from us and how we talk about it.
- General Principles
  - DO NOT 3rd Party the union
- Examples: (put up the bad statements on the flip chart and have people discuss why they are not good and then the group comes up with a better answer)

1. Bad = "Thank you" as a way to end a conversation
   a. Better = Good talking to you/See you later/Look forward to seeing you soon
2. Bad = We need you to get a schedule for us.
   a. Better = It's important that you and your co-workers know who works at the facility, what days and when, so that you can be effective and efficient in building your worksite structure.

The 1199 nursing home campaign in 2014 that Baril was describing above was a textbook implementation of the *Advice to Rookie Organizers* (see below), including postulate #20, "We lose when we don't put workers into struggle." Even with a neutrality agreement, the organizers understand that if the workers don't do the work of building their own union—including preparing for and having a fight—their leadership will not be tested or developed to the level of strength needed for a solid union, one where the rank-and-file workers themselves can govern the workplace after the election victory.

The list below represents the key postulates taken from the characteristic 1199 organizing "manual"—a handwritten, dated, single sheet of paper that hangs on the door or is pinned on the bulletin board of most 1199 organizers' offices. It is often covered with coffee stains and marking-pen notes and is called, simply, "Advice for Rookie Organizers."[34]

1. Get close to the workers, stay close to the workers.
2. Tell workers it's their union and then behave that way.
3. Don't do for workers what they can do.
4. The union is not a fee for service; it is the collective experience of workers in struggle.
5. The union's function is to assist workers in making a positive change in their lives.
6. Workers are made of clay, not glass.
7. Don't be afraid to ask workers to build their own union.
8. Don't be afraid to confront them when they don't.
9. Don't spend your time organizing workers who are already organizing themselves, go to the biggest worst.
10. The working class builds cells for its own defense, identify them and recruit their leaders.

11. Anger is there before you are—channel it, don't defuse it.
12. Channeled anger builds a fighting organization.
13. Workers know the risks, don't lie to them.
14. Every worker is showtime—communicate energy, excitement, urgency and confidence.
15. There is enough oppression in workers' lives not to be oppressed by organizers.
16. Organizers talk too much. Most of what you say is forgotten.
17. Communicate to workers that there is no salvation beyond their own power.
18. Workers united can beat the boss. You have to believe that and so do they.
19. Don't underestimate the workers.
20. We lose when we don't put workers into struggle.

Realistically, only one of these postulates—#14—could be practically adopted by an organization like Local 775, and even if 775 did adopt it, it would be applied to external political campaigns in the midst of a machine-like, staff-run 'Get Out the Vote' (GOTV) campaign moment. The team running 775 does heed *"Every worker is show time—communicate energy, excitement, urgency and confidence."* Professional staff make use of those qualities when driving hard to win a political race or ballot initiative.

But taken as a whole, these 1199 postulates can be seen as defining features that separate the organizing approach from the mobilizing approach. For example, most people who call themselves organizers in the New Labor model would probably adhere to the list below during the unionization phase, but abandon them soon after:

> [1] *Get close to the workers, stay close to the workers.*
> [11] *Anger is there before you are—channel it, don't defuse it.*
> [12] *Channeled anger builds a fighting organization.*
> [14] *Every worker is show time—communicate energy, excitement, urgency, and confidence.*

Each postulate expresses a core value and reflects 1199's roots in the CIO era. Starting with the first one, a close relationship with all or a majority of the workers can only be formed in a majority-worker approach

and by working through the organic leaders. And there are other postulates—the most important ones in terms of worker agency—that can
only manifest in a model that vests primary power in the workers themselves. Postulate #2, "Tell the workers it's their union, and behave that
way," is significantly worded: *behave*, not *act*—no pretense allowed. That's
a commandment, and in the 1199NE tradition, it's a commandment with
teeth: An organizer can be fired for *not* behaving that way. Similarly, postulates #17 ("Communicate to workers there is no salvation beyond their
own power") and #18 ("Workers united can beat the boss—you have to
believe that and so do they") conceive of workers as the primary leverage
in their own liberation. A professional organizing staffer trying to play
Bruce Lee—the lone hero outmaneuvering the boss in a series of high-
flying karate moves—cannot replace the workers' army when it comes
to the long march. Real organizers never underestimate the true fighting
value of workers; workers' struggle is key to the pedagogy.

With the kind of endless anti-union warfare waged by employers, for example—documented and superbly described by Kate
Bronfenbrenner—there's little question that workers need coaching
on the employer offensive that they will face and on how to stay ahead
of and beat the professional union busters. According to the 1199NE
method,[35] falling behind the employer's war is usually fatal; it is crucial
that workers know how to build a majority before the first skirmishes
begin, and especially before the union busters start threatening workers. For that, you need excellent teachers who can school workers on
the stages of an employer fight and coach them through what the workers' side must do before and during each stage of it. If the fight were
easy, if workers didn't need good coaches, the vast majority of them
would already be in unions, based on the consistently high number
of workers in the United States who say they want a union. It's when
the boss converts the workplace into a war zone and starts intimidat-
ing and firing people that this number drops, and drops considerably.
Good organizer-coaches are needed to circumvent that attrition by
preparing workers to face and fight the worst that management can do.

The Union Difference: What Being a Unionized Nursing Home Worker Means in Washington and in Connecticut

As shown in Table 3.1 below, a nursing-home worker in New England,
where the minimum wage is lower than Washington's, earns substantially

TABLE 3.1 Contract Comparison: CT vs WA

	Starting CNA Wages October, 2014	Access to Health care	The Right to Retire	Able to Stay Home if Sick	Contract allows for wage reductions when state funding declines?	Union commits to no strikes after contract ends.
1199NE						
A= 41% of all contracts	$14.39	Family coverage, employer contributes 23% of gross wages to union-run insurance plan (up to $8,750 per worker).	Employer contributes 8% of gross wages to union-run, defined-benefit fund.	Up to 12 paid sick days per year; can cash out unused days.	NO	NO
B=48% of all contracts	$13.88	Workers pay a fixed portion of his or her insurance premiums, from $18.26 for individual to $55.02 per week for family coverage as of 2011; maximum annual increase to workers is capped at 15%.	Employer contributes from 8% to 8.5% of gross wages to union-run, defined-benefit fund.	Up to 10 paid sick days per year; up to 8 accrued days can be cashed out per year.	NO	NO
C=11% of all contracts	$14.95	Before 2015, workers paid up to 15% of their premiums ($13.90–$35.36 weekly in 2011). After 2015, workers entered employer-run plan.	401(k) plan.	Up to 9 paid sick days per year, can be cashed out, with a 10% added premium, each December.	NO	NO

(continued)

TABLE 3.1 Continued

775-WA

	Starting CNA Wages October, 2014	Access to Health care	The Right to Retire	Able to Stay Home if Sick	Contract allows for wage reductions when state funding declines?	Union commits to no strikes after contract ends.
EmpRes Healthcare (covers six Washington state nursing homes)	$10.75–$12.00, depending on employer	No coverage for spouses or families. Workers pay 20% of premiums to company-run plan. Same plan is offered to nonunion employees.	401K plan (no employer match)	6 paid sick days per year, but must use vacation time for first three days of any illness.	YES	YES
Extendicare Homes (covers four homes)	$10.70–$11.10, depending on employer	No coverage for spouses or families. Workers pay 20% of premiums to company-run plan. Same plan is offered to nonunion employees.	401K plan (no employer match)	No provisions for paid sick time, must use vacation time.	NO	NO
Avamere (covers two homes)	$10.95	No family coverage; spousal coverage ended; current enrollees grandfathered. Workers pay 20% of premiums to company-run plan. Same as offered to nonunion employees.	401(k) plan, which employer "may match" up to $500	No provisions for paid sick time.	YES	YES

more pay on her first day of her first year, and in every year of her working life compared with her counterpart in Washington. Three-quarters of 1199NE-unionized nursing-home workers in New England have employer-paid health care for themselves and their families, with minimal copays and deductibles. A majority also enjoy a real, defined-benefits pension ("DB" pension). All employees have the right to take sick time that doesn't draw from their vacation time. Finally, they retain the right to strike at the end of each contract. Through sustained collective action, including the strike weapon, nursing-home workers in New England have transformed their workplaces and the quality of their lives.

In Washington state, where the minimum wage is higher,[36] negotiated contractual wages in most nursing homes are considerably lower than in nursing homes in New England. In addition, the contract at many of Washington's locals allows the employer to decrease negotiated wages if Washington decreases Medicaid reimbursement rates—guaranteeing operators a fixed percentage of revenues from the state while passing the risk of lower revenues on to the workers. Moreover, the majority of unionized nursing-home workers in Washington have health-care coverage for themselves *only*, not for their spouses or children. These "bargained-for" health-care plans, as explicitly stated in the 775 union contracts, are to be *identical to those of all nonunion workers* employed by the same owners. Nursing-home workers in Washington also have little opportunity to build retirement savings; they do not enjoy a pension or even an employer match on their 401(k). Their contracts specify that their retirement provisions, like their health-care plans, shall be "*identical with those of nonunion employees* working for the same operators."

In Washington, 775's alliance with the employers for a fair election process is controlled by the employers and contingent on the union's making significant financial and other regulatory gains for the employer in the legislature. It places severe limits on the collective bargaining and representation process; it was negotiated with no workers in the room; it was confidential; and it has yielded less than half as many nursing-home elections as the 1199NE has achieved in Connecticut. An article in *The Seattle Times*[37] quotes the Washington union's president, David Rolf, as saying, "Wouldn't it be something if people thought unions weren't about creating problems but they were actually about working with management to solve problems? Where is it written that the thing we need to do most is have fights?"

Washington's Approach: Three Sides as Three Sides;
Connecticut's Approach: From Three Sides to Two

In nursing homes in Washington State's local 775, the employer, the union, and the workers are three distinct entities. The union remains a third party, different from the workers, advancing its own interests through negotiations with the employer to meet the employer's primary objectives: increased revenue and status quo management rights. In turn, the union, as a freestanding entity, separate from the workers, meets its own primary objective: growth. The objectives of the third group, the workers, enjoy the least consideration in the negotiations. In this model, there are three sides to the bargain, but two sides have interests that lie closer together—the union and the employer. These two oppose the primary needs of the workers: stronger shop floor protections, a meaningful voice in shop rule making, and benefits that, even more than increased wages, might lift them out of poverty.

Jonathan Rosenblum is an experienced organizer who got his initial training in 1199NE's CIO-style nursing-home fights, and then moved to Washington, where he eventually joined and worked on the early stages of the Washington Nursing Home Alliance, but resigned from his position in the Washington local over his frustration with their program. He would later go on to be the campaign director of the nation's first successful $15-an-hour campaign, the SEA-TAC airport campaign that gave rise to the subsequent Seattle $15 campaign. He sums up his experience with the early implementation of the Washington Alliance as follows:

> We went to a nursing home where there was a joint labor-management presentation on the Alliance plan to lobby the [Oregon] legislature for more money (a related program that launched before Washington). Per the plan, there wasn't clarity in the presentations that if we were successful then the union would obtain card check recognition at certain facilities. I remember the workers being generally unresponsive to the presentation. Sort of apathetic, low energy. These were not like any other nursing home workers I'd ever seen. What was different? We weren't speaking to their issues. I remember talking to one worker on the side after the meeting. She was uninspired. The meeting didn't address her concerns. They were short-staffed, *today*. She

was poor and mistrustful of the boss. The idea of going to lobby for more money didn't meet her needs, which were both immediate and different. She saw the problem as the boss and we were not inviting her to build an organization that met her needs.[38]

In strong contrast to the Washington experience, 1199NE today continues to run a successful NLRB election program. The workers routinely strike and win contract standards better than those of any other nursing-home workers in the country; they have converted lousy jobs into fairly decent ones. The only reason that 1199NE was not placed in trusteeship in 2004—when, on being presented with the framework of the Nursing Home Industry Alliance, they told the national union, "Go fuck yourselves"—is that in 1989, when members of 1199 voted to join SIEU, they forced the national union to sign very strategic and legally airtight affiliation language. Under Sal Rosselli, California's health-care workers' local did not have such language when its own dispute with the national union began over this very issue, the Nursing Home Industry Alliance, and so Rosselli's local was placed in trusteeship. I asked Jerry Brown whether he thought his union would have been trusteed without the presence of legal affiliation and jurisdiction language that stipulated that the local union could not be placed in trusteeship without the consent of three-quarters of its own elected executive board. He said:

> If we didn't have strong affiliation language, we would already have been forced to merge with the New York mega local right now. The national union would have made deals with the nursing home bosses without us. They would have created a new local in Connecticut and taken our nursing home jurisdiction away. They'd rearrange everything, set up new locals, eliminate jurisdictions; they did whatever the fuck they wanted. And they were great about having votes, but they rigged every vote to work in their favor by who was allowed to vote. There's no way we would not have been trusteed.[39]

The 1199 tradition—the CIO tradition based on identifying *preexisting* worker-leaders and connecting with them and coaching and apprenticing them through the employer fights is a winning tradition. Organizers in 1199NE understand that real fights for life-changing gains can be won only by the workers themselves, led by organic worker-leaders. By contrast, the 775 tradition, based on the principles of Stern and Rolf, does not build worker agency, worker leadership, or worker strength. The union picks leaders based on community organizers' criteria: likability and charisma, commitment to the organization's agenda, attendance at meetings, and ability to speak with the media and chair meetings. In the 1199NE model, none of those factors matter. The only factor that *does* matter is that coworkers trust and respect the worker-leader, who might not—and often does not—display the public qualities sought in the 775 model.

According to Brendan Williams, the former head of the Washington Health Care Association (WHCA), the employers' lobbying group, "One challenge for the [775] union is [that] they could never get the big players on board, those guys with the most homes, the national players, who have so much money they can afford their ideology and ignore the union's partnership offers." Williams explained that even though he assured the nursing-home owners that David Rolf was a decent guy, he could not move them. He encouraged the owners to see "the entrepreneurial aspect to it, to set aside ideology and look at the union, they aren't being ideological, they don't want to bring about the destruction of capitalism, they want to grow just like you want to grow." But by 2007 it was apparent that the Washington union ceased "growing" in nursing homes because the state legislature had voted to lock in a multi-year reimbursement rate that was set to last until 2015. Because Rolf could no longer increase this rate for the owners, he couldn't draw down more election "victories."

Shallow Advocacy versus Deep Organizing

Local 775, operating on an advocacy model, cannot help private sector nursing-home workers form unions unless they are able to cut a deal with the employer of each home. Private-sector nursing homes are a hard test of social movement work; even Williams, the employer lobbyist, saw clearly that Rolf's local had no lever to move employers who didn't want to engage in the Alliance. In 1199NE, the union has a long track record of winning very hard fights. They've done it by teaching workers to build their own organizations: The workers are their own lever. Their union is built for a struggle. Rolf of 775 replaced class struggle with what the 1199NE team slyly calls class snuggle, not class struggle. David Pickus, 1199NE's current president, says:

> What I understand about our work is that people want a better life, and that's about the relationship between workers and the boss. When I started out, people were afraid to talk about this as an ideological issue. Understand me: This isn't some ultra-left issue, or hard left. This is what capitalism is, you work in it, you sell your labor, they don't need *you*, they need *all of you*. And if you accept that, you'd better get everyone together, because if you want a better life, you need a plan to do that. People have a tremendous respect for you when you talk to them about the truth and where their power comes from and what they will have to do if they want to win.[40]

In New England today, as everywhere, workers and their unions are having a harder and harder time—the ongoing decimation of labor unions across the country and the nearly complete acquiescence to the employer-alliance model have made the higher-participation model increasingly challenging. According to Pickus, "The employers have got it down now, it takes them about ten full days to replace the entire staff of a nursing home for good during a strike." And so 1199NE, like most unions in the service industries, will have to make a choice about which strategies to embrace to garner the additional power needed to con-tinue winning in today's conditions. Their parent union, SEIU, beats the drum loudly about deal-making strategies, and may yet drown out 1199's other clear, far better choice: adapting each postulate from their own *Advice to Rookie Organizers* to an approach that goes as deep into organizing their members' communities as it does into organizing their members in the workplace.

4

Chicago Teachers: Building a Resilient Union

We'd done our homework; we knew that the highest threshold of any bargaining unit that had ever voted one way or another on a collective bargaining agreement was 48.3 percent. The threshold we were arguing for was three-quarters. So in effect, they wouldn't have the right to strike even though the right was maintained. And so in the end game, the CTU leadership took the deal misunderstanding and probably not knowing the statistics about their voting history.[1]

Jonah Edelman, *cofounder, Stand for Children,*
"On Their Plan to Cripple the Chicago Teachers Union"

I thought to myself, they are fucked. When the legislature passed SB7 saying the teachers needed a 76 percent turnout for a strike authorization vote, I thought, They are so fucked.

Keith Kelleher, *president, SEIU Healthcare Illinois*

I remember waking up the first day of the strike and thinking what was all the deafening noise? It was incredible, and it was the sound of cars three blocks away honking and beeping in support of the teachers' picket line at my neighborhood school. We could suddenly visualize that this was our city, our streets; Chicago had never felt this way in my lifetime.

Amisha Patel, *parent and executive director, the Grassroots*
Collaborative, Chicago

ON SEPTEMBER 10, 2012, CHICAGO's teachers walked off the job in the largest strike of the new millennium. Against the backdrop of a well-funded effort at the national and local level to demonize teachers and their unions as authors of the ills of public education, the union enjoyed unprecedented backing from parents, students, and the broader Chicago community.[2] Over nine days, teachers and their supporters in the community trounced one of the best-known big-city mayors in the country, former White House chief of staff Rahm Emanuel. With the parents of more than 400,000 school-age kids scrambling to keep up with their own jobs and schedules and a mayor appealing to the parents in paid ads and press conferences to turn against the teachers, the teachers sustained majority support throughout the strike.[3] Not only that: Two years later, two major polls found that the head of the Chicago Teachers Union was significantly more popular than the mayor.[4]

U.S. unions have all but abandoned the strike,[5] so what explains the popularity of this strike with teachers, parents, and the broader public? Does the success of the teachers' strike during a period considered hostile to all workers, and brutal to teachers and public-service employees, suggest that other U.S. workers could effectively use the strike weapon? What lessons can be drawn from the example of the Chicago Teachers Union?

As Francis Fox Piven and Richard Cloward have found through their own analysis, the ability of workers to withdraw their cooperation from the interdependent relationships of power is, in part, contingent on workers understanding their contribution to the interdependent power equation. Teachers and educators (including paraprofessionals; clinicians, such as social workers and school nurses; and more), do understand their contribution to the education and development of today's K-12 children. I argue that teachers and all educators are what I call are mission-driven workers. Surely, they labor for a material reward that enables them and their families to pay the bills, but they also labor for something deeply purposeful; they are called to their labor. Enabling mission-driven workers to strike requires a very particular set of circumstances, a special context, because mission-driven workers understand that the withdrawal of their labor has an immediate, direct impact on those they are called to serve—in the case of teachers, America's children, teens, and young adults.

When Chicago's teachers and educators went on strike, the strike authorization vote was 23,780 in favor of a strike to 482 against, out of a total universe of 26,502 union members.[6] One of the most dominant themes arising in my interviews with rank-and-file teacher leaders was their disbelief, after twenty-five years of never having been on strike, that their students, and, their students' parents, would fervently lend them support. When Chicago's teachers struck, it was a total disruption of the "production process," not a merely symbolic action of the kind so common today. Sociologically speaking, the Chicago strike brought a major United States city to a grinding halt. The strike impacted over 400,000 people in 180,000 households, snarled traffic for days, and put an end to business-as-usual. It was a massive exercise of power.

The American Federation of Teachers was born in Chicago, in 1916, when four teachers' local unions in the region merged to form a national organization. Two decades later, in 1937, the Chicago Teachers Union (CTU) was founded; it would remain the largest and most influential local union in the AFT until the 1960s, when the New York City local eclipsed Chicago's in power and influence over national union policy.[7] Chicago was an early leader in teacher unionism, and a signature legacy of the CTU during its many decades of dominance in the national union was its defeat of the Communist Party in its own ranks and in those of the national union. Smashing the Communist influence was a CTU preoccupation during the 1940s up until the early 1960s. Charges, hearings, expulsions, and purges were common.[8]

By the late 1960s, the Communists were out of the union, and in Chicago other things were changing, too. The second Great Migration saw waves of African Americans moving to the city. The number of black teachers expanded along with the growth of Chicago's black population; these educators faced systemic racism inside the Chicago public schools (CPS), through certification and testing requirements designed to keep blacks on the rolls as substitutes but effectively barred from full-time teaching positions. In 1968, the momentum of the civil rights movement and the rise of black power emboldened black teachers to mount a wildcat strike that would shake up the union and bring together two key constituencies for the first time: African-American substitutes and Irish-American staff teachers, who aligned to form the United Progressive Caucus (UPC). The UPC controlled the CTU for decades, and during that era, Chicago's teachers went on strike nine times.[9]

The 2012 Chicago Teachers Union strike was the CTU's tenth since 1969, but its first in twenty-five years. During the administration of Harold Washington, the nation's first black big-city mayor, the union, which had helped to elect him in 1983, led four strikes, including its longest strike ever: twenty-five days[10] in 1987, just six months into Washington's second term. As George Schmidt, the union's unofficial historian, tells it:

> Harold Washington was the most anti-CTU mayor in Chicago history, if we measure his years by the number of strikes we were forced to go on. We first elected Harold against the white supremacists and racist attacks, but the minute he became mayor, he began establishing policies and appointing people who would force us to strike in defense of our rights.[11]

The teachers' union had endorsed Washington, but as is common today, this endorsement was not a guarantee of friendly labor relations between educators and his administration.

From Militant to Milquetoast

The twenty-five years between that marathon 1987 strike and the strike in 2012 saw the CTU's steady decline from a once mighty and militant union to a weak, concession-prone union-in-name-only. The CTU began surrendering its members' rights under a wave of anti–teachers' union legislation—much of it Chicago-specific rather than statewide— that presaged the national attack on teachers' unions, including the subsequent federal law called No Child Left Behind. Chicago's students and teachers became the guinea pigs for a relentless barrage of efforts to "reform" both education and unions—few of which changed actual outcomes in student achievement or teachers' morale.[12]

In 1988, on the heels of the 1987 strike, the first of a series of legislative changes was approved: the Chicago School Reform Law. The law was sold as a pro-community decentralization effort, and in many respects it was. It resulted in several key changes to longstanding policy: Local school councils (LSCs), consisting of one principal, six parents, two teachers, and two community members, were created and empowered to hire school principals and make budgetary decisions; principals no longer received tenure; and principals were empowered to hire and fire teachers. Hiring principals, hiring and firing teachers, and setting budgets had previously been centralized functions of the Board of Education. The law explicitly barred teachers from running for the council as either parents or community members, despite the vast number of teachers who were both. Part of what makes teachers and teachers' unions so interesting in the educational production process is that they are also parents, meaning community members with children of their own. The law, therefore, redefined them as "only" workers, denying them of their full status in society as worker, parent, community member, stripping them of parenthood, stripping them of neighborhood—a new constraint in the name of community control. Despite this, the LSCs were considered a radical approach to representative democracy in the schools.[13]

The slow downhill slide of the union's relevance became an avalanche after the death in 1994 of Jackie Vaughn, an African-American teacher, UPC leader, and CTU president. Tom Reece, who stepped into the presidency from his number-two spot in the hierarchy, was strike *and* conflict averse.[14] Reece's candidacy was opposed by a slate called the Caucus for a Democratic Union, or CDC. Most members of the CDC had also run in 1988, when they were called the Teachers Action Caucus Two (TAC2). Despite their lackluster leadership, their very presence as an internal opposition caucus is important: Robert Michels[15] suggests that the absence of internal parties, or caucuses, is a symptom of oligarchy. The opposing slate alleged the vote was rigged,[16] but it was really entrenchment and low voter turnout that helped the UPC incumbents retain their positions. Meanwhile, Reece got busy increasing pay and expanding the payroll, but not doing much else.

Chicago has never had an elected school board. The 1988 Reform Act merely created a nominating committee to guide mayoral appointments—though even guidance interfered with Mayor Daley's ability to control decision-making at CPS. Additionally, the grassroots reform groups who had been proponents of the 1988 Chicago School Reform Act concluded that the law hadn't led to greater parental involvement, one of their goals. Finally, a fiscal crisis—which some in the union allege was completely manufactured—prompted a new effort in the state legislature to "fix" Chicago's schools—one more sweeping and more explicitly aimed at weakening the union.

In 1995, the Amendatory Act, aimed at amending the Chicago School Reform Act, had its bull's-eye the teachers and their union.[17]

In the name of the alleged fiscal crisis, and with Illinois having trifecta Republican control—the governor and both legislative chambers belonged to the same conservative party—permitted privatization within the Chicago public school system for the first time, encouraging the private subcontracting of many functions, including the cafeterias, janitorial services, and more. This legislation laid the groundwork for a concept that was then brand-new: charter schools. (At the time, only two states had adopted charter schools: Minnesota, in 1991, and Texas, in 1995.)[18] Under the provisions of the Amendatory Act, teachers lost the right to collectively bargain over the length of their day, their schedules, and class size, conditions long considered central to the quality of their work and home life.

Daley reasserted total mayoral control by abolishing the nominations commission and shrinking the board of education, which the earlier law had expanded, changing its name from the Board of Education to the Reform Board of Trustees. The education model had shifted decidedly to a business model, one that entirely eliminated pedagogical experience from the requirements for the CPS's top staff positions. A chief executive officer (CEO) replaced the superintendent; similar title changes across the hierarchy changed the language of school governance to that of business administration. Finally, Mayor Daley took defensive action against a struggle that was unlikely to emerge in that era of the teachers' union: he had language added to the law that for the first time made strikes illegal. The actual wording banned strikes for eighteen months; that was the period of time the mayor thought he needed to implement the whole law, with its radical curtailment of teachers' rights.[19] Reece, the new union president, wasn't yet a well-known quantity—if he had been, Daley might have realized that the anti-strike provision was a waste of ink and political capital. Reece got busy claiming that the dissolving of PATCO—the Professional Air Traffic Controllers Organization—by President Reagan's order in 1981 meant that workers should never strike again.[20] Daley had given Reece an opportunity to galvanize teachers to fight for their right to strike, but instead Reece took this as political cover for his own anti-strike orientation.

Several years passed under the new pro-privatization, pro-charter, anti–teacher and teachers' union CPS administration before a serious challenge to the UPC and Reece emerged inside the union. In the 1998 union elections, a caucus calling itself the ProActive Caucus of Teachers, or, PACT, ran a slate, headed by Deborah Lynch, to take control of the CTU, winning the union's high school seats but failing to win the officerships and other executive board positions. Still, a challenge to the UPC had been launched. Meanwhile, the first Chicago public school CEO, Paul Vallas, made changes in the schools that were as swift as they were sweeping and took advantage of every corner of legislative permissibility, cutting deals with CTU leader Reece along the way.

The teachers were getting contracts with reasonable raises but not much else. This was in part, if not entirely, because the price of their raises was their acquiescence to the creation of charter schools in 1996; the mass privatization of many other city services that had previously provided non-teachers with decently paid union jobs; and Vallas's assumption and implementation of monarchical powers—to disband local school councils, fire principals, and fire teachers en masse in schools he deemed to be failing. Soon, he changed the justifying term "failing school" to "educational crisis school." By 1996, he'd changed that term to "on probation," adding to his powers the ability to fire a probationary school's entire staff. In 1996, he put 109 schools on probation, creating the first reserve pool of teachers in the district. Though initially these displaced teachers were paid for up to twenty months if they remained in the pool, the move marked the beginning of a challenge to teachers' seniority. Then Vallas changed the name of his game again, to "intervention," and the reserve pool grew as he claimed the power to selectively fire teachers inside a school and to cut the reserve-pool pay period from twenty months to ten.

Remarkably, this entire era is considered an era of labor peace with the Chicago Teachers Union.

In 2001, the year of No Child Left Behind, two changes set the stage for yet more upheaval: Mayor Daley grew disgruntled with Vallas, whose assumption of so much power publicly challenged his own. Daley preferred "his" people to genuflect, and Vallas had to go. Also that year, the PACT caucus finally succeeded in wresting the union from the control of the UPC. According to George Schmidt, "Reece was double-dipping by this point, because he was serving as president of the Illinois Federation of Teachers and the president of the CTU. It was to the point of corruption." In May of 2001, Debbie Lynch and the PACT slate swept all the top offices and executive board seats in CTU—the first time that UPC had been out of office since the late 1960s. The difference between the slate she ran in her failed bid in 1998 from her slate in 2001 was Howard Heath, a black teacher she picked as her number two. The addition of Heath, along with the mounting chaos being created by Vallas, all but assured PACT's election success. One month later, Mayor Daley would nominate Arne Duncan, Vallas's chief of staff, as the new CEO of the Chicago school system. Duncan was a Harvard grad who had been playing professional basketball in Australia for four years. His experience in the field of education was minimal: He'd once been the director of a small nonprofit that worked on educational achievement issues.[21]

Duncan's strategy with the union was to foster collaboration with Lynch, its new leader—courting her, calling her often, and immediately bringing her into his fold. By 2002, the Civic Committee of the Commercial Club of Chicago, the most powerful big-business group in the city, had released a report titled "Left Behind: Student Achievement in Chicago's Public Schools." The report identified "school unions" and "politics" as the *chief* factors in poor student performance in a school system where 85 percent of the students participated in the school lunch program[22] and only 9.4 percent were white. The report made two key recommendations: merit pay for teachers and the creation of 100 new charter schools in Chicago. CTU president Lynch's comment to the press was "Collaboration is best done with, not outside of, the CPS."[23] As a reward for the new union leader's commitment to collaboration, Duncan cut a deal to bargain over the school day, and almost immediately got Lynch to agree to *lengthen* it. By 2003, Duncan, like his predecessor CEO, had renamed the program by which the authority of the local schools council was to be undermined: "renaissance schools." "Renaissance" described a school that was closed and whose staff had been fired, that was then "reconstituted" in the same building, with selective firing or keeping of teachers—at Duncan's will. Lynch brought a contract before the teachers that fall that was initially voted down, overwhelmingly (more evidence that Michels's oligarchy did not exist in the CTU). When the members trounced her contract, she was sent back to the bargaining table to come up with more. The teachers narrowly approved her second settlement, a marginally better deal.

By the spring of 2004, teachers were fed up with Lynch's collaborationist model and decided that the change they had voted for had been ineffective. They handed the leadership back to a UPC slate, headed up this time by an African-American special-education teacher named Marilyn Stewart. Schmidt recalls that Stewart talked a good line and said the things teachers wanted to hear—an apparent improvement over the one-term PACT-Lynch experiment favoring collaboration over confrontation—but Stewart didn't *act* tough. Shortly after Stewart's election, in June of 2004, Duncan announced the Renaissance 2010 plan, whose centerpiece was lifted from the pages of the Commercial Club of Chicago's 2002 report and which called again for the creation of 100 new charter schools.[24] The plan would be paid for by the closure of twenty of the twenty-two schools on Chicago's south side. The union did not protest. In fact, Marilyn Stewart, its president, officially refused to even comment.[25]

Change Begins, From the Outside In

Two longtime community organizations in Chicago weren't waiting for the teachers' union to sort out their internal affairs or opinions at the end of a decade of massive disruptions in the lives of Chicago's students, parents, and teachers. The first to take action was the Chicago Coalition of the Homeless (CCH), which attempted to thwart the charter plan, or at least stall it, by filing suit in Circuit Court in September of 2004, generating headlines as they linked the effort to privatize schools to broader gentrification and the demolition of Chicago's public housing. Two months later, ACORN (under the leadership of Madeline Talbot, a longtime, successful community organizer in Chicago); Parents United for Responsible Education (PURE); and the Kenwood-Oakwood Community Organization (KOCO), a direct-action organization founded in 1965 by religious and community activists, started a fight-back, bringing hundreds of parents and students to a CPS board meeting to protest the plan to close all but two of their twenty-two neighborhood schools. KOCO's members, like ACORN's and CCH's, had already experienced displacement of one sort, as many of Chicago's public housing apartments were being torn down. At that November 2004 meeting, after being completely ignored by the CPS board, KOCO's chair, Jitu Brown, announced loudly to the packed room and to the board, "Oh, now it's on! We were trying to be civil, but now it's going to be civil disobedience!"[26] The resistance campaign led by Chicago's community-based organizations succeeded in getting the plan moderated, shrinking the initial closings from twenty to twelve, but it was clear more battles were coming. By 2006 Brown, already seen as a leader in the struggle against the school closings, went from chairing the board of KOCO to being a full-time, paid education organizer.

Ten schools on Chicago's South Side had been saved, but by the 2005-2006 school year, more than a dozen had been closed, along with another two dozen throughout the city. Each closing provoked site-based protests, but there was no effective citywide challenge. Chicago's long history of Alinskyism had created strong neighborhood-based organizations, but these had a political and policy vision that stopped at their tightly drawn and highly turf-conscious neighborhood boundaries.[27] The organization that was citywide and crossed all neighborhoods, the teachers' union, was barely audible in them. But among the ranks of the teachers being impacted by school closings, a new generation of activists had arisen who were individually aligning with various neighborhood groups across the city. When Englewood High School and De La Cruz Middle School were threatened with closure, and Senn High School with a complete revision of its mission, individual actors among the teachers—Jackson Potter at Englewood with his friend Al Ramirez; Norine Gutekanst at nearby Whittier; Kristine Mayle at De La Cruz; and eventually Jesse Sharkey at Senn, who was mobilizing a Save Our Senn (charter threat) effort—began to coalesce into a broader teacher's movement. Potter was on the board of directors of another of Chicago's important neighborhood groups, the Pilsen Alliance, and Gutenkanst was an active member of it. The Pilsen Alliance was based in and identified with the Mexican neighborhood, just as KOCO had a black base and leadership. Ramirez and Potter devoted 2007 to making a handheld amateur video about the school closings, going around the city interviewing teachers, parents, and kids. By late 2007, these teachers had formed a citywide study group on the closings, inviting other teachers to join through informal activist networks.[28]

The Caucus of Rank-and-File Educators (CORE) Forms

Evolving out of the study group, whose first collective read in 2008 was Naomi Klein's *The Shock Doctrine*,[29] two more important groups were developed: the Caucus of Rank-and-File Educators (CORE), inside of the Chicago Teachers Union, and soon after that the Grassroots Education Movement (GEM), a CORE-inspired coalition created with community-based organizations to fight school closings, gentrification, and racism.[30] *The Shock Doctrine* had just been published, and Klein was shaping an analysis about mass school closures, capitalism, and racism. According to Kristine Mayle, a middle and elementary school special education teacher and currently the CTU's elected financial secretary, "We were going to neighborhood groups and saying, Look, we are talking about little human beings, about kids; we are teachers and you are our natural allies; we can't do this alone."[31] With each school closing, the ranks of teachers frustrated and angered were growing. By the time CORE was formalized in early 2008, many more were actively participating in the study groups, including Jesse Sharkey and Karen Lewis.

At this point, rather than fighting school closings or challenging the CPS, Marilyn Stewart, the union president, was focused on a single goal: taking total control of the union (just as 1199's Bernie Minter describes it, in Chapter Three). Stewart had been reelected in the spring of 2007 partly because of her tough talk in public, but mainly because of the absence of any coherent challenge. PACT, the one caucus that had defeated the UPC in 2001, was engaging with Stewart in internal union politics. Petty cronyism and self-absorption ruled the day. Stewart had already brought her vice president up on internal charges and removed him from office, and now she was bent on removing other potential future challengers to her seemingly entrenched position.

According to Jackson Potter, CORE's initial mission was "to do what the union should have been doing all along, acting like a union in the face of massive upheaval."[32] The CORE study group was now being augmented by other activities. Potter's school had been converted to a charter (half became a charter and half a charter-like "team" school); taking advantage of the ten months of paid "reserve" time provided by CPS, he decided to study history at the graduate level.[33] The forced break led to many other important developments for Potter. He began to work with a group called the Collaborative for Equity and Justice in Education, where he met Pauline Lipman, an education professor. It was Lipman who encouraged Potter to attend an important annual gathering of teachers from Mexico, the United States, and Canada called the Trinational Conference. That single conference introduced Potter to the *concept* of progressive teachers forming caucuses. He met Alex Caputo Pearl, a progressive teacher caucus leader from Los Angeles who would himself later go on to win the presidency of the United Teachers of Los Angeles, UTLA. And, he heard a talk by and met with Jinny Sims, the leader of the British Columbia Teachers' Federation (BCTF). The BCTF was fresh off an illegal strike in 2005 widely considered to have been won *primarily* because the teachers had spent several years developing mass support among community-based groups before they walked off the job. The strike had been mounted in defiance of a recently passed provincial law that defined teachers as "essential employees," eliminating their previous legal right to strike.

Substance News, the longtime newspaper of CTU's internal opposition—another challenge to Michels's iron law of oligarchy—was also publishing stories about the British Columbia strike. The paper had long publicized not only opposition activity in the CTU but also militant teacher activism from around the world. Potter raised the idea to CORE that they should pool their money and buy a plane ticket to bring the head of the British Columbia Teachers' Federation to Chicago for a day to educate CORE members about how the Canadian union had won their strike, beat back court injunctions, and more throughout the 2005-2006 school year.[34]

The CTU had officially disbanded their committee on school closings in 2007, clearing the path for CORE's ascent as the place to go for those concerned about Arne Duncan's plans. The teachers, many of whom had already engaged with local neighborhood groups in site-based fight-backs, saw CORE and GEM as an extension of their foundational understanding of "what a union should be doing." According to Mayle, "We shared an underpinning, a common analysis about class, race, and public education, and that common analysis lets us work it out when things get tricky." GEM and CORE formed, grew, and developed simultaneously while the official union bureaucracy was unraveling. There was no initial plan to contest for union office. The new caucus was rather seen as an actor that could make the existing union leadership do what it was, in these activists' minds, "supposed to do." In the fall of 2009, CORE teacher activists and GEM nonteacher activists attended every single school board meeting, each time amassing more recruits to their cause and challenging the school board. Meanwhile, the union bureaucrats were busy bringing each other up on charges.

GEM decided to organize a public community forum on school closings, to be held at the end of 2009, when the CPS planned to release the school closings list. CORE activists would use the forum to deepen their fight against school closings and to strengthen and expand their ties with the broader Chicago community, and also to recruit and expand their base among the teachers. Chicago's community groups had long lived in the legacy of Saul Alinsky and provincial neighborhood isms, so GEM and CORE taking this effort citywide signaled a change in the Chicago norm. Their momentum was building nicely, but one external factor wasn't cooperating—Chicago's weather. On the day of the forum, a blizzard struck. There was a debate about whether or not to cancel the event, but its organizers decided to move forward. More than 500 people turned up, despite the storm. Several weeks later, the Chicago School Board trimmed back the planned closure list. Expectations were suddenly raised: Teacher-and-community coalitions could beat city hall.

That spring, CORE members held a convention and began to solidify their structure. They set affordable dues: $35 per person per year. They ratified a mission statement. And they continued attending CPS board meetings. They began discussing the possibility of filing a discrimination charge against the CPS administration based on the fact that most of the teachers being impacted by the closures were black. The number of African-American teachers was declining rapidly as the turnaround schools hired Teach for America recruits and younger teachers, changing the demographics of Chicago's teaching force, bringing down the pay scale, and, perhaps most importantly, rupturing the tradition of teachers living in the neighborhoods where they taught. By June, CORE had decided to file a formal complaint with the Equal Employment Education Commission (EEOC). Though this challenge would later be dismissed, the organizing and media around the EEOC complaint increased CORE's base among black teachers and helped CORE build a relationship with the union's black caucus. The EEOC complaint and several other school and teaching profession–specific fights that CORE led during the summer of 2009 were part of CORE's ever-expanding reach into all aspects of the union, pushing beyond the school-closings battles.

In October of 2009, a union-wide election was held for the union's pension board trustee seats. Potter and a few others decided to use the campaign as a test of CORE's ability to mobilize enough of a citywide school-based teacher vote to win an internal union election. This was a smart low-risk structure test. The CPS's CEO, at that time had previously headed the Chicago Transit Authority—never before considered a stepping-stone to heading the schools—and had taken a wrecking ball to the transit workers' pension, so having smart and fighting teacher leadership on the pension board mattered in and of itself and could be used as a test of CORE's mobilization capacity. When the CORE candidates narrowly won both trustee seats in a tight race, caucus members began to have a very different discussion about how to challenge the Arne Duncan Renaissance 2010 plan: This time, they would first challenge their inept union leaders for top offices.

The Slate of Candidates Emerges

In August of 2009, CORE held a nominations convention so that caucus members could decide who among them would run for the union's higher offices. According to George Schmidt, there was internal competition for each position, and members were allowed to listen to candidate speeches and ask questions of the potential candidates. Schmidt recalled, "My only question that day in 2009 was to ask how are you going to prepare the union for the strike we are going to have to have in 2012 to get a contract?" Then CORE members chose their slate: Karen Lewis for president, Jackson Potter for vice president, Michael Brunson for recording secretary, and Kristine Mayle for financial secretary. In response to a credentials challenge from the old guard of the union, Potter had to withdraw: The union's constitution states that no member can run for elected office who has not been a continuous dues-paying member in the three prior years; Potter had a lapse in his dues from the year he'd taken off after his school had been closed. Though some in the union and active in the caucus, like Schmidt, thought Potter should challenge the ruling, Potter decided not to give the old guard any potential negative talking points about the CORE slate in general. And although he was off the slate officially, he never faltered in his role as a key strategist and chief influence in the union. He was replaced on the ticket by Jesse Sharkey.

The architects of the slate paid close attention to developing a team that would represent the broad diversity of the union, in grade level and type of teacher; race and ethnicity; age and experience; untenured and long-tenured status. The top of the ticket, Karen Lewis, was a woman whose black father and white Jewish mother had both been public school teachers in Chicago (as is her husband). Lewis herself had been the only black woman in her 1974 graduating class at Dartmouth. She had taught chemistry in Chicago high schools for twenty-two years.[35] She had been a member of the union's black caucus prior to getting involved with CORE, but she had no deep experience with the union. With the exception of Chicago's mayor, Rahm Emanuel, it's hard to find anyone in Chicago who doesn't have great things to say about Lewis. Schmidt, CTU's informal historian and a longtime leader who himself once ran for president in an unsuccessful bid to rid the union of the UPC, describes the Lewis appeal:

> Karen is half Jewish and half Black. She speaks better Yiddish than Rahm. She's a Nationally Board Certified Teacher. She's so intense and so thorough; the level of her intelligence is incredibly high. When Jean Claude Brizard became the CEO of the CPS, there was this policy forum organized by the Chicago *Tribune,* with one of those backdrop banners 'Chicago Issues Week.' I was taking pictures for the magazine, and Brizard, who speaks with a Haitian accent, comes on stage and Karen rattles off some long greeting in French to him, and he just stares at her, turns out she knows more French than him. It's just Karen stuff, so complex and so intelligent.[36]

To become a National Board Certified Teacher, the highest possible certification available in K-12, teachers subject themselves to a rigorous process of exams over several years with an intense focus on best practice and pedagogy. Lewis is the only teacher union leader anywhere in the United States with this distinction.[37]

Jesse Sharkey, the new vice presidential candidate, like Lewis an early member of CORE, was also raised by a teacher, his single mother. Also like Lewis, Sharkey had been a top student and graduated from an Ivy League school, Brown University. Unlike Lewis, Sharkey is white and grew up in one of the whitest regions of the U.S., rural Maine, where his mother was a back-to-the-lander. Sharkey was in high school during one of the most contentious strikes in the latter half of the last century, at the Jay Maine Paper Mill. The strike made a big impression on him; he later wrote his undergraduate thesis on it. He was a student activist in college and upon graduation went to work as a union organizer. His first move was to attend the AFL-CIO's Organizing Institute (OI), a program that taught the fundamentals of how to win a National Labor Relations Board (NLRB) election. Successful graduates of this three-day program are placed with a union to apprentice their skills, and Sharkey was placed with the United Steelworkers of America. He worked as a young organizer on the ALCOA campaign, one of the larger union victories of that era. The mentor who led his apprenticeship was Bob Callahan, who would go on to become the national organizing director at SEIU under Andy Stern.

Sharkey tired of the hot-shop model at the Steelworkers, which followed easy but often pyrrhic wins rather than strategic and power-building organizing. In 1993 he quit and moved back to Providence, Rhode Island, where he had lived as a student at Brown. He was then hired as an organizer and went to work for the local union, 1199 New England, where he was mentored by a long-respected organizer named Stan Israel. Eventually, he returned to school to get his teaching degree, and soon after moved to Chicago, where his fiancée had been offered a job at *In These Times*, a progressive magazine. He began teaching high school social studies in the fall of 1998. In March of that year he was stricken by a massive brain hemorrhage and hospitalized in critical condition. Sharkey says that this experience changed his view of life and of the things that matter. After returning to work, he became a union delegate, but despite this title, he was not particularly active until 2005, when his high school, Senn, was targeted to become a charter school.[38]

Jackson Potter, the strategist whom Sharkey replaced as vice presidential nominee, was raised by activist parents. When Potter was growing up, they were considered left-wing and identified themselves as Reds. His father is a labor lawyer, his stepfather worked with the Teamsters for a Democratic Union (TDU), and his mother is a lawyer who has long worked on progressive causes.[39] Their son went through K-12 in the Chicago public schools, and while in high school helped lead a school walkout for more equitable school funding. He attended the University of Illinois at Urbana, and then transferred to the University of Illinois in Chicago; he did his graduate program at the University of Chicago. He was a student activist all through college, working with Students Against Sweatshops and on anti–Iraq War efforts, campaigning against the UI mascot (an Indian chief), and working for increased minority student recruitment. When he returned to the Chicago area to finish his university years, he got involved in anti-gentrification campaigns around campus, working with the Pilsen Alliance, the neighborhood group that later allied with the teachers against school closings. Potter became a history teacher and, like Sharkey, a union delegate turned serious union activist when his school (Englewood High) was threatened with a closure. Arne Duncan won that campaign, leaving Potter and many others out of a job. Potter and a colleague, Al Ramirez, are widely credited with being the cofounders of CORE, and Potter is often referred to as the group's lead strategist. ACORN's Madeline Talbot has often called him "brilliant"—a word she uses sparingly.[40]

Michael Brunson and Kristine Mayle had much less union contact or experience than the others before they were elected to top union office. Brunson, who is black, was an elementary school teacher on Chicago's South Side and was better known for his activism on and with the Local Schools Councils (LSCs). His first union involvement, like Mayle's, was with CORE in 2008. Though he had been teaching for many years, his education activism had been with community groups, not with his teachers' union. Brunson met the CORE activists because the community organization he was working with at the time began getting involved in GEM. Mayle is white and is the youngest of the Lewis team. She had barely begun her teaching career when her school, De La Cruz, was targeted for closure. She hadn't had long experience suffering under a bad union, and she emerged as a top leader in CORE, known for her tenacity, smarts, energy, and a commitment to building the kind of union that could stop school closures.

These CORE candidates had ten months to campaign before the triennial union election in May of 2010. CORE's strategy was to continue what the members had been doing: contesting the Renaissance 2010 plan, working through GEM with the community, and building a more systematic approach to developing their potential teacher voting base. With 600 schools, a universe of almost 30,000 voters, and few financial resources, they strategically focused on the biggest schools, those that would have the most votes in the election. In January of 2010, CORE, working with GEM, hosted its second wintertime forum on school closings, with 400 in attendance. As the May election neared, the union's old guard was both fracturing into sub-candidate slates, weakening their position, and throwing one obstacle after another in the way of the competition—including asking the administration to ban teachers from campaigning in any way in or near Chicago's schools. A different slate, the PACT slate, took the CTU leaders to court to get them to stop interfering in the election, but it was CORE that benefited the most from PACT's legal victories, as CORE had the most extensive grassroots operation by the spring of 2010. In part because of all the shenanigans taking place, all of the caucuses running against each other and against the current office-holding party, the UPC, met before the election and agreed that if the UPC did not win on the first round—which would require 51 percent or more of the vote—all other slates would line up behind the first runner-up in an effort to remove the UPC from office. And on May 21, that is exactly what happened. With nearly 18,000—more than half of Chicago's teachers—turning out to vote, the UPC got 32 percent of the vote to CORE's 31 percent, and the other three competing slates dropped their campaigns and unified behind CORE.[41]

Reflecting the smart strategy and careful planning CORE had displayed since its founding, the group had planned a Save Our Schools (SOS) rally for May 25, between the first election and the planned runoff date. CORE members decided to move this rally through the union's house of delegates, to make it officially a CTU rally, and this was a master stroke: The literature for the SOS rally was covered with CORE's logo, giving the slate additional visibility beyond their own campaign literature leading up to both elections; the universe of activists who would be motivated to recruit attendees for the SOS rally would be larger than the typical universe of people involved in an internal union election; the rally cemented the image of CORE members as the people who were fighting for real change in the education system, not just electoral power; and, in case of a runoff, the rally would give them a huge visibility and credibility boost just days before teachers returned to the polls. The SOS event was the biggest rally in Chicago in many years, drawing more than 5,000 marchers. According to Madeline Talbot, "Some teachers organized this rally to fight school closures, in May of 2010, and I couldn't get to it, and then I started hearing from people that it was the best fucking rally they had ever been to, and that was CORE."

On May 31, CORE posted a 2½-minute video clip of the rally, encouraging all of their supporters to take to social media to share it. In the clip, Lewis and Sharkey are seen among the thousands of marchers to downtown Chicago. At the end, text comes up reminding teachers to vote in the runoff on June 11.[42] On June 11, the online version of *Substance News*, the Chicago Teachers Union's alternative weekly newspaper since the late 1960s, posted the results:

> CORE not only won the top four offices in the union, but the other nine citywide offices and all of the vice presidencies for high schools (six) and elementary schools (17). By the time the final vote counts were announced in the early hours of June 12, it was clear that CORE had completely defeated the United Progressive Caucus (UPC) and the six-year CTU president Marilyn Stewart.

In her acceptance speech, Karen Lewis framed the crisis in a way no union president had since the 1988 Chicago School Reform Act, the act that began the attack on the schools:

> Corporate America sees K-12 public education as $380 billion dollars that, up until the last ten or fifteen years, they didn't have a sizable piece of. This so-called school reform is not an education plan. It's a business plan ... fifteen years ago, this city purposely began starving our lowest-income neighborhood schools of greatly needed resources and personnel. Class sizes rose, and schools were closed.

Then, standardized tests, which in this town alone is a $60 million business, measured that slow death by starvation. These tests labeled our students, families, and educators failures, because standardized tests reveal more about a student's zip code than a student's academic growth.[43]

Lewis was reclaiming the identity of teacher as not just worker, but teacher, parent, community member, citizen activist.

From Milquetoast to Militant

The *Chicago Sun-Times* telegraphed the changed union with this headline: "New CTU President is a Fierce Foe of Daley's Agenda." On June 15, just four days after the reform slate swept into office, the Chicago School Board held an emergency meeting and voted unanimously to give the CPS's CEO unilateral authority to lay off teachers and increase class size. The new union interpreted this move as the first in a long series of welcoming gestures that would continue all summer. Within two days of the board's meeting, racing the clock against summer vacation, the new leaders sent out an urgent alert that read, in part, "The Board will work overtime this summer to ensure their demands are met. They assume that teachers, PSRPs, parents, and students will be 'on vacation.' The last thing the board wants us to do is to continue organizing." Attached was a sample Excel spreadsheet and a plea that members gather the name, email, and phone number(s) of not only every teacher but also *every parent*, with instructions to send the completed spreadsheet to the new leadership.[44] The newly elected slate hadn't yet taken the reins of office—that wouldn't happen officially until July 1, per the union constitution[45]—but they were immediately shifting the vision and work of the union by including parents as a core constituency.

The union did not have an organizing department, but it did have a lot of staff, as well as plenty of field representatives. One of the first acts of the new officers was to reduce their own salaries considerably, aligning them with teachers' salaries; they also eliminated the excessive personal spending accounts of the previous officers. These savings alone freed up enough money for them to begin to cobble together their union's first organizing department. But unlike such departments in most unions, this one was created only for the purpose of internal organizing, to work with the existing members and help rebuild the union. The new leaders were keenly aware that they had less than two years before the union's current contract expired, and even less time than that—eighteen months—before they would be sitting at the negotiating table; unions typically begin contract negotiations many months before a contract expires. They had inherited a vast organization—albeit one untested and unassessed—of teachers from each school. Hundreds of these were elected delegates—what most unions call shop stewards. The delegates function as problem solvers at the shop floor (or individual school) level. But because the CTU had been mostly consumed by internal warfare for years, no one really understood the quality of the delegates the CORE leaders were inheriting. Plus, the workers who are often attracted, or at least recruitable, for these kinds of positions in unions tend to be activist personalities—people who tend to work alone, who often have been in trouble with management before in their own work lives, and who may not have the respect of many other workers. (This is why CIO-style unions like 1199NE try to recruit the organic leaders, not the activists, for these positions. There is a radical and crucial difference between delegates who approach problem solving as a group effort and those who operate as lone wolves.)

The role of organizing coordinator was given to Norine Gutekanst, who left teaching to head up the new department. Though Gutekanst had been a key CORE activist, unlike Sharkey she had no formal training as a union organizer. She quickly hired an organizer from outside the CTU, Matthew Luskin, who had been the organizing director from 2003 to 2010 at SEIU's public sector in the state, a local of mostly homecare and childcare workers, known for most of those years as SEIU Local 880 (later turned into a megalocal now called HealthCare Illinois, representing the same classes of workers in Indiana, Missouri, and Kansas). According to its president, Keith Kelleher, 880 was "always considered one of those ACORN locals"—a reference to the local unions inspired or formed by Wade Rathke. Kelleher, however, was never aligned with Wade Rathke, nor did he get his initial training from Rathke.[46] Even so, Kelleher describes their model as a "community organizing model, very grassroots based, with a lot of door knocking, workers being responsible for their drive and not just in name only, but with heavy preparation and training."[47] This is not an organic leader identification model, but it is democratic and activist oriented. This was Luskin's background, and because of his experience, he and Gutekanst functioned not as subordinate and boss but as co-coordinators in the design of the new department.

They saw their chief work as focusing on the existing delegates: Winning them over to the new strategy would be key to their union's immediate future. They recast the function of delegates from "information conduits" to school leaders—leaders who would need to very quickly begin mobilizing in the schools. According to Luskin, "Our model wasn't about the staff picking leaders, it was about winning the debate about our future with the existing leaders in each school; we had to win the debate about our new strategy among the rank and file." The fight was being positioned as an all-out, high stakes, high-risk battle royal.

Organizers went from school to school attending as many school meetings as they could and blowing the debate about strategy wide open. Luskin recalls that they'd start by saying, "If any of you think the next contract is about a percentage-point raise, tell us, because we think we know it's about the future of public education as we know it: that's what's on the table."[48] If the labor movement's instinct has been to reduce demands in order to sound reasonable, the new CTU took the opposite approach: They led every meeting with school-based discussions of billionaires, banks, and racism. (*Note to other teachers' unions*: they got reelected.) Mass political education of the existing base was their *primary* focus. Along with all of CTU's leaders, they were creating a sense of urgency, a burning platform, and framing the choice ahead in very clear and unambiguous language. They were being as mindful with semantics as 1199NE.

Because CORE had won a commanding victory, every single officer was a CORE slate member, including the many lesser ones—area vice presidents, vice presidents for every type of school and grade level. All of these newly elected officers were on the same program, unified in their vision, making the work of "winning over the delegates to the new strategy" a union-wide effort at every level. CTU delegates meet on the second Wednesday of every month to make union policy. Under the previous leadership, by design, these meetings had had low attendance—so low that they wouldn't always make quorum (by the design of the old leadership). It was a way of doing little, of maintaining a trouble-free status quo. And when they did make quorum, often the old UPC leaders would talk for so long at the microphones during the "officer reports" that began the meeting, the delegates would leave in frustration, which was just what the leaders wanted them to do. Verbosity was a useful tool for keeping inconvenient delegates—such as CORE members—from raising inconvenient issues from the floor. Then came CORE's clean-sweep election, and, by the time the new school year began in September 2010, the meetings were packed, with 800 teacher delegates walking in, hoping to better understand their new union and to begin to implement an entirely new program. Because of their sheer size, and the number of teachers lining up at microphones around the room to ask questions or speak to a resolution, those monthly meetings came to resemble what for many unions would be an entire union convention.

Union vice president Sharkey explains that CORE had an activist rather than a shop-floor model. Sharkey understood the difference, having been trained at 1199NE. The activist rather than organic leader approach was consistent with the model Luskin brought from his years at SEIU, a union that functioned more like a community organizing group, by Kelleher's own description, and from his ACORN training. Some of CORE's members had been elected as delegates in their schools, but most were just free radicals.

> I would defend that model at the time because during that period there were a lot of political defeats," Sharkey says. "We needed to create a space that was inspiring, where we could co-think and where we could get excited together, so at the end of a meeting it wasn't just telling people to go back to your buildings and work with your coworkers. People were learning politics, people were getting excited; we did a lot of things in early 2010, in 2011, and leading up to 2012 to get people excited about taking back Chicago.[49]

During the first year, eight of the long-serving field representatives left, most of these resigning or retiring. These changes gave the new leadership yet more resources for creating new departments in the union and re-creating old ones, such as communications and politics departments.

That September, the teachers' union was experiencing revolutionary changes on the inside, throwing off the shackles of the UPC, which had held union office in a one-party rule for thirty-six of the previous forty-two years. Outside the union, the entire city was hit with the equivalent of a massive earthquake when Mayor Daley announced he would not seek an eighth term.[50] Mayors named Daley had held the office for forty-two out of the past fifty-five years. As Amisha Patel, executive director of the Grassroots Collaborative in Chicago, recalls it:

> When Daley announced he wasn't running, we had a window where everyone began excitedly discussing what we could do in this new moment in our city. We had a mayoral forum called New Chicago 2011, and 2,600 people showed up and the energy was rocking. Even though Rahm's announcement a few weeks later crushed that moment, we had cracked open the idea that Chicago could be different.[51]

Getting 2,600 people from across the city to attend a mayoral forum is even more impressive when you consider that not only had the mayor's office been functionally a family-run business for generations, but also that the long history of Chicago's community organizing sector was steeped in the traditions of Saul Alinsky. No city has been more impacted by Alinskyism than Chicago, and the resulting culture for more than a half-century was one of racially segregated, community-based organizations existing inside tightly drawn neighborhood boundaries, all political imagination choked by the idea that one's own little ward was the universe. ACORN's Talbot says that some of this negative Alinsky impact had been shaken off in the few years leading up to the CTU leadership change, and she was an active part of challenging that culture. But the residue remains.

"The Daley legacy was so deep because people thought Chicago could never change, so having even a little space of time where there was uncertainty allowed groups to cross old lines and sit down in one big room and imagine a different kind of Chicago," Patel says. Patel, a Chicago native, had left the city to attend Stanford University on a full scholarship. Her parents were both born in India, and she represents another aspect of the changing Chicago. After becoming a student activist involved in progressive issues in the San Francisco Bay Area, she'd settled into the idea of never enduring a Midwestern winter again. Then one day, while she sat enjoying the warm California sun and contemplating various career options with progressive groups around the Bay, she had an epiphany, one that felt to her the way people have described feeling the call to religious duty. "I thought, Wait a minute, why not Chicago? Why not go home where there's so much work to be done? The Bay Area is full of progressive activists." So Patel did go home, and went to work for SEIU's Chicago government workers' union—a different local from the one Luskin worked for, although Patel and Luskin who were from two different SEIU locals met many times. At SEIU, Patel was constantly trying to build coalitions with Chicago's communities in an effort to develop fairly traditional union-community labor alliances. In 2006, along with others, including members of ACORN and a few unions besides the major player, SEIU, she took part in the unsuccessful campaign to pass Chicago's 2006 Big Box ordinance, which would have forced warehouses like Walmart's to substantially increase base pay to $9.25 an hour—an early forerunner, idea to local living-wage laws. In 2007, she was ready to do something focused more on shifting Chicago's community-organizing sector from turf-based to citywide thinking. By 2010, when the teachers' union and city hall were opening up in new ways, her Grassroots Collaborative was perfectly situated to become a key partner in that change.[52]

Throughout the fall of 2010, the CTU's new leadership was engaged in endless skirmishes with the Chicago public schools' CEO Ron Huberman, including a successful campaign to reverse most of the 1,700 layoffs the CEO had implemented in direct violation of the union contract. Using the powers vested in him by the emergency meeting held just after CORE swept into power at the teachers' union, he had ignored contractually negotiated seniority, and the union won in court. There were plenty of hints that the stakes in the next contract were going to be dialed to "highest risk." And when Rahm Emanuel resigned from his post at the White House in mid-October, returned to Chicago and quickly mobilized the signatures he would need to file by November for the February 2011 mayoral election, hints of high risk turned to something more closely resembling a visit from the Angel of Death. For two years, Emanuel had been deeply involved with a fellow

Chicagoan, Secretary of Education Arne Duncan, the original architect of Chicago Public Schools Renaissance 2010, the program that had in many ways provoked the birth of CORE. Within weeks, Emanuel's campaign team developed a television ad in which the candidate took aim at Chicago's teachers, chiding them for not working enough hours in the day and promising that as mayor, he would make it a top priority to lengthen Chicago's school day. It later became known that this anti-teacher TV spot had been scripted in part by the fiercely anti-union Stand for Children campaign. Jonah Edelman, that group's founder, was later caught snarkily boasting in a video clip from the 2011 elite annual gathering called the Summer Aspen Institute that Stand for Children had "duped the Chicago teachers into accepting a deal that would mean they could never go on strike."[53]

Meanwhile, the union was functioning nonstop at a dynamic, exciting, and frenetic pace, trying to shift the CTU's twenty-five-year-old bureaucratic administration, which had long since stopped functioning in any meaningful way. Behind the scenes, as they tried to rebuild themselves while putting out fires like a fall 2010 legislative assault on public pensions—including those of teachers—Emanuel was home campaigning and putting a bull's-eye on the CTU with what Edelman called "the talking points we wrote," which Emanuel "repeated about 1,000 times." Stand for Children had also begun a stealth strategy of working to buy off the Democratic state legislative leadership, aiming to introduce a bill that would severely curtail the activities of the teachers' union before Emanuel took office and before the teachers' current contract expired. When Emanuel won on the first ballot in February 2011, averting a runoff, it was as if Stand for Children had won the office, in a city with total mayoral control of the school board.

Emanuel Ups the Ante, Shifts the Power Equation, and Doubles Down the Challenge

Political parties and people who sweep into office with something of a mandate hit the ground running: They begin asserting their agenda during the outgoing administration's lame duck period. CORE did it at the teachers' union after trouncing the entrenched old guard. And Emanuel did it after winning the mayor's seat in a one-round fight. As Edelman tells the story, in his workshop on how to bust teachers' unions even in Democratically-controlled states: "So in this intervening time, Rahm Emanuel is elected mayor, he won on the first ballot, and he strongly supports our proposal ... that was another shoe that dropped on the Chicago Teachers Union because they didn't support him."[54]

The Stand for Children legislative proposal would again strip teachers of the right to collectively bargain over schedules—an item that had been negotiable historically, had been stripped away by the 1995 Amendatory Act, and then reinstated in 2001 as a negotiable item, but under a compliant union that quickly negotiated a deal to lengthen the teaching day. Now, because a less compliant teachers' union was in power, it was taken off the table again. And the Stand for Children legislation did far more than that: It included a frontal assault on tenure that would empower principals to hire and fire teachers, and mandated that at least one-quarter of the decision to fire be based on student test scores. Each of these measures took aim at unions. The final provision of the proposed legislation attempted to bar teachers from striking. Stand for Children started the bargaining with an outright ban, and counted on "compromising" with a deal that would allow a strike, but dependent on what they believed would be an impossible criterion: 75 percent of all teachers would have to show up at the polls for a strike authorization vote to be valid (a rather amazing criteria given that turn out in typical elections in the United States hovers in the 20 to 30 percent range).

Edelman's description of this deal making is illuminating, revealing not only that Emanuel was using all his muscle behind the scenes, but also that the two statewide federations of teachers were in some way working against the new Chicago leadership. The Illinois Federation of Teachers (IFT) and the Illinois Education Association (IEA) dominated suburban and rural Illinois, which was largely white. Their leaders, who found strikes an unappealing concept at best, were selling out the kids of Chicago, who were mostly black, and the union that ultimately protected those kids' interests. Karen Lewis was known for her intellect—she had taught chemistry and was a master of pedagogy—but she is human, and as head of the CTU she quickly made her first serious gaffe.

Set down in a climate of backroom deal making, counseled by the statewide teachers' lobbyists, Lewis was told to take the deal. The biggest error she made, as she fully admitted later, was going into these meetings alone, without having sufficiently consulted CTU or CORE. With all the other teachers' unions signing on, she went along. The CORE caucus essentially censured Lewis for this breach, publicly and privately, challenging her authority and forcing her to announce that she had made a mistake and that there was no way the Chicago Teachers Union supported the deal, but the damage was done. The legislation, called SB7, passed unanimously just before Emanuel's swearing-in ceremony, measurably shifting the power equation of the coming fight.

This was CORE's first exercise in holding union leadership accountable to the platform they ran on, union democracy, and it was a breakthrough of sorts. Most union caucuses that engage in electoral work inside of their unions either disband until the next election cycle or toe the party line once their party is in power. But CORE didn't start out as an electoral caucus; it was formed by progressive teachers to pressure the CTU to "act like a real union," and they felt that their new leader had just violated this principle in a way that was likely to have dire consequences for the rank and file. It was an important lesson: for Lewis, for the executive officers, for CORE, and for CTU members. Lewis's willingness to publicly apologize to those members was something of a novelty and is still unusual among union leaders at her level. And CORE's powerful message that she should never make such an error again helped the caucus reestablish itself as a voice independent of the leadership, including the leadership that had emerged from CORE itself. Meanwhile CORE and Lewis were able to quickly mend their relationship and return to the business at hand, staying focused on building their power against the threat from Emanuel, which now loomed larger than ever.

Emanuel wasted no time in using his victory. By June of 2011, he had appointed an all-new Chicago school board and a new CEO of schools. The board's first action was to vote to repeal that year's 4 percent raise, the final annual raise stipulated by the contract that had been agreed to before CORE took the CTU leadership. That contract was often referred to as the *Olympics* contract, because Mayor Daley gave it to the teachers when Chicago was under a public microscope in its bid to host the Summer Olympics. (Chicago would eventually lose the bid, but not before several Chicago unions, including CTU, had seized the moment and got their deals done.)[55]

If any of the teachers still doubted that the new mayor was coming for them, the unilateral repeal of the scheduled raise made their future crystal clear. Emanuel's arrogance erased almost all memory of the setback Lewis had suffered in the SB7 negotiations, and though nobody in the new leadership wanted to see the teachers lose their raise, the repeal unified Chicago's teachers behind the new leadership in a way they could never have dreamed of before. The anger and the unity became palpable inside and outside of the union. Emanuel looked like a schoolyard bully right out of the starting gate. And his behavior would only get more aggressive.

In early September, he made good on his campaign ad, launching his promised push for the longer school day, basing his argument to the public on the hours Chicago's teachers spent with kids in the classroom without mentioning the hours they worked outside it, preparing lessons, grading homework, attending meetings, and performing other tasks that benefited their students. He then summoned Lewis to his office to discuss extending the school day. It was her first closed-door meeting with the mayor.

Lewis may have erred in the SB7 negotiations, but what she did after this meeting was considered a stroke of genius. When she left Emanuel's office, the press asked what had happened. Lewis did what she has come to be known for doing: told them exactly what they'd asked to know. As ACORN leader Madeline Talbot tells the story:

> Lewis . . . said Emanuel said, "Well what the fuck do you want?" And Lewis said, "More than you've fucking got." People were really angry that Emanuel started off the cussing, that a white man shouldn't talk to a black woman leader that way, but they were really happy that Karen continued it—that Karen gave it back was just great.[56]

That fall, the CTU began to signal that they would be trying out a different kind of contract negotiation. Through the house of delegates, they launched a survey and invited union members to participate in drafting the union's contract proposals. Negotiations had been scheduled to start in early 2012. Union members hadn't experienced a contract campaign in several decades. According to Sharkey:

The old guard were Shankerites, basically unrepentant business unionists who thought that contracts were tough sometimes but we could
win them by having a big hand on the table and making deals by talking tough, but we began to ask aloud, How's that going to work with
Rahm? He's not coming to make deals, he's coming to fight.

The new leaders were changing the conversation about how a contract
should be won, and they were acting like a union by involving all the
members in the discussion. The Occupy movement had just surfaced
on the heels of the spring 2011 uprising in Wisconsin, which was led by
Midwestern teachers with many ties to Chicago. Every month, the CTU
and CORE mobilized activists to attend the CPS school board meetings
and to challenge the board during the period of open public comments
on the agenda, which is required by law. The fall of 2010 had been col-
ored by CPS administration-prompted skirmishes, but by the fall of
2011, the skirmishes were prompted by the CTU and aimed at socializing the teachers into taking harder and more frequent direct actions,
building their confidence in their ability to win. At the December 2011
meeting, the teachers used the #OWS (Occupy Wall Street) tactic "mic
check": One person says something and everyone else repeats it, as into
a megaphone powered by human voices. After the mic check began—
"These are our children, not corporate products!"—the school board
left the room and shut the meeting down.[57] The teachers and their allies
were successfully finding their voice and practicing direct action; business as usual would not be happening.

Mass Political Education and Structure Tests

In January of 2012, with the start of contract negotiations imminent, it
was time for the teachers to do a very thorough structure test, to assess
their internal strength after eighteen months of new leadership. Sharkey
describes the strategy:

We decided to hold a mock strike vote and we did it over three days.
We had charted the entire union; we had charts all over the walls
taking up entire rooms in our offices. We had a forty-person team

working the vote, and the union's district supervisors were the key people in the room with the staff [there were forty-nine district supervisors, appointed teachers who earned a small stipend for the job, which was to stay in touch with the delegates in their turf between meetings],[58] and we planned it so that right in the middle of it was our monthly house of delegates meeting, so we could announce how it was going on day two and give out assignments to every school delegate for the third and final day of voting.

Staging the three days of voting around the house of delegates meeting, when 800 teachers from across the city come together, was part of the ongoing campaign by the union's leaders to both teach and empower their members to own the union, to take responsibility for it, to see themselves as the leaders of the union, all 800 of them. Sharkey adds, "Coming out of the mock vote, we did identify the schools where we had weaknesses." This knowledge prioritized the union's task for the next few months, letting the leadership zero in on areas where schools presented one of three scenarios: the delegate wasn't an organic leader, clearly the case when the teachers in a school didn't turn out to vote; the delegate was opposed to the idea of a strike, requiring the development of different leadership beneath the elected delegate; or the school was missing a delegate altogether. Once the need for internal structure work was laid out, the CTU moved on to its next potential base of support, the general public.

In February, the union released its opening salvo, a policy paper that framed its demands for the coming contract negotiations and also clarified its public message. The report was titled "The Schools Chicago's Students Deserve, Research-based Proposals to Strengthen Elementary and Secondary Education in the Chicago Public Schools."[59] Its top ten recommendations were:

1. Recognize that Class Size Matters (countering the message that size doesn't matter)
2. Educate the Whole Child (stressing the importance of art, gym, theater, dance, music, and other key electives and activities)
3. Create More Robust Wrap-around Services (such as free transit fares and more school nurses)

4. Address Inequities In Our System (described as de facto apartheid)
5. Help Students Get Off To A Good Start (calling for access to pre-kindergarten and all-day kindergarten)
6. Respect and Develop the Professionals (lift all salaries, hire more classroom aides)
7. Teach All Students (addressing the need for bilingual and special education)
8. Provide Quality Facilities (citing the need for asbestos abatement and other repairs, especially those affecting health and safety)
9. Partner With Parents
10. Fully Fund Education (improve funding formulas and increase funds available)

The media received this report with open arms, primed by their respect for Lewis, who had established herself as a credible media source. Even more important, so did Chicago's general public. In the eight months since that memorable "fuck you, well fuck you" revelation to the press, pitting the image of Emanuel, snarky white male graduate of a rich suburban school, against that of Lewis, strong, confident, black, female teacher and student from the same inner city schools, Lewis had used her national board–certified pedagogical expertise to turn all of Chicago into her classroom and teach her entire community the ABC of what was really happening to the city's school system. She had created a master narrative, issuing daily press releases that the media were gobbling up. As Madeline Talbot put it:

> Karen was black, smart, and bold, and that alone made her newsworthy in a city not known for straight talkers; she was taking Rahm on every day on every topic; she had earned the media's trust as a person who told the truth; and for more than half a year she had been putting out an analysis, a frame about the schools that was never there before, and Chicagoans began to understand education differently.[60]

Lewis also had an email blast list and would send out a short fact about education every day. The list was for anyone who wanted to be on it; it included media, civil society leaders like Talbot, and, of course, teachers.

Negotiations were already under way. The CTU leadership hadn't merely given the members the right to participate in developing the contract proposals, they had also greatly expanded the size of their bargaining team and the rules for negotiations. Traditionally, the bargaining team had consisted of the union's president, a lawyer, and just a few others. The union's constitution and bylaws are virtually silent on collective bargaining, except to say, "During major negotiations, [the president] shall be accompanied by at least one other officer or member of the Executive Board."[61] Lewis described launching her team in an article for the education blog Rethinking Schools:

> We said, "OK, but we're bringing 50 people with us." They said, "Oh, no, we don't do that." But we told them this is a new administration and we do things differently—we don't do things under cover of darkness. We want people to see and hear what really goes on so they can make good choices and so they can communicate back to our members. The difference is we're rank and file—we feel the members should make the decisions about what we should do.[62]

That wasn't the only change the new leadership made in the negotiations game. In the past, the CTU, like most unions, had agreed to a formal set of ground rules; these had included a gag rule that had prevented the union team from talking with union members about what was going on at the bargaining table. Such ground rules are typical even though they are not required by labor law; they cover what are called *permissive* but *not mandatory* subjects of bargaining; they reflect a business unionist approach to collective bargaining.[63] CTU signed off on some ground rules, but they eliminated the gag rule. (As noted in Chapter Three, the highly successful union 1199 New England has never agreed to ground rules at all and doesn't believe in them. I have also always refused them when leading contract negotiations.)[64]

In the early stages of the Chicago negotiations, neither the CTU nor the CPS was bargaining very seriously, and there weren't many meetings set; each side believed that slowing the process down would work to their advantage under the new rules passed in SB7. Management, Jonah Edelman's extensive videotaped comments at the Aspen Institute made clear, was sure that the union didn't really understand the new rules very well, an incorrect assumption that perhaps made the employer overconfident. Meanwhile, the union was still methodically working to shore up the weaker schools identified by the mock strike vote, and also working with parents and community allies, making sure everyone was on the same page.

Exercising Workers' Most Powerful Weapon

In May, the union began to prepare for the real, not mock, strike vote. The contract was set to expire on June 30, 2012. The old guard inside the union was leading an interesting campaign against the strike vote. They formally challenged the vote at a meeting of the union's rules commit-tee, charging that holding such a vote over three days was a violation of the union's constitution. They were grasping at straws. According to union historian Schmidt, who was a member of the rules committee, the old guard understood something few people did:

> The old UPC folks were fighting this so hard because they knew something important: that if the new leaders led workers through a successful strike, they would likely stay in power for a very long time, because that's what happens when you lead people through a tough fight, they give you their trust.

Eventually, Schmidt said, the lawyers had to be brought into a rules committee meeting before the new leaders could establish that a three-day strike vote was in fact perfectly legal. In the past, more than twenty-five years back, the CTU hadn't taken strike votes that seriously because they hadn't had to. Delegates called for a strike vote, and without much fanfare, over the course of a morning, the union would take a vote and declare a strike as needed.[65]

Now, while the rules committee debated the procedure for a strike vote, a momentum-building structure test was playing out on the streets of Chicago. The union called for a rally on May 23 to show support for their negotiations team. They reserved a location downtown, the Auditorium Theater, at the corner of Wabash and Michigan. This the-ater is a national landmark, its great arches lined with 24-karat gold leaf;

it has hosted many of Chicago's most famous performances. The CTU's turnout—some 7,000 teachers, all wearing their red T-shirts—far surpassed the theater's 4,000-person[66] maximum capacity, and the rally spilled out into the street.[67] A sea of red below and vaulting gold above created a spectacular visual, and the Chicago media made the most of it. Footage from the many clips on YouTube reflects a crowd electrified by their newfound power, the power of unity and purpose.

After this rally, with the rules committee clear about the union's right to conduct a three-day strike vote, planning was under way for June. The union leaders knew they had to complete the vote before school let out or they'd lose their chance of getting the high turnout they needed. The vote was held June 6–8, and by the end, 24,000 union members had voted, far surpassing the percentage required by SB7's anti-union law. Ninety percent of all teachers cast a ballot, and of them, 76 percent voted to authorize a strike. The vote count each night was conducted by local religious leaders, working with the religious group ARISE, adding moral authority to the teachers' decision and a validation that strengthened the workers' courage.

But SB7 also had language mandating that the union and the CPS would first have to go through a byzantine but typical labor process called "fact finding" and recommendations of a fact finder had to be reported, and at least one side had to reject the fact finder's report before a strike could commence. In late July, the CTU and the CPS both rejected the fact finder's report, and everything was in place for the first teachers' strike in twenty-five years. The union was running a Summer Organizing Institute, and had hired a few dozen extra teachers to do parent and community outreach throughout the summer vacation. By August, the union was debating whether to strike on day one of the new school year, or to wait, let the schools open, and then strike in week two. They decided the latter plan would be more effective. Their strategizing took into account that there would be brand-new teachers coming in who hadn't been a part of the mobilizing efforts, and many other teachers who'd been away on vacation and would need to be briefed about how the summer's events had unfolded. Walking out on kids and parents is a difficult act for mission-driven workers, such as teachers, and many in the rank and file would have to be shown that there really was no other option, that every attempt to reach a fair settlement had been made in good faith.

On September 9, the union called a press conference, and Karen Lewis announced that the strike was on, starting the next morning. From September 10 through September 18, the Chicago Teachers Union closed the Chicago schools, under a limpid sky. Schmidt noted gleefully, "God gave us nine of the most perfect-weather days in Chicago history!" On day one of the strike, an estimated 35,000 teachers and their allies marched through the heart of Chicago, effectively shutting not just the schools but the entire downtown and marking the largest rally in the city since McCarthyism first chilled the voice of Chicago labor. Not since the declaration of the end of World War II had Chicagoans showed up in such force to let their voices be heard.[68] Each day, the teachers would picket their schools, then join together in downtown marches. Three days into the strike, the CPS management had consolidated 600 schools into 120 designated cluster schools, desperately trying to keep enough classes open to reduce the number of parents demanding that they settle with the teachers. Then the teachers' union and their allies consolidated their pickets too, sending them only to the cluster schools, maintaining strong lines during the school day wherever the CPS tried to keep classes open, before moving downtown for daily direct actions. Teachers at almost every consolidated picket line felt the validation of the parent committees, many of which were even cooking meals for them, keeping the picket lines well fed during their long school-day vigils. This food for the teachers went way beyond shiny red apples. Parents grilled barbecue and cooked giant pots of traditional stews and soups representing every ethnic group in that diverse city.

Many parents had been placed in a tough position by the strike. "We talked about child care for the working parents," Sarah Chambers, a teacher at Saucedo Academy, a public elementary school, recalls. "It was really tricky, because you want the parents pressuring the CPS and the mayor to settle, but we knew it was really hard for a lot of people. Some parents came and cooked for us, and we just took their kids on the picket lines and the marches all day, meeting them later."

The strike passed its fifth day and continued into the weekend, and the pressure to settle was indeed rising. Everyone wanted to avert a second week. The teachers were hearing it from the parents and the mayor, and city leaders were hearing it from them even more loudly. Up to this point, CORE members had forcefully exercised their power as the rank-and-file caucus only once, when they made Karen Lewis do an about-face on SB7. Now they again felt strongly the need to hold their leaders accountable as the time for a settlement drew near. The bargaining committee, which in previous decades numbered in single digits, had been enlarged to forty-five people. Among the forty-five sat Sarah Chambers, teacher leader and co-chair of the CORE caucus:

> I was the only rank-and-file person in the room, and I was already a CORE steering committee member. Karen came in and said, "We are close to an agreement," and I said, "There is no way 'we' can come to an agreement without the members who are walking the picket lines getting a chance to discuss this . . . our members feel like they got to write some of those proposals for the first time; they own this fight; the entire membership has to decide to call this off, not you or us." The leaders said we were being too radical. People were screaming and crying and saying no, the members have to make this decision, not you, not the house of delegates.[69]

This moment, when Lewis and the CTU leadership agreed to extend the strike, against the *intense* pressure of the media and growing numbers of parents demanding they settle or go back to the table and try again, was decisive for CORE and for the new leadership's decision to genuinely empower the rank and file. Tammie Vinson, a teacher who had hated the old union and then became a very active rank-and-file leader through CORE, helping to make her union *her* union, said:

> It's so different now. I remember when Marilyn Stewart was president, we would just find out about contract settlements. She didn't even give members the right to vote on them. I was so proud of CORE because we forced the leadership to make the time to let the members decide to come off the picket lines, to go from not even voting on our contract to being allowed to come off the picket lines and set up group readings by school and by picket line. It was so important.

For two more days, the strike continued, as teachers sat in the unusually warm Chicago sun reading the proposed contract line by line. They
found that concessions had been made in the negotiations, but not
many. Considering how much effort had been spent by the mayor and
the political elite to pass a state law that they believed would prevent the
teachers from ever striking, the mere act of going on strike was the first
and perhaps biggest victory of this struggle. In the face of an all-out war
declared by an ideologically driven mayor, where the cost of settlement
was high, teachers, parents, and students had taken over the city. The
mayor did win a longer school day, but the union exacted a pay raise
in exchange. And on Emanuel's second major objective, merit pay, the
union defeated him, maintaining the system of raises based on years of
service (called steps) and educational skills (called lanes). Finally, the
mayor was defeated in his attempt to gut tenure.[70]

It had been a defensive fight for the teachers' union, and defend they
had. Throughout the strike, parents and students had stood arm-in-arm
with them, squaring off against the man some called the bully-in-chief.
Emanuel's real objective had been to destroy the teachers' union, and
instead he had unified a group of workers who had been suffering insults
for years—on top of a ferocious attack on their profession and on the
reason most teachers teach: their kids.

After the Strike, Challenges

Official Chicago's class warfare against those who occupy its classrooms
went into overdrive with the passage of the Amendatory Act in 1995.
In the years that followed, Chicago public schools became a laboratory
for privatization and the charter program, and results were devastating,
especially for inner-city students, most of them poor and black. The
2012 strike did not end those troubles. In 2013, Emanuel announced the
single largest public schools closing in history anywhere outside of New
Orleans after Hurricane Katrina; he shuttered forty-seven schools in a
gesture that many interpreted as part payback for the rank and file's 2012
victory and part message that this victory had been futile. His proposal,
launched in the dead of winter, overwhelmed the city. Once more, the
teachers' union locked arms with their community allies in a site-by-site
fight to save the marked schools, but their protests were weakened by

battle fatigue, and the mayor won the round. Amisha Patel—whom Chicago's media had nicknamed the shadow bargaining-committee member for her visible role in coordinating the community support during the strike—was in a position to see that clearly:

> The hearings around the school closings were amazing, hundreds of people taking over hearings, throwing down, but the effort went back to being a site fight. Of the 50 sites proposed for closure, if it wasn't your school, you didn't get involved. Contrast this with the strike, which was a citywide fight and showed us how to lead a citywide effort for really the first time—but the narrative on these closings went back to a site fight and we got totally diffused.

Despite the massive amount of organization required in 2012 to get a moribund union ready to fight hard in an all-out war, permanent systems for capturing the parent contacts and broader community hadn't been developed. Neither had the internal tracking systems been developed enough to make the kind of assessments the CTU is going to need for future contract and school-closing fights. Interviewed about the situation in October 2014, Sharkey said:

> A shortcoming to our work now is that the leader of the union in each school is the delegate, and we are very dependent on the delegates. Traditionally many delegates ran their schools like they were servicing them, not organizing or mobilizing members onto committees so that teachers could be the union in the school. And even though we've put a lot of emphasis on a leadership development model to help shift our delegates to acting like leaders, not just servicing, if you asked me how many we have at a first-tier leader level, how many at a second-tier leader level, and third tier, and so on, I could only give you a low-quality number; we just haven't gotten to that level of assessment.

Shortly after this interview, Sharkey, the union's vice president, would become its acting president, when the dynamic Karen Lewis was diagnosed in late October 2014 with advanced brain cancer—a massive tumor. Overnight, she was completely out of the picture, dealing with urgent medical needs.

Prior to her diagnosis, she and the teachers' union had planned to announce her candidacy for mayor, on November 5, the day after the fall elections, which in Chicago is the traditional day for candidates to begin gathering the signatures required to qualify for office. Polls showed her *beating* Emanuel. The mood among the teachers was electrifying. The idea that a black woman teacher would and could challenge the most anti-teacher mayor in the nation's third-largest city, during an era of massive, coordinated assault on unions and the teaching profession, had everyone in Chicago buzzing. When her unexpected diagnosis closed that possibility, a collective gasp seemed to sound across the region. Lewis had been the main topic in coffee shops, on public buses, on street corners, and most definitely inside the union.

As part of the evolution of the union's work, and Lewis's decision to run, CTU leadership decided to jump feet first into city-level politics, too, running for seats as aldermen, something they had never done before. The transformation of their identity from teachers, to teacher-leaders, to union leaders, to candidates for city council was remarkable. Sue Garza, upon deciding to run for alderman in her ward on the South Side—a seat she would go on to win—said:

I am not a politician and it's really scary; my mouth has gotten me into trouble, my life has gotten me thrown into jail, but everything in my life has gotten me ready to run for office. When we started talking about running people for office, I said no, but my father (himself a famous union leader) literally read me the riot act; he said, "When did you ever back down from anything in your life?" And these people have backed us into a corner, but we can't let a few people ruin the entire career of teaching.

The future of the resurgent Chicago teachers' union has yet to be written, but their efforts have demonstrated that teachers are willing and able to fight back and win against even their biggest foes. Teacher Tammie Vinson looks at the immediate future:

The question of the ages right now is "What is the role of CORE?" How does a bureaucrat not become a bureaucrat? The majority of CORE's founding leadership is now downtown (meaning the union's headquarters). Now Jackson Potter is the guy sending out mandates from downtown, and he might be way more friendly than the people before, but how do you not let leaders get too far removed from the rank and file?

Note to Michels, your law isn't ironclad.

CORE members are currently debating a resolution on term limits for union officers. They are also struggling together with the question of how best to do electoral work. After Karen Lewis was knocked out of the mayoral race, the union scrambled and even fumbled a little to quickly figure out whom from among less great alternative candidates they could endorse on such short notice. They found Jesus Garcia, the progressive Cook County Commissioner, and though Garcia was defeated on the second ballot, they'd succeeded in achieving something no pundit, and almost no person, predicted: preventing Emanuel from gaining the nomination on the first ballot, as he had in his first mayoral race, and forcing him to fight hard for his reelection. Sue Garza won her race, but most of the other teacher candidates did not. Even so, Jackson Potter says, every teacher knew it was the teachers' power that had forced the mayoral runoff, and that the union had, in fact, had a stellar plan, only derailed by Lewis's health crisis.

The fact that the union forced the runoff has been making Emanuel think a little harder about his actions; his venomous rhetoric has vanished for now, but the next contract has yet to be negotiated. Of far greater concern, the behavior of some other key unions in Chicago during the race proved the biggest obstacle to defeating Emanuel. So-called progressive unions in the private sector, unions that don't need to deal with him as their employer, cut deals with him to gain other advantages in regional power politics. SEIU Healthcare Illinois remains a staunch ally of the teachers, which is encouraging, but without other union support, the future of the now-mighty teachers' union is threatened by a right-wing, hedge fund governor who wants to wipe out *all* public service unions, on top of a mayor who would be satisfied by merely decimating one of them, the CTU. Jackson Potter, reflecting on the post–mayoral race period, said, "Our ability to connect with the community has been key for us. But I worry about our ability to have much success over the long run if there aren't other worker-led insurrections. Chicago's labor scene is disappointingly lonely."[71]

But Chicago's teachers have proved that a broken union can be rebuilt in a *very* short time—less than two years. They've demonstrated not only that the strike remains the working class's most powerful weapon, but also that its successful deployment is *contingent* on first developing deep relationships with the wider community. And they've demonstrated the crucial importance of broad democracy in the union, beyond the formal vote—the democracy that let the rank and file read the proposed contract settlement line by line on the picket lines, and helped the teachers take full responsibility for their own liberation. In the process of that liberation, inevitably, there will be compromises on the way to more substantive victories. But the Chicago experience has shown that when workers are empowered to make the decisions in real-life fights, their union becomes stronger, not weaker.

The union speeds on the way to a better future when it slows down to allow broad democracy to flourish. The working-class teachers of Chicago are struggling *as* a class.

5

Smithfield Foods: A Huge Success You've Hardly Heard About

Once the union understood that we had to run a campaign where race was a central issue, where race and class were given equal weight and the intersectionality of the two was lifted up, and we reframed the fight as a moral fight, we won in just two years. People trying to win these fights with morality or race off the table, versus front and center, are starting fights with one hand tied behind their back.

Rev. Dr. William Barber, Moral Mondays[1]

KING COUNTY, WASHINGTON, HAS A population of 2 million. Ninety-three percent of its people are city dwellers; most of them live in Seattle. At the time I am writing this, the median household income is $71,175, and the average rent for a two-bedroom house is $1,123 per month.[2] In 2014, there was a successful campaign to increase Seattle's minimum wage to $15 an hour by the year 2022 (by which time, incidentally, that $15 will not be $15; it will be worth less, since Seattle didn't index it to inflation). The story was *banner news* worldwide in print and broadcast media, and a cause célèbre for many liberals.

Meanwhile, without the fanfare of a single national headline, another kind of contract in a very different region also introduced a wage of $15 an hour. Bladen County, in southeastern North Carolina, has a population of 35,843. Ninety-one percent of those people live in the countryside; the rest are in the county's few small towns. Thirty-five percent are African American. At the time of writing, the median income is $30,031, and the average rent for a two-bedroom house is $637 per month.

In 2008, in the county's tiny town of Tar Heel, 5,000 workers at the Smithfield Foods pork factory voted to form a union with the United Food and Commercial Workers (UFCW). It was the single largest private-sector union victory of the new millennium.[3] And it happened in the South, in the state with the lowest rate of union membership in the entire country: 3 percent.[4] The new, ratified contract not only guaranteed a $15-an-hour wage but also paid sick leave, paid vacation, health care, retirement benefits, overtime pay, guaranteed minimum work hours, job security through a "just cause" provision, and tools to remedy dangerous working conditions. The wage alone far outranks Washington's; given the dollar's buying power in Bladen County, King County workers would have to earn $26.40 an hour to equal it.[5]

Because the union signed a 'gag order' as part of the final deal to reach a 'fair' union election process, little has been said or written about the campaign since the workers won it, depriving other Southern workers of a very important example of how labor can win in the new millennium in the many manufacturing plants that have moved to the region. In Chapter Two, I discussed the negative effects of gag orders during collective bargaining, a staple imposition of the New Labor era (and labor writ large). The Smithfield gag order may well have hampered workers in the U.S. South from believing that they, too, can win, like the workers in rural North Carolina.

In this chapter I highlight the decisive moments in the campaign when the decisions of the key individuals made the difference between winning and losing. I identify these decisions as embodying the organizing strategy that differs from New Labor's mobilizing approach.

The Global South Within the Global North

Smithfield Foods is the largest pork producer in the world. It is a vertically integrated company that owns tens of thousands of acres of land where Smithfield farmers and contractors raise hogs that are taken to company-owned plants for slaughter, production, and packing, and then shipped to all 50 states as well as exported to China, Japan, and Europe. In the U.S. alone, the company markets twelve distinct brands, including Healthy Ones, Margherita, Farmland, and Armour. They have another fifty brands globally. Smithfield's land ownership and farms were historically concentrated in the Deep South, because of that region's lax environmental laws and lack of unions. But by the 1980s, Smithfield Foods had begun expanding out of the Deep South. The first mechanism that facilitated their expansion was a rash of acquisitions of existing smaller pork producers, mostly in the Midwest. The second was the passage of the North American Free Trade Agreement (NAFTA) in 1994. NAFTA's success, if not its key objective, depended on many domestic rules in the United States, Canada, and Mexico being changed to facilitate global capital's mobility between the three countries.

One such change was a mandate that Mexico amend its constitution to allow foreigners to own Mexican land; previously, this had been against the law. Mexico after NAFTA would prove useful to the Smithfield company because it had basically no environmental laws and even less enforcement of what laws there were than the U.S. South. Typical hog farms concentrate thousands of animals in small spaces, creating lake-sized waste pools containing a toxic brew of blood, bones, and guts mixed with poisons that at least theoretically stop the waste pools from generating or spreading deadly mosquito-borne or other diseases. The combination of low to no laws, zero enforcement, and a second NAFTA requirement, permission for Mexican trucks and truckers to move their rigs across the U.S. border, would make Mexico a new, strategic enclave for Smithfield.

In the late 1980s, prior to NAFTA, Smithfield had viewed North Carolina as a mini-Mexico inside the U.S. The workforce had darker skin and spoke English. A big international ocean port, a plantation legal culture, and lax laws advantaged southeastern North Carolina when the company decided to build the biggest hog plant in the world. *New York Times* columnist Bob Herbert described the place in a 2006 column: "Spending a few days in Tar Heel and the surrounding area—dotted with hog farms, cornfields, and the occasional Confederate flag—is like stepping back in time. This is a place where progress has slowed to a crawl."[6] And the pork plant in Tar Heel opened for production in 1992. Today, 32,000 hogs *a day* are slaughtered and processed in this single plant. Five thousand workers staff departments with names like the Kill Floor, the Gas Chamber, and the Hanging and Rehanging Rooms. Meat production is considered one of the most dangerous jobs in the world, and a Human Rights Watch report in 2005 listed six factors that make meat factories deadly to the humans as well as the hogs: Line Speed, Close-Quarters Cutting, Heavy Lifting, Sullied Work Conditions, Long Hours, and Inadequate Training and Equipment.[7]

Failure Round I

In 1993, the United Food and Commercial Workers Union, the UFCW, decided to help workers at the new Tar Heel plant form a union. The UFCW was founded in 1979 through several mergers of four older unions, including the Amalgamated Meat Cutters and Butcher Workmen of North America, chartered by the American Federation of Labor in 1897, which in 1937 was reformulated by the Congress of Industrial Organizations, (CIO), into a new union, the Packinghouse Workers Organizing Committee (PWOC).[8] The PWOC, a union heavily influenced by Communists and socialists in its heyday,[9] was the union that Saul Alinsky partnered with in Chicago in his first community organizing effort, the Back of the Yards Council.[10] Upton Sinclair described the conditions in the Chicago meat-packing plants in his 1906 novel *The Jungle*.[11]

The UFCW had other Smithfield Foods plants in several Midwestern states that had long been under union contract. But the union presence in these Midwestern plants was not the result of contemporary organizing by the UFCW, but rather of Smithfield Foods' aggressive acquisition during the 1980s of smaller companies like John Morrell and Farmland, plants and companies that had been unionized by the PWOC in its more radical days, in the decades prior to the election of Ronald Reagan and Reagan's campaign to deunionize America. But the Tar Heel plant dwarfed all other facilities in size, workforce numbers, and production output. The union understood that its ability to hold or set decent standards in its older Midwestern meat-packing contracts would be eroded or threatened if it couldn't organize a union in the shiny new factory, the biggest such facility in the world. The Tar Heel plant was so massive that its arrival instantly altered the balance of power between the union and the company. The plant had been open for one year when the UFCW first attempted a unionization drive, in 1994. The UFCW approached the drive as if it were still the early 1970s, following the standard union playbook, which requires that the union get 30 percent of the workers to sign union authorization cards, then file for an election at the National Labor Relations Board (NLRB).

The company also followed a standard playbook, the employer's, but unlike the union's, theirs had been updated for the post-Reagan era and systematically broke almost every law on the labor books, with tactics that included intimidation, threats, and even violence. The company beat the union: 704 votes for the employer, 587 for the union, in a low-turnout election. But Smithfield had violated the National Labor Relations Act so egregiously that the underfunded and understaffed NLRB actually managed to prioritize an investigation into the election abuses and reports that had been filed by workers through the union. Three years later, in 1997, the NLRB concluded their investigation and found that the company committed a series of flagrant violations in 1994, and ordered a new election to be held.[12]

The union in those years could gently be characterized as inept. Its leadership seemed to have missed Reagan's election and big business's clarion call to wipe unions out of the private sector through union busting, trade deals, automation, and plant relocation to nonunion states. Joseph Luter III, the third-generation family CEO at Smithfield, met with a senior official of the UFCW shortly after the NLRB ruling and made a personal promise in writing not to break the law as union and company headed into the second round.

Round II, New Labor is Elected at the AFL-CIO

By the 1997 election, one substantial factor affecting workers had changed: The first contested election ever at the American Federation of Labor-Congress of Industrial Organizations (AFL-CIO) had brought new leadership to the top of the house of organized labor. The UFCW had campaigned vigorously against the winning slate, clearly aligning itself with an older generation of unionists who seemed resigned to the status quo of slow union death. Now the new team at the AFL-CIO was beginning to make changes at the state level in the State Federations of Labor, and also in the county and municipal Central Labor Councils

(CLCs). The national AFL-CIO is a constitutionally weak federation; it can't dictate policy to national unions, but it can have a significant impact on more local federations of labor. The AFL-CIO in North Carolina, seeing the handwriting on the wall coming into the 1997 Smithfield election, as a last-ditch effort persuaded the UFCW to mobilize some community support for the workers. To help the union in its Smithfield drive, they sent in Roz Pellas, a well-known North Carolina activist who had recently been hired as part of the new wave of reform at the AFL-CIO, and assigned to the North Carolina Federation of Labor. Pellas recalls:

> We were called in six weeks before the election, and even though we were able to broaden the campaign beyond the plant gates in 1997, by talking to Black ministers, and tribal chiefs, it was too little, too late. They (the union) had never done this before, worker organizing and community organizing at the same time. It was simply too late; the approach was right, but it has to be from the beginning, not slapped on in the end.[13]

Because the union approached the second election with an only slightly modified playbook, with the modifications coming too little and too late, the result was a second and even more disastrous election defeat: 1910 votes for the employer, 1107 for the union.[14]

Pellas, the only woman who was allowed into the National Labor Relations vote count in 1997, described in horrific detail the scene during that second election, conducted over three days:

> It was a defeat in many ways, not just the numbers, we were being chased down the stairs by goons, the NLRB agents were hiding under the voting tables, the company was having people arrested outside as they tried to come in and vote, Smithfield had hired and deputized their own police force dressed in riot gear and stationed them all around the plant for the election, forcing workers to do something like walk the plank if they attempted to vote in the election.[15]

More than 100 labor law violations were filed by the union against the company resulting from the 1997 "election." Pellas described it as something beyond a loss—more a beat-down of epic proportions; the kind of drubbing intended to drive what professional union busters call futility, along with fear, into the hearts and minds of workers, so they'd never again think about forming a union.

It should have been blatantly obvious from the scale of the violations of the first election in 1994 that the company would repeat, if not double down on, their behavior in the 1997 election. The notion that the leader of the UFCW accepted a personal promise from the boss is unimaginable. Although the NLRB investigators had found in favor of the union after the 1994 election, the board had imposed no fines or penalties on the company for its illegal behavior, so there was no incentive against a repeat performance. One of many examples of the union's poor judgment was its decision to hold the 1997 election at all. One tool a union can use heading into an election is to deploy a tactic called blocking charges: The union gathers evidence from workers that the "laboratory conditions for the election" have been so tainted as to render the possibility of a fair election moot. The NLRB has to react immediately to "blocking charges" and determine whether or not to suspend the election. Assessing the more than 150 violations filed by the union after the 1997 election—the sheer number and types of charges that took nine years to investigate—it seems clear the union's staff leadership, had they been experienced, should have discussed with the worker leaders an alternate route, filing charges to block the election itself, rather than risk putting the workers through what union lingo calls a death march.

After its drubbing in 1997, the union turned back to its legal fight with Smithfield, walking away from the 1,107 Tar Heel workers who had voted to unionize, abandoning contact with them. Meanwhile, over the decade that followed, there was an explosion of Mexican immigration into the region, the direct result of NAFTA as Smithfield scooped up hog farms in Mexico. The company displaced Mexican workers on previously Mexican-owned lands, then helped persuade them to cross the border to work in the big new plant in North Carolina. This was a perverse and extreme extension of the concept of Smithfield's vertical integration.[16]

What began as a legal battle over the 100 labor law violations that had taken place during the 1994 election became a case study in how the laws are stacked against workers. At every turn, the National Labor Relations Board would rule in favor of the workers and against the company. And every time this happened, the company dragged out and stalled resolution by an appeal to the next level. This legal fight went on for nine years, from 1997 to 2006, until the case reached the U.S. Court of Appeals, which also ruled in favor of the workers and against the company. Facing the Supreme Court as their last option, and, with the likelihood that the court would decline their case based on the pile of evidence produced against them, Smithfield finally stopped their appeals. After more company stalling on other grounds—delaying a hearing with pleas of scheduling conflicts, company lawyers calling in sick—the U.S. Court of Appeals issued an unusually strongly worded demand that the company reinstate workers who had been fired during the 1997 election, and once again ordered a new election.

Round III, Leadership Changes in the National Union Lead to Different Strategies

By the time of this third attempt, a significant change had taken place at the UFCW. Joe Hansen, originally a rank-and-file meat cutter from Milwaukee, had been elected UFCW president, in 2004. Hansen represented a significant departure from his predecessor, Douglas Dority, the union's second president, who had initially been appointed to his position by the union's executive board. Dority was strongly aligned with the business unionist old guard of the national labor movement. During the AFL-CIO's tumultuous 1995 election, the first contested election in the organization's history, he'd acted as chief campaigner for Thomas Donahue, the union's establishment candidate. In 2003, five unions formed a coalition inside of the AFL-CIO called the New Unity Partnership (NUP). The NUP represented a group of unions that were demanding changes in the direction of the AFL-CIO, pushing it toward more effective organizing. Dority again had refused to ally himself with the opposition team. But the union's third president, Joe Hansen, immediately signaled a change in the UFCW's image and actions by realigning its position in the debate and joining the NUP leaders. By 2005, Hansen went from merely aligning with to becoming the leader of the NUP unions, which would soon break away from the AFL-CIO to form the rival national labor federation, Change to Win, arguing that much more aggressive organizing was not only needed but urgent. Some observers think the real motivation behind Hansen's decision to align with CTW had more to do with not wanting to pay per capita dues owed to the AFL-CIO, but whatever the reason, these were big changes for the UFCW in a short time period.

It was late in 2004, not long after Hansen was elected to his new post, and seven years after the second attempt at a union election at Smithfield in 1997, that the National Labor Relations Board issued its 175-page decision in favor of the workers and against the company.[17] Smithfield immediately appealed, again, but, Hansen began sending organizers down to North Carolina, confident that at some point Smithfield would exhaust its court options. The organizers he sent were inexperienced, with the exception of one skilled lead organizer. Though they wasted no time in sending this team, the national union then impeded their own progress for the next year, which they spent in a kind of schizophrenic quandary about whether or how to commit to a new campaign on the ground. They opened up a small worker center, aimed mainly at mutual assistance efforts for the now majority-Latino workforce in the plant. By providing basic immigration legal services and responding to other, largely non-workplace issues facing the new Latino population in the area, they began to make worker contacts.

The change in the national union leadership set up the context for the UFCW's decision in 2006 to go all out to win at Smithfield, and to do it by radically changing their strategy. As a newly elected national president, Hansen had *publicly* led his union out of the AFL-CIO on a pledge to organize the unorganized; now he was under pressure to deliver a big organizing win for the union. In January of 2006, four months before the U.S. Court of Appeals issued its strongly worded order compelling Smithfield to follow the National Labor Relations Board's legal order, Hansen began a new round with Smithfield, with urging and some support from the new Change to Win federation. In some ways, the CTW alliance removed internal obstacles—including staffing decisions—within the union that might have slowed the campaign at Smithfield. A new campaign director was hired to run the Tar Heel organizing drive, under the aegis of the CTW but with heavy funding from the UFCW.

The Staff Leadership

In campaigns to help workers form new unions where none exist, the full-time staff of the union determines how union resources will be used, as there is not yet a local union run by rank-and-file workers. The staff at this stage, therefore, plays an outsize role in encouraging or discouraging worker activism, participation, levels of militancy, and more, in addition to setting the framework for what a union will mean to workers who have never had one. In North Carolina, the state with the lowest union density in the United States, just 3 percent, no workers interviewed for this investigation had had any prior involvement in—or in many cases, even any knowledge of—such a thing as a union. Under such circumstances, how the staff talks about the union, literally the semantics used, in addition to key decisions made, will condition the future and set the terms for what kind of union will be created by the workers. In Chapter Three, I discussed how and why union organizers pay very close attention to semantics. In the case of the Smithfield fight, set in a rural region of a state where few unions have ever existed, workers really were literally learning about unions for the first time, so every word of these conversations mattered.

In the previous attempts to unionize the factory, in 1994 and 1997, the union staff had proved inadequate for the task. No matter how many workers wanted the union in the beginning of the campaign in 1994, few of them had understood how the employer would respond. How could they? Had they been in a union stronghold, like the health care workers in New York City, they might have. But in rural North Carolina, as workers later described it, many had never even heard of such a thing as a union. The situation demanded organizers who had sufficient know-how to be able to teach and coach worker-leaders through what was obviously going to be a *very* hard fight.

Overcoming the two prior defeats at Smithfield would surely signal a new day at the national union. And the new union leadership understood that the conventional approach that had failed twice would fail a third time, if they didn't change the *strategy*. Based on the repression level deployed by the employer in the first two attempts, they knew they would have to bring pressure from both outside the workplace—to help create room for the workers to first develop and then sustain a strong worker-led campaign on the inside. By chance, the first person they chose to run the new Smithfield campaign, an internal candidate, had to back out of the role for family reasons. Their second choice was Gene

Bruskin, a longtime and respected union campaigner. Bruskin's main role for decades in the labor movement had been as the elected secretary treasurer at the Food and Allied Services Trade (FAST) department of the AFL-CIO, where he was mentored by Jeff Fiedler, FAST's elected president.[18]

In his book *Restoring the Power of Unions*,[19] Julius Getman credits the leaders of FAST generally and Fiedler specifically, with helping to invent the modern strategic campaign, experimenting through the 1980s on deploying campaigns that both sought high levels of worker engagement and agency (known as "the ground war") and also sought to exploit any type of vulnerability a corporation might have outside the workplace (called the "air war").[20] The strategic campaign model that FAST was developing in the 1980s was not simply a corporate campaign. Corporate campaigns typically underuse or entirely bypass the workers and concentrate efforts on a leverage strategy focused on vulnerabilities in the supply chain and the regulatory structure of an employer. Strategic campaigns, by contrast, place at least some emphasis on the inside strategy or the ground war, and the outside strategy, meaning other forms of leverage.

Bruskin is a working-class Jew raised in Philadelphia. "I definitely describe myself as a leftist and have since the '60s," he told me in an interview. "I am a child of the '60s anti-war, anti-racist, anti-sexist movements. I didn't get involved in the labor movement for ideological reasons. In 1977 I was driving a bus because I was doing community theater and needed an income, and we went on strike to demand a union election and they put me in jail. My politics were central to everything I have done in the labor movement."[21] By the time Bruskin was hired to run the Smithfield campaign, he had had the experience of founding another workers' organization, U.S. Labor Against the War, formed in 2003 to oppose George Bush's war in Iraq. He had worked on Jesse Jackson's Rainbow Coalition campaign effort in the early 1990s, and done extensive solidarity work with liberation struggles in Central America, South Africa, the Middle East, and the Philippines. I argue that Bruskin's left-wing politics *significantly informed the organizing strategy he used*, a strategy that kept the focus on the workers themselves engaging in class struggle.

He describes his entry into the Smithfield fight:

I came in as an outsider. I didn't know meat-packing. Fiedler said,
'Give it to Bruskin.' So I made a deal with them [the UFCW], which
was I will go on loan to the UFCW if you want me to do this, I am
going to hire my own staff, put together my own Smithfield team,
control my budget, and you can't take my people away from the campaign for any reason, I don't care if you have nine decertification campaigns going someplace else, you can't touch my team.[22]

When he met with Joe Hansen, Hansen told Bruskin, "Luter
(Smithfield's CEO) will never give in; I've talked to him, he will never
give us a deal."[23] In reply, Bruskin thanked Hansen for "giving me
the chance to organize the biggest meat-packing plant in the world.
I wanted to say, 'I'd do this for free,' but I didn't. I just thanked him."
Bruskin's years of work with Fiedler oriented the subsequent campaign,
a campaign in which Bruskin would at times have to beat back the
union's attempts to downscale, downsize, and diminish the workers'
role. It was Bruskin's long experience in unions that gave him the fore-
sight during his personal hiring negotiations to place a fortress around
his staff and negotiate the autonomy that conditioned the subsequent
campaign.

Workers as Primary Actors, aka Worker Agency

They pissed off the wrong motherfucker.[24]

Keith Ludlum, Smithfield Employee Fired for Union Activism

Bruskin was put in charge of this campaign at the height of the
debate between unions in the AFL-CIO and the breakaway unions
of the Change to Win federation. The debate is the one I discussed
in Chapter Two, the debate between mobilizing and organizing, and
about whether or not, as Peter Olney said, "workers get in the way of
growth deals." Some of CTW's leaders were being heavily influenced
by SEIU, especially when it came to central questions of worker agency
in campaigns. There was growing pressure on Bruskin to stop focusing
so much on the workers. But as the story of this fight will show, the

intensity of the previous fights had made some of the workers' leaders extraordinarily skilled, because of their experience in *struggle*.

The nine-year legal battle over the 1997 election violations culminated in early 2006. On May 5, the U.S. Court of Appeals, D.C. Circuit, issued an order for the "Enforcement of an Order of the National Labor Relations Board."[25] The strongly worded eleven-page ruling affirmed the NLRB's 175-page order issued on December 16, 2004. The December 2004 NLRB order was itself a result of the employer appealing the *initial* decision in favor of the workers, a more-than-400-page decision by the NLRB's administrative law judge, or ALJ, on December 15, 2000. Administrative law judges hold hearings that are much like a trial, but within the National Labor Relations Process, in which both sides present their case, with witnesses, lawyers, evidence, and so forth. Though the workers "won" at this first stage, which the employer had already slowed down by obstructing the scheduling of hearings, delaying providing required documents, and other tactics, the employer appealed. Four years later in 2004, the workers won again. And the employer appealed again. Two years later, the workers won for the third time, and still no election or other worker action was possible, as the company stalled through other legal delays.

In 2002, long after the initial trial was concluded, after the case had been heard and was working its way through the many employer appeals, a whistle-blower emerged. A manager quit, a manager who had been in the human resources department at Smithfield and who had been part of the team that had disciplined and fired the union supporters because they were union supporters. Though the trial had been wrapped up two years earlier, the union cleverly engineered for this manager to present testimony, under sworn oath, before a congressional committee. She gave alarming details in her testimony, including that Smithfield told her to engage in illegal activity or she herself would be fired.

This former human resources manager, Sherri Buffkin, told the U.S. Senate Health, Education, Labor, and Pensions Committee in 2002,

> "I'm here because Smithfield Foods asked me to lie on an affidavit and made me choose between my job and telling the truth. I'm here today to tell you how Smithfield Foods sought out and punished employees

because they were union supporters, and that the company remained true to its word that it would stop at nothing to keep the union out."[26]

Although this evidence came outside of the earlier trial court process inside the NLRB, because it was sworn under oath before Congress, and because the manager testified that her own affidavits used by the employer in the trial were falsified, this testimony was referenced by the subsequent legal orders.

The contents of the eventual order covered 175 pages because the employer had violated so many laws, each one of which was investigated. For example, in section one of the document, the company was ordered to "cease and desist" a series of behaviors so lengthy that in listing them the NLRB judge exhausted the letters in the alphabet, starting over after "z" with "aa." They began on page 14, starting with a: The employer shall cease and desist from "threatening employees with plant closure if they select the Union as their collective bargaining agent," and going all the way through to ee: "In any other manner interfering with, restraining, or coercing its employees in the exercise of their rights." In particular, x through aa offer sobering insights into and evidence of what the employees had faced in the 1997 election: the company is to "cease and desist from"

x   Threating employees that wages would be frozen if the Union were elected as the collective bargaining representative;
y   Assaulting employees in retaliation for their union activities.
z   Causing the arrest of employees in retaliation for their union activities.
aa Threatening violence in retaliation for employee activities.

In language related to y, the document reads:

In the cafeteria after the ballots in the 1997 election were counted and it became apparent that the Union had lost, [manager] Null and Plant Manager Larry Johnson told Anthony Forrest, an observer for the Respondent, "to go kick Chad Young's ass." Forrest then approached Young, and pushing and shoving began in the cafeteria.

Young had been an observer for the union and the employers physically beat him in public, just to make the point that not only would the workers lose the election, but union supporters would be physically beaten in front of coworkers, in addition to losing their jobs. The judge also describes how each of ten workers was illegally fired, and stipulates the terms for their rehire, with an order to "make them whole," meaning pay them back wages from the nine years since their dismissal. Most of these fired workers had long since found alternative employment, died, or moved, one of the objectives the employer's strategy of stalling was calculated to achieve.

By June 27, 2006, Smithfield was forced under threat of the U.S. Court of Appeals to post a legal "Notice to Employees, Posted Pursuant to a Judgment of the United States Court of Appeals, Enforcing an Order of the National Labor Relations Board." This document was posted at every time clock and in every break room. In view of the company's glaring violations, the NLRB also made Smithfield mail it to every single worker who had been employed in the company from 1997 to the present. In addition, the NLRB ordered the company to have an actual NLRB agent enter the factory and over the course of several days read the order aloud in employee meetings. The court also ordered a new election, but the union understood by now that a third election undertaken without some form of preagreement for employer neutrality, union access to the inside of the facility, and an accord limiting company antiworker behavior would be a disaster. The union's first goal became securing a "card check and neutrality agreement," requiring the employer to legally recognize the union as the certified collective bargaining agent once a majority of workers had signed union authorization cards.

The conditions at the Smithfield Tar Heels factory were so bad before the union came that some workers joked that there was 100 percent turnover every day. A New York Times reporter, Charlie LeDuff, went undercover and worked in the Smithfield factory in 2000, for what became part of a Pulitzer Prize–winning series on race in America. LeDuff wrote, "Slaughtering swine is repetitive, brutish work, so grueling that three weeks on the factory floor leave no doubt in your mind about why the turnover is 100 percent. Five thousand quit and five thousand are hired every year."[27] LeDuff reported that blacks and Latinos got the dirtiest jobs, with the Latinos at the absolute bottom of the dirty jobs ladder, along with convicts in full prison uniform, who were often allowed to work there just prior to their release (a 2008 spin on wage slavery). According to union reports, all joking aside, the turnover at Smithfield actually was nearly 100 percent each year. Three times the UFCW at Tar Heel had received the Excelsior list, the list of employees that employers must give to the union when the NLRB has declared an election will take place. Five thousand employees were different each time, save for some 200 names that overlapped. In the first election in 1994, a majority of the plant's employees were black. By the 1997 election, some 35 to 40 percent were Latino, the rest being variously black, Native American (Lumbee, mostly), and white. The Center for Immigration Studies reported that during the 1990s, the Latino population in North Carolina ballooned faster than in any other state, a 394 percent increase from 76,726 to 378,963.[28]

By the time the union received the Excelsior list again in 2006, as part of the court order, roughly 60 percent of the plant's workers were Latino.[29] By the time of the election, the Latino number, remarkably, would fall again, back to 26 percent.[30] High turnover is often used as an excuse for union defeat, or union inaction, but high turnover had little to no effect on the results in these elections. The primarily African-American workforce in the first election did not produce a yes vote, though research indicates that blacks vote for unions.[31] According to Buffkin's congressional testimony, it was the employer's intent to replace blacks with Latinos with two objectives in mind: to keep the workforce divided through both instigations of racial conflict and overt segregation, and to create an undocumented immigrant workforce that the employer believed they could more easily control.[32] While the employer succeeded at driving racial divisions between 1997 and 2005 in the absence of an effective union campaign; a key to the union's success in 2006 would be first earning legitimacy with each major constituency in the plant, and then bridging the divisions between them, creating unity and solidarity despite the extraordinary efforts by the boss to systematically pit worker against worker.

Gene Bruskin learned early in his tenure as campaign director that the employer's calculation on the timidity of Latinos was wildly off base. Immigrant rights organizations had declared May 1, 2006 to be a national "strike" day for immigrant workers. A few weeks before May 1, Latino worker leaders approached the union to tell them they planned to participate in the national strike. This would be the first walkout on the new staff director's watch, though the second in three years for the plant. "The workers decided to strike and asked for our help to organize a large march, and we did what they asked," Bruskin recalled. While this meant union organizers were encouraging the May 1 walkout, there's no doubt that an earlier wildcat walkout in 2003 by the plant's Latino cleaners had been on the workers' own initiative; the union had had no presence at all during the 2003 action.

For May 1, 2006, the union was laying low, waiting for the U.S. Court of Appeals ruling. Even so, the UFCW assembled a meeting with workers, the DJ of the main Latino radio station, Catholic priests in the area, and the local soccer club president, to make a plan. Bruskin set the stage for many subsequent responses to such actions by directing staff to order 5,000 T-shirts that said, "Immigrant rights are worker rights." They also made a leaflet linking Cesar Chavez to Martin Luther King, Jr., to distribute along the march. On May 1, over 2,500 Latino employees at the Smithfield plant refused work and joined even more immigrant workers in a march that by local standards was the largest people could remember in Tar Heel. They returned to the plant the next day, and the employer, hoping to not alienate them just as the courts were sputtering out their legal orders for a new union election, actually waived employer action against them. By late June, after the NLRB had forced management to post, mail, and discuss their many violations of the law, direct actions by workers inside the plant would pick up where the May 1 action had left off, and slowly escalate for the next 18 months.

As noted above, included in the U.S. Court of Appeals ruling, after the first order of cease-and-desist came the order that the employer offer ten workers illegally fired in the campaigns in the 1990s their jobs back. It also stipulated making the workers "whole," that is, financially compensating them for loss of wages:

2. Take the following affirmative action necessary to effectuate the policies of the Act.

(a) Within 14 days from the date of this Order, offer Lawanna Johnson, Keith Ludlum, George Simpson, Chris Council, Fred McDonald, Larry Jones, Ray Shawn Ward, Margo McMillan, Tara Davis, and Ada Perry full reinstatement to their former jobs or, if those jobs no longer exist, offer

them substantially equivalent positions, without prejudice to their senior-
ity and other rights or privileges previously enjoyed.

Of the ten employees named, nine accepted the financial compensation offer and never returned to Smithfield. One worker, Keith Ludlum,
wanted his job back.

Ludlum had been fired from the Smithfield plant during the 1994
election, and had been taken out in handcuffs.[33] The NLRB ordered that
he be reinstated in time for the 1997 election; the company refused.[34]
His termination and the company's refusal to follow the first order for
reinstatement were rolled into the longer legal battle. Ludlum is white,
a North Carolina native, and a Desert Storm veteran who shocked
just about everyone, by accepting the offer of his old job in 2006. By
then he had a new life and was making good money as a construction
contractor—much better money than he would make walking back into
nonunion Smithfield. But Ludlum had unfinished business at the plant.
As he put it, "They pissed off the wrong motherfucker." After a pause, he
added, "Not sure I should be quoted saying that? But when you escort
people out with sheriff's deputies, in handcuffs, we tend to not accept
that real well. They really pissed me off."[35]

On his first day back inside the plant, in early July of 2006, Ludlum
had a sense of confidence that came with a court order from the U.S.
Court of Appeal, D.C. Circuit reinstating him:

> When I first went back in, there was no inside campaign, so we
> started it. The company wasn't reacting. First I figured out some rela-
> tionships inside, who was relating to who, then I had to make the
> company react. I had to scratch their underbelly. I wrote *Union Time*
> across my hard hat. I had a mission. They had a mission. The next
> day, I did it on my raincoat, and they came after me for that. I had to
> do things so that the other workers could see me winning the battle
> against them. I had a federal court order and I knew the company
> had to be careful.

Within weeks, Ludlum began leading direct actions with dozens, and
then hundreds, of his coworkers, including a collective sit-down action
to demand clean water for the workers inside the plant. From my interviews with him, it was clear his knowledge of labor law, gleaned from

the first organizing campaign and the subsequent legal fight over his termination, was an incredible asset.

"I remember everything, his hat, his raincoat, I remember it all," coworker Ollie Hunt says. "I came to work at Smithfield right after Keith was reinstated. I was right there running hogs, stationed right next to Keith." Ollie Hunt is a Lumbee Indian who grew up in Rowland, North Carolina, about 40 miles from the factory. His father is pure Lumbee; his mother is white. "I grew up in a town with one red light, and as a kid I worked cropping tobacco and picking cucumbers," he told me. He has two daughters and one son: "My first girl is named Miami Raynie Hunt after my wife, Amy's, favorite country song; 'Miami, My Amy.' The song, by Keith Whitley, was once #14 on the country charts and remains their favorite. Amy, also Lumbee, is a youth development specialist who has gone back to school to become a guidance counselor. Ollie notes, "Where I was from, I never heard of a union."[36]

Within days of Keith Ludlum's return, Ollie, Keith, and a third emerging union leader, Terry Slaughter, all stationed together in the livestock department, began to plot their course to a union victory. Livestock was a key department, because if workers in Livestock stopped letting the hogs off the trucks, not only would it stop the production line, it would also cause a massive traffic blockade on a major interstate highway. The Livestock workers all talked about how easy it would be to block that highway. With 32,000 hogs a day coming in on the trucks, the tactic was guaranteed to work.

Terry Slaughter was the crew shift leader in Livestock, assigning who took which station and where, and generally keeping an eye on the flow of the hogs. This wasn't a management position, but it did mean he knew a little more about hog flow, workers' schedules, and more. Slaughter is black, born in North Carolina but raised in New York City. Unions weren't a foreign concept to Terry, and before moving back to North Carolina he'd gotten to know people in New York's health-care workers' union and in city government unions. He'd left New York to try his fortunes someplace more affordable, where he might get a little house.

Slaughter, Hunt, and Ludlum would build an inseparable bond during the campaign. As Ollie said, "Me, Slaughter, and Keith, we had a tight relationship. People would see the white, the black and the Indian, and management knew trouble was coming." In the Smithfield factory, workers were isolated to an unusual degree, segregated by department, room, race, language, and more, with incredibly loud machines running at all times, drowning casual communication. But Livestock workers had to walk the entire length of the plant to get to their jobs. This gave them a second privilege as power workers: They could see people, and talk to them, as they walked into and out of the plant. It took almost 40 minutes for Hunt, Slaughter, and Ludlum to get from the parking lot to their station.[37] They would soon turn that already long walk into a saunter, doing union work along the way, work only the worker-leaders themselves could do, since union staff were barred from going anywhere near this factory. More than one hour of face-chat time each day.

Bruskin says that once the leaders established this first small team of worker activists inside the plant, they began to physically map the entire factory, something the union had never attempted in the earlier campaigns. The sheer size of the plant—973,000 square feet, with a maze-like layout—was daunting. Drawing a literal map is step one for workplace organizers, but charting which workers worked where, with whom, when, and who related to whom and *why* is the most important step, the chart is a hallmark of a good organizing campaign. The peripatetic Livestock workers were key in drawing the map and charting social networks among the workers. They also spent the summer and fall escalating "in-plant" direct actions and beginning to build a statewide community support effort, as well as a national coalition that would soon launch a consumer campaign against Smithfield, all under the banner of Justice@Smithfield, complete with a website, facts about the employer's track record against its workers, an exhaustive litany of the company's environmental law violations, CEO profits—just about as good a profile on a company as any ever done in such a campaign. Top-notch research and strategic leverage had been among Bruskin's areas of expertise coming into the fight, and FAST had already conducted years of in-depth research on every aspect of this company. Workers and their allies were marching at shareholder meetings, creating online petition campaigns, and more. The Justice@Smithfield campaign was generating not just local but also national newspaper headlines. Workers were constantly challenging the company's authority inside the plant, including sitting down in the plant, backing up the line, blocking the highway, and more.

By the fall of 2006, there were strong pro-union worker committees being built within the plant's Latino and black departments. Bruskin was trying to figure out how to begin to build solidarity between these groups, and this was harder than usual, because management had almost perfected the science of fomenting racial hatred inside the plant. The three weeks Charles LeDuff, the *New York Times* reporter, spent undercover in the Tar Heel factory led to a searing journalistic indictment of company-inspired hate. LeDuff wrote that the whites and Indians hated the blacks and Mexicans; the Mexicans hated the blacks; the blacks hated the Mexicans; and the boss drove this hate *systematically*.[38] Bruskin decided it was time for a Black-Brown weekend picnic among the groups' key leaders. People were ready to meet and talk as one factory, to emerge from their departmental ethnic enclaves. And just as the plans for the weekend BBQ were launched, Smithfield launched an "air strike."

In October, the employer sent several thousand letters to Latino workers, saying that they needed to prove their immigration status by providing Social Security numbers that matched their birth certificates—one of the more common employer tactics today.[39] The letters, according to Smithfield, were a response to Immigration and Customs Enforcement (ICE) officials contacting Smithfield and requesting that the employer verify the legal status of the employees on payroll by verifying their Social Security numbers. It's surely not a likely coincidence that in the middle of a renewed, and clearly more successful, union organizing drive, this employer, known for rogue behavior since the plant opened, took a sudden interest in complying with a law—when the law was one to sow fear in the hearts of more than half the plant's workforce. By early November, the employer had sent out 550 "no match" letters, informing workers that their Social Security numbers could not be verified from the documents provided. Next, they fired two dozen workers based on charges of bad paperwork. The 550 letters sent a signal that mass firings of Latinos were coming.

On November 17, 2006, more than 1,000 Latinos staged a wildcat strike and walked off the job, temporarily shutting the plant down, again. Bruskin's deeply rooted values are perhaps best depicted by his response to this action: "I am on the job for seven months, and about to drive down to North Carolina to meet with some workers when I get a call from an organizer freaking out, 'Gene, they've just shut the plant down, the Latinos walked out. What should we do?'" Bruskin's reaction to the call underscores the central importance of top staff leadership. He could easily have said, "Get them all back to work as fast as you can," which was exactly what Bruskin's supervisor demanded he do, or "Run the other way," or, worse, "Hold a press conference condemning the workers' behavior." Any of these responses would be fairly typical of many unions today. Instead, Bruskin guided by his leftist principles, ordered his staff to get "1,000 bottles of water and 100 pizzas to the workers, *fast!*"[40] It's still hot in southeastern North Carolina in November.

A handful of non-Latinos had also walked out in solidarity, workers like Ludlum. According to Slaughter, "These firings and then the walk-out was a wake-up call to us blacks in the plant. Watching brown people get taken off the line and fired and then others walking out over it sort of shook us, like, Hey, what are we waiting for? What are we doing about the conditions here? It was almost embarrassing how little we were doing."[41] The walkout generated headlines throughout North Carolina, and also in *The New York Times*, which declared how unusual it was for nonunion employees, let alone employees with documentation issues, to wildcat in the United States.[42] As soon as the walkout began, creating a crisis for the employer, Bruskin and the worker leaders decided to dispatch a priest, Father Arce of St. Andrew's Catholic church, to mediate and negotiate with the employer. Smithfield had refused to meet with union staff or union-identified worker leaders, so the union found a perfect alternate to handle the negotiations: a religious leader who had credibility with the Latinos but was not seen as an associate of the union. In fact, Father Arce was receiving coaching from the Latino members of his parish who were also now union leaders, the workers themselves acting as brokers between the union staff and the Catholic priest.[43]

The workers' demands were that everyone who walked out be allowed to return to work the next day with no reprisals, that the company stop firing people, and that the immigrant workers be given more time to prove their status. When Father Arce first came out of the meeting with a "promise" from the employer to meet all demands, the Latino parishioners turned union leaders sent him back inside to get it all in writing. They were schooling the priest that the company was not to be trusted. Bruskin understood at the time the pivotal importance of the fact that for the first time ever the employer was actually *negotiating* with employees—the fact that it was through a Catholic priest was immaterial. The mere act of getting recalcitrant employers to begin to learn to bargain with employees can be an important first step towards later negotiations: The concept has been established.

On the heels of this walkout, Bruskin and key worker-leaders, the very ones who had just met for the Black-Brown BBQ, agreed that they needed a way to get the black employees activated and working together with the Latinos. Their idea was to demand that Martin Luther King Day be an official holiday at the plant, with paid time off for those who requested it and double time for everyone who had to work shifts that day. The union immediately began to produce literature in Spanish and English, with King's picture on one side, Cesar Chavez's on the other, describing the common values and the liberation efforts of these two leaders. Additionally, the demand that Smithfield honor Martin Luther King Day was one that union activists could use to rally the broader community to their cause. When the nationally recognized holiday arrived, a majority of workers had signed a petition demanding a paid day off, and the company's refusal generated press headlines sympathetic to the workers.[44]

Smithfield then reversed its decision, but did so in a manner that denied the workers' victory; the company announced a new policy to give all workers in all their facilities nationwide the holiday, effectually denying their decision had anything to do with local worker demands. The workers felt vindicated nonetheless, but their euphoria was short-lived. Two days after the holiday, on January 23, the employer let Immigration and Customs Enforcement into the plant, and the uniformed officials took twenty-one more Latino workers off the lines, in handcuffs, clearly headed for deportation. Anxiety seeped throughout the plant. By the weekend, news that the workers had been shipped to deportation facilities far from North Carolina had spread, along with the fear that any one of hundreds, if not thousands of employees, might be next.

Rather than see people slink away one by one, worker-leaders decided to shut the plant down, *again*. It was an act of defiance as well as a move to avoid getting dragged off to a for-profit U.S. detention center for eventual deportation. On Sunday, January 28, more than 2,000 Latino employees walked off the first shift, which shut the plant down immediately.[45] But this time, the workers had packed up and left for good. There were no parking-lot negotiations between Catholic priests and the employer. "La Migra," Immigration, was clearly returning soon to deport more workers. Whatever trust the employer might have earned with its November decision to allow the workers back into the plant had been permanently destroyed.

There were so many employer-inflicted casualties in this particular class war, the rather stunning fact that 2,000 individuals lost their jobs in a single day because they had wanted a union can almost get buried in the long list of other outrages. That they chose to leave by engaging in a massive wildcat strike that would hurt the boss, if only for several days, speaks to their deep sense of human dignity, and their bravery. By this time, there were almost daily daring actions by workers on the inside and vicious responses from the employer, and the fight was shifting outside, where it would generate more support.

Additional Power Source: The North Carolina Community

> *The first time I remember getting called from the union was when the ICE had just raided and deported some Smithfield workers. I was driving back from Tennessee that day, where I had just been part of starting a new faith formation called the Word and the World, an effort to bring together the seminary, the sanctuary, and the streets. To make "The Word" more meaningful to the world we live in.*[46]
>
>   Reverend Nelson Johnson, Beloved Community Church, Greensboro, N.C.

The pace of the worker campaign inside the plant was overwhelming the union staff, but it was still insufficient to bring the employer to the table. Bruskin sought out national allies to launch a national consumer campaign branding Smithfield Pork as the white meat that came with human blood through human sacrifice. A young North Carolina organizer named Libby Manley had been an intern on the campaign, and Bruskin decided to make her position full-time, assigning her to engage the North Carolina community. Because the UFCW had pulled out of the national AFL-CIO, the AFL-CIO wouldn't lend them Roz Pellas again, but Pellas was committed to the workers and the campaign, no matter what official fissures appeared at the national level. Back in 1997, Pellas had tapped any and every religious leader she knew in North Carolina. Reverend Nelson Johnson had attended college with Roz Pellas two decades earlier, and they were still friends. Reverend Johnson would emerge as a central player driving North Carolina religious leaders' response to the workers' campaign. He understood that framing (how to contextualize the fight when discussing it) was going to be key if the workers were to stand a chance, and his earliest objective was to shift the frame of the story as it was unfolding:

> First of all, I think community is a framing for all the issues we face, and in this case the leading edge of the issue at Smithfield was labor. By calling this a community struggle, we began to change the frame and break down the structural division and set it up so that if justice is the issue here, than everyone in the community is invited to be a part of the campaign. So labor isn't an "other," some "Northern-based" thing, some "anti-Southern" thing; it's actually people in our own community.[47]

Reverend Johnson decided that the Smithfield workers' campaign would be a good North Carolina project for his new program, the Word and the World. He hosted a meeting of religious leaders from around the region and invited a longtime North Carolina farmworker leader, Baldemar Velasquez,[48] to come to the meeting to educate the religious leaders about two issues: unions and Latino immigrants. Reverend Johnson's network was almost exclusively a black preachers' network. Immigration was so new that people in the region didn't understand it. Sarita Gupta, the head of Jobs with Justice, the group that would coordinate the national consumer boycott, reflects on this:

> It seems hard to believe now, but in 2006, we'd try to talk about the immigrant rights sub-struggle taking place in this union fight, and people would look at us and say, "Huh? Immigrants, in North Carolina, in a factory?" People weren't quite processing the rapid growth of the immigrant workforce in the U.S. South. And, the union was struggling with how to manage the conversation around immigration. The Smithfield management was as sophisticated as any we've seen in pitting people against each other.[49]

Reverend Johnson understood, as Gupta and Velasquez did, that the Smithfield fight could be a breakthrough in many ways for North Carolina in black-brown relations, in addition to being a potential breakthrough for the national union in the meat-packing industry and also the South. Rev. Johnson made a point of inviting a longtime colleague of his to attend the weekend meeting, a little-known pastor from Goldsboro, the Reverend Dr. William Barber. Today, Rev. Barber is regarded as the founder and a key leader of North Carolina's Moral Mondays movement. Back then, he had just made a successful run for president of the state branch of the NAACP. He beat a do-nothing incumbent who had routinely accepted financial contributions from Smithfield Foods during the horrific period of deportations, firings, and racist company shenanigans.

One of Rev. Barber's first public acts as president was to refuse a check for $10,000 from Smithfield, informing the company that the NAACP would no longer be complicit in the company's abuse of their workers' human rights. He became a key figure supporting the Smithfield workers in their unionization effort and used the campaign against Smithfield to help renew a moribund NAACP chapter. Suddenly the workers had a historic civil rights group with considerable legitimacy in North Carolina helping to lead the charge, in addition to the emerging religious leader's coalition.

Rev. Johnson, intent on making the Smithfield campaign a North Carolina community fight, proposed that the first action by religious leaders inside the state would be to hold twelve simultaneous pickets at North Carolina's homegrown and very successful grocery store chain, Harris Teeter.[50] He and the team of religious leaders picked these dozen Harris Teeter stores based whether or not they had large numbers of black customers, and on whether they had a willing partner in their religious network, a partner who could bring out sufficient people to lead the protests. Harris Teeter's current website reflects the image-conscious nature of the grocery store, something the local pastors already understood. The site displays page after page of "famous celebrities" who shop at Harris Teeter stores, including Dick Cheney, Tiger Woods, Tom Brokaw, and Wayne Newton. The picketers declared that Harris Teeter needed to stop selling Smithfield's products until the company began to treat the community right. The decision to target North Carolina–based Smithfield pork in North Carolina's home-bred and popular chain grocery with North Carolina preachers calling on the company to treat "the community" with decency was an instant success. Harris Teeter, which had a board dominated by evangelical conservatives, immediately began calling Smithfield to demand they "get these people out from in front of our stores."

According to Bob Geary, a veteran North Carolina journalist who filed more than two dozen stories about Smithfield[51] and is currently a columnist at the North Carolina *Indy Week*, "Nothing made a difference with the union campaigns all those years until they brought the campaign to Raleigh [the state capital]. No one goes to Tar Heel, it's all by itself, this giant plant in a tiny town. Smithfield had no incentive not to fight. When they [the union] made it statewide, and made it a broad political fight, they won."[52]

To Win in Manufacturing in the South, Still More Leverage Is Needed

The workers inside Smithfield were firing on all pistons. The North Carolina community was engaged and upping their involvement in the fight. The company still wasn't moving. By this time, the union had abandoned any real hope for securing the card check agreement they had set out to win, because the employer had cleverly announced publicly that they were willing to hold a union election. Smithfield bosses understood what is so very difficult for almost anyone who has not been involved in this type of effort to understand: Just because you hold an election, it does not mean it is free or fair. Most liberals, including those in the U.S. mainstream media, readily understand that when a repressive regime somewhere in the world calls for an election to add a fig leaf of legitimacy to its continued rule, the election is in no way free or fair. Yet these same people cannot seem to grasp that an employer like Smithfield, which effectively got rid of 2,000 immigrant workers (pro-union voters)—many of them encouraged by the company to come to the U.S. illegally in the first place—and was systematically driving a race war inside the plant, is not likely to hold a "free and fair" union election. Bruskin discussed how difficult this moment in the campaign was: being suddenly forced to argue against an election. He "lost" some key sympathetic journalists over this issue, including the *New York Times* columnist Bob Herbert, and decided to all but abandon the card check effort and shift to accepting that there would have to be an election, but with *enforceable* neutrality of some sort, actual terms in writing, with observers (picture Jimmy Carter), guaranteeing that the company wouldn't violate the workers' rights again.

Bruskin wanted an all-out national escalation of the union's campaign. His first request was to the UFCW, which represents the retail
workers in some large grocery stores across the country.[53] Bruskin
thought that if the fifteen biggest UFCW grocery locals across the country began to take action, the company would understand that the fight
was leaving the North Carolina border. But there was a problem. The
UFCW local unions basically did nothing (a remarkably common challenge most U.S. unions have been unwilling to take on, lest they lose
votes for their leadership at future conventions). A few tried to help;
most took no action at all, no matter what the request. According to
Bruskin, "I just wanted the heads of the fifteen biggest locals to write a
Dear Grocery Store letter to the grocery store owners saying, 'We want
to talk about this one product,' but the retail locals were weak, always
trying to make nice with the employer, and they were siloed internally
from the meatpacking division. So we gave up." Bruskin decided to turn
to Jobs with Justice (JwJ) to lead the field mobilization of the national
escalation.

Sarita Gupta, JwJ's executive director, said that it was in part Gene
Bruskin's style, in addition to Joe Hansen's arrival at the helm of the
UFCW, that allowed local North Carolina leaders and groups like hers
to take *ownership* of the effort together: "The campaign was really different in the sense that the union actually turned entire pieces over
to allies, invited us to the table, and challenged us to get it done."[54]
After the Taft-Hartley Act was passed in 1947, unions in the United
States were barred from calling boycotts or secondary boycotts (one of
so many examples of how fundamentally anti-democratic the workplace is under United States laws). But community groups, religious
organizations, and other nonunion groups are able as consumers to call
for consumer boycotts. [*Note to unions*: workers are also community
members, religious, and consumers—see Chapter Two on the vastness
of the potential army.] One of the most effective tactics that Jobs with
Justice deployed in the national consumer strategy was its campaign
targeting Food Network celebrity chef Paula Deen. Deen, wildly popular at the time, written up in *The New York Times* and elsewhere for
her butter-heavy Southern cooking, had been hired by Smithfield to
promote its products. The effort to get Paula Deen to drop Smithfield's

products and sponsorship unfolded. It was the kind of opportunity creative activists look for.

Deen was on a national tour promoting a brand-new cookbook. Jobs with Justice tracked Deen's schedule of public appearances and began mobilizing their activist network in the places where they had enough strength for folks to picket and handbill Paula Deen. According to a Jobs With Justice internal report and evaluation of the Smithfield campaign, the JwJ coalitions publicly confronted Paula Deen at events in Washington, D.C.; Portland, Oregon; Seattle; Louisville, Kentucky; and Chicago. The group also intervened in numerous Deen radio interviews by having community allies call in and ask specific questions about the situation with Smithfield workers at the Tar Heel plant, including, most notably, during the Diane Rehm show on NPR.[55] When Deen came to promote Smithfield products in Chicago, the city where Oprah Winfrey produced her show, more than 200 union sympathizers turned out to protest, generating a good headline for the campaign in the *Chicago Tribune*. The header, "Deen Appearance Has Lots to Chew On," was followed by these opening lines:

> If Paula Deen were everybody's grandma, every meal would hit the spot, puppies would get along with kittens, and there'd be peace in the world. The genial face of Southern cooking on television's Food Network, Deen conveys a country-fried charm that seems to solve our ills with a slice of peach cobbler, although that probably wouldn't have worked with the band of union protesters who dogged her Chicago appearance.[56]

That headline would persist, and the bird-dogging the protesters engaged in at an event for Deen that drew 3,000 fans, according to the article, wouldn't end in Chicago. According to the Deen public appearances website, the union knew she was headed for Oprah Winfrey's television show. As Bruskin described it:

> We had Leila McDowell, an experienced communication strategist with a social justice perspective, she's this really smart and radical Black communications consultant; she was so radical I couldn't get the union to hire her, and, she was incredible. So she takes the

headlines we got from the *Chicago Tribune*, with 200 people protesting Paula Deen, and starts faxing it to Oprah Winfrey's people till
finally she gets someone on the phone. She says, basically, "Hey, I
want to tip you off, I don't want Oprah to get in any trouble, but if
Paula Deen comes on and promotes Smithfield hams, Oprah's wading
into the biggest labor fight in the country, and we all want Oprah to
help Obama win, not get caught up in this big labor fight."

Though the union wanted Deen's appearance canceled, the compromise was that the *Oprah Winfrey Show* forbade Deen from saying the
word "Smithfield," and they prevented her from using Smithfield products. The reason Smithfield was underwriting Deen was for her to use
her biggest public appearances to promote their hams. There was nothing bigger than the *Oprah Winfrey Show* using its clout to shut down the
Smithfield's promotion. According to legal documents, the company
had preordered 10,000 special hams for the show, none of which were
sold. In fact, these same legal documents identified this one event as
crucial to their exaggerated claim that the "union effort" was costing
them $900 million.[57]

The RICO Suit and the Election Procedure Accord

The union had endured and managed a nine-year legal fight that had
finally culminated in 2006. But the company found yet another way
to attempt to use the law to destroy the workers legally. On November
27, 2007, eighteen months after the U.S. Court of Appeals ordered the
company to cease and desist on more than an alphabet's worth of listed
illegal behavior, ten months after a third ICE immigration raid that led
over 2,000 Latino workers to stage a wildcat strike and shut the plant
down as they quit en masse in a defiant action,[58] Smithfield filed a rack-
eteering lawsuit against the union and the union's allies, opening up yet
another new legal front on which to defeat the workers. Smithfield had
found an unusual angle, deploying a set of laws originally devised to
prosecute organized crime and the Mafia: the Racketeer Influenced and
Corrupt Organizations Act, or RICO. The company asserted that the
national consumer boycott of their products amounted to "economic
warfare."[59] Smithfield further alleged that the union had mounted this

war in an attempt to "extort" from the company a card check and neutrality agreement. With the help of discovery and subpoenas, the union deduced that the plan had been hatched by Richard Berman of the website The Center for Union Facts, which later became a leading proponent of the effort, begun in 2013, to legally label worker centers and other community-based organizations essentially as "unions." Bruskin reports:

> Smithfield hired the person that drafted the original [RICO] law in the 1970s as their consultant.[60] They spent, according to them, $25 million on legal work against us. In one year, from when they filed the RICO suit until when we settled, there were over one million pages of materials subpoenaed from us; we had to take our hard drives from our desktop computers and our laptops and hand them over. Berman described the tactic in a memo as "the nuclear option." In one year, which was being expedited by the judge, all the depositions, pre-trial motions all happened. The case was ridiculous, but every time we tried to get the suit dismissed, the judge let the company continue.[61]

The contrast between the pace of activity (warp speed) of Smithfield's legal team on the RICO suit and that of their team on the nine-year NLRB suit is like the contrast between a modern race car at Indy and a horse and buggy in the rain. The RICO judge drove a fierce timeline for Smithfield, an unusually short timeline for cases on the scale of the RICO allegations. The RICO suit made many claims, an example of which was the company's allegation that the union had been particularly effective in the Paula Deen campaign. Smithfield said the union had "deprived Smithfield of an incomparable marketing opportunity" when it convinced the *Oprah Winfrey Show* to refuse to allow Paula Deen to "promote Smithfield's products before millions of viewers."[62]

Because RICO suits were designed to shut down individual family members involved in organized crime, and their organizations, RICO suits name and sue individuals, not just organizations. The Smithfield suit was filed against the key people and groups the company decided were the linchpins in the effort, including UFCW, the United Food and Commercial Workers Union; CTW, Change to Win Federation, at that

time a new rival to the AFL-CIO; Research Associates of America, the
501(c)(3) organization that was formed after CTW split from the AFL-
CIO to house the research team; FAST, the Food And Allied Service
Trades, Bruskin's employer; Jobs with Justice; Gene Bruskin; Joseph
Hansen; William T. McDonough; Leila P. McDowell; Patrick J. O'Neill;
Andrew L. Stern; and Tom Woodruff, the organizing director at CTW
and at SEIU.

The suit had an instant chilling impact on the campaign. The high-
level players inside the UFCW who were uncomfortable with the
intense and militant workers' activism on the inside of the plant used
the RICO suit as an excuse to damp down direct actions in the plant.
The more traditional thinkers inside the UFCW used the RICO suit
to attack Bruskin's strategy at every level. Tensions were rife. Bruskin,
the workers, and their allies wanted to ramp up action in response;
the old-guard types wanted to pull field resources and shift them to
nonworker leverage strategies. Concurrently, the individuals named in
the RICO suit were all coming to terms with the reality of significant
personal liability if they lost the case, as the purpose of RICO is, in
part, to bankrupt corrupt individuals. Bruskin pushed hard against
the effort to shut the campaign down, arguing they clearly had the
company feeling desperate. These decisions about pedal-to-the-metal
versus full-brake aren't uncommon in big union campaigns, and in this
case, the strategy to fight on and uptick the pressure was being driven
by an avowed leftist, as the old guard in the union took a position of
surrender.

Complicating matters more, a new generation of unionists born at
Change to Win but schooled originally in Andy Stern's SEIU[63] took a
position somewhere in the middle: continue the corporate campaign
but shut down worker organizing and shut down the community campaign in North Carolina. This reflected their view, discussed in Chapter
Two, that campaigns can be won without workers, and that workers
(and in this case also the workers' community) might just get in the way.
Bruskin had an absolutely different philosophy and sense of strategy,
namely that the campaign was *only* winning *because of* the high levels
of worker agency. He further maintained that any union win without
worker agency in the right-to-work South—where dues are voluntary
and employer behavior is closer to the year 1815 than 2015—would soon

collapse from a lack of battle-tested worker leadership. Now Bruskin's early individual negotiations about the terms under which he would accept his campaign position—that the union wouldn't control him and couldn't fire him—were paying off. But his opponents inside the union were succeeding at pulling back some financial resources, and his daily battle became not just fighting Smithfield, but also fighting people inside the union.

For the next half-year, there was internal dissension over strategy and months of time lost, once again, to subpoenas and evidence gathering. The "heat" in the campaign was being ratcheted down, against Bruskin's better instincts, but it wasn't being closed down. During this time the campaign managed to pull off a big "inside-outside" action day at the Smithfield Foods annual shareholder meeting: workers protesting on the inside, ministers and community supporters from across the country demonstrating on the outside.[64] On the eve of the start of the RICO trial, in an all-night negotiation that ended thirty minutes before the courthouse opened its doors, the union and the company reached an agreement to hold a union election with prenegotiated rules, the most important of which would be the union's right to have access to the inside of the plant, and the naming of a "monitor" with strong enforcement mechanisms whose job was to be at the plant during the election cycle to referee the period leading up to the vote. Each side agreed to cease certain activities; for example, the employer dropped the RICO case and agreed to take down an anti-union website it had created, Smithfieldfacts.com; and the union surrendered the words "Justice@ Smithfield" and along with them suspended the national consumer campaign. The deal on the courthouse steps was signed and "ordered" as a settlement by the RICO judge on October 27, 2008. The nation's presidential election was eight days away. The election in the plant was set for the week of December 8.

By the time of the court steps settlement, the tea leaves, including all polls, were showing a Democratic presidential victory. Big, vertically integrated multinational companies, often with a history of supporting Republicans, sometimes find unions helpful when Democratic administrations take office, using them as conduits to the administration on key issues.[65] For the once-again-majority black workforce in the plant, the fact that on November 4 a black man became the first Democrat in

36 years to win the popular vote in North Carolina was a huge validation: It showed that black people in North Carolina really could overcome stiff odds and a plantation culture. After the presidential election,
one worker wore this hand-printed T-shirt: "If we can change the White
House we can change the hog house."[66] The union ramped up that
"against all odds" message between the nation's election day and their
own. And on December 10—incidentally the United Nations' annual
International Human Rights Day—the workers voted "yes" to unionize the plant, 2,041 to 1,879.[67] Obama barely won North Carolina, and
made history. The Smithfield workers barely won their election, and
made history, too, one month later. Their win represented the single
largest private sector unionization effort of the new millennium.

Struggle Builds Resiliency and Leadership In and Outside the Factory

> It's been a busy year in the hog market. Pork prices way up, bacon seems to be
> everywhere, ice cream, milkshakes, even Las Vegas martinis.
>
> Kai Ryssdal on NPR's *Marketplace*, December 26, 2013

According to UFCW national executive vice president Pat O'Neill, the
most important long-term development from the Smithfield campaign
is that today in Tar Heel there is a local union that is already helping
nonunion workers in a nearby poultry plant to form their own union in
Bladen County. "What's important is that we have a local union that's
actually organizing unorganized workers," he says.[68] At least equally
important is the internal organizing work spearheaded by that local
union, a program that has achieved a steady membership of 80 percent
in this right-to-work state. And, they've done it because, in the words of
the once-fired-worker Keith Ludlum:

> We've created an organizing culture. I meet every single new
> [employee] hire at the orientation and talk about the struggle to win
> the wages, benefits, and rights we've won. I tell every worker that
> the first thing the boss knows going into our contract negotiations
> is what percentage of workers are in the union—anything less than
> 80 percent and the employer won't be taking our concerns very seri-
> ously. Keeping our internal membership high isn't just my job, it's

everyone's job here, just like helping the workers down the street at the Mountainaire poultry plant, where 2,000 workers work under horrible conditions. The first thing those workers say when we talk to them is, "*We want the Smithfield contract.*"[69]

By defeating the company, the Smithfield workers achieved much more than a contract. They won confidence in themselves—including the confidence to go down the street to a chicken factory to help teach 2,000 unorganized workers exactly what they need to do to beat *their* employer. Through the vicious fight inside the pork plant, the workers learned also to take on controversial right-wing wedge issues like immigration and even gay marriage. These 5,000 workers are now key to the effort to help change the political conversation among thousands of workers in rural North Carolina. Reverends Barber and Johnson both note with home-state pride that the Smithfield workers are regular and consistent participants in the protest movement he founded in 2014, Moral Mondays. Barber believes the fight at Smithfield helped lay the groundwork for North Carolina's newly elevated consciousness about the urgent need for unions:

> We learned to trust each other during the Smithfield fight; we deepened our ties considerably, like when we held simultaneous actions in twelve cities in North Carolina all at once, something that could only happen because the leadership of the union campaign at the time trusted the NAACP and Black Church network to lead the effort. The union had no capacity on its own to do anything like that without us.[70]

Sarita Gupta of Jobs with Justice says,

> The Smithfield campaign was our campaign as much as the UFCW's, the NAACP's, and the North Carolina religious community's. JwJ felt that way—that campaign was really our victory in a deep way, in a deep-heart way that you don't always feel on campaigns. Gene Bruskin was really smart in creating and structuring the fight in such a way that groups could feel ownership and get credit for the work we were doing. It felt like a real joint campaign, and that often doesn't happen.[71]

Ollie Hunt became a full-time staff organizer in the new local union and subsequently began helping the Mountaire poultry workers form their organization. Hunt says, "I know people, cousins, who work at Walmart distribution centers, and I am telling them all about it. My parents wanted me to go to college, I want my kids to go to college, too. But what if they don't? If you've got kids, you expect the best for them, but things don't always work out the way we think. The workers in the poultry plant, who could be my kids in the future, they drive two hours a day to earn $250 per week with no health insurance, and the company is building a $5 million expansion in their plant." Delcia Rodriguez from the Dominican Republic, a former worker at Mountaire, was fired by her employer when she had an industrial accident that caused her to miscarry. Now 23, she's been hired by the local union to help her former colleagues. She reports that everyone in the poultry plant is scared, but they all want "what Smithfield workers got."

The workers at Smithfield won $15 an hour, in rural North Carolina the equivalent of a $26.40 wage in Seattle; Seattle's low-wage nonunion workers, who won $15, got far less. The Smithfield workers also developed a worker-led unified movement among previously warring ethnic factions. They've become a base of workers in a key national electoral swing state that still has the lowest unionization level in the United States, and they are taking on political wedge issues not as outsiders, but as home-grown North Carolinians, and they are helping their next-door neighbors form a new union of their own.

That almost no workers elsewhere in the U.S. South know this story is a travesty.

6

Make the Road New York

THE ROOM WENT UNCHARACTERISTICALLY SILENT after the two leaders in the front of the room, Amador Rivas and Augusto Fernandez, posed the question, "What do you think it means?" The leaders seemed at ease with the nervous looks and fidgeting that often accompany silence in a large group. Then, from the back of the room, a commanding voice boomed out, "I think it means us. We are the ones who are an army of the good. Every day we fight to hold politicians and bosses accountable for the wrongs they inflict on our community." A round of applause and head-bobbing followed, signaling that the woman in the back of the room was speaking for everyone.

The scene was a meeting of Trabajadores en Acción ("Workers in Action") at the office of Make the Road New York (MRNY), in the Bushwick neighborhood of Brooklyn. More than fifty people were present for this gathering, a weekly event where MRNY members and prospective members meet to analyze the previous week's activities and plan future actions. Those at this meeting had just been asked to interpret the meaning of a quotation from Juan Bosch: "*No hay arma más potente que la verdad en los manos de los buenos*" ("There is no weapon more powerful than the truth in the hands of the good.")[1] Such prompts are a regular feature of MRNY's public meetings, which are conducted in Spanish. First, all those present introduce themselves, stating whether they are first-time visitors or members (and if so, how long they have been part of MRNY). Then the leaders open the discussion with a prompt designed to spark a discussion that everyone can participate

179

in—longstanding members and newcomers, old and young, men and women. The prompt is also intended to ensure that the meeting agenda includes a "big picture" question along with quotidian details such as taking volunteers for leafleting (a key form of outreach for MRNY) in the coming week; evaluating what did and didn't work at the last big public event or direct action; asking who would like to cook for the next meeting.

About two hours after this meeting began, Augusto, who was co-chairing as part of a leadership development assignment, called for "*silencio*" and then approached each person in the room to ask them, "*Que le gusta sobre este reunion and que no le gusta?*" ("What do you like about this meeting and what do you not like?") When he got to the third person, the front doors to the room opened and a few members began to carry in enormous pots of rice and beans.

The fragrant smell wafting through the room was a challenge for Augusto at this point—almost two hours after the meeting began—but he pressed on with his questions undeterred. The answers he got were all variations on a theme: People liked being able to participate in the discussion and having a clear agenda; what they didn't like was "that this meeting is going on too long, look—see—our dinner is here and we should be eating it." This exposed the time-intensive aspect of MRNY's "high-touch," participatory decision-making process.

MRNY is the largest nonunion membership organization of immigrants in New York City, with more than 15,000 dues-paying members, an annual budget of over $13.5 million, and 155 full-time staff.[2] Membership requirements include a one-time dues payment of $120 for those members over 21 years of age, and newly established annual dues of $20.[3] Members who have paid their dues can participate in meetings. MRNY has experimented considerably over the past decade with what constitutes being eligible to be a voting member and what, if any, requirements there should be for those wishing to take advantage of MRNY's legal services and ESL (English as a Second Language) classes—which also include political education and leadership skills. As the organization has evolved, most of what they call their "survival services" have become free for the entire working class, not just their members. MRNY deputy director Deborah Axt, an attorney and former union organizer, points out, "In addition to realizing that because much of our survival services are supported with public money, that requires them to be open to anyone in need, we also see this as our contribution to the broader working class."[4] Requirements are higher for voting members: to qualify, a member must attend at least two meetings a month, and must participate in a series of workshops during his or her first year in the organization. Workshop topics include "Understanding Sexism," "LGBTQ Tolerance," education on each issue area in the organization, and a session on effective recruitment. (This last workshop is crucially important, since MRNY members do most of the recruitment of new members.)

MRNY is what I call a self-selecting group, one that works on many different kinds of issues. The organization was formed in 2007 when two earlier organizations—Make the Road by Walking and the Latin American Integration Center—agreed on a merger. Make the Road by Walking had been founded in 1998 by Andrew Friedman and Oona Chatterjee to advocate for immigrant welfare recipients in Brooklyn. Friedman and Chatterjee had met as law students at New York University, and both were frustrated by the idea of legal work that involved defending poor people one at a time. "We thought if poor people had power, they would need fewer lawyers," Friedman recalled.[5] At the time of the merger, Make the Road by Walking had a $2.5 million budget, 43 full-time staffers, and the office in Bushwick.[6]

The Latin American Integration Center (LAIC) had been formed in 1992 by a group of Colombian immigrants in Jackson Heights, Queens—New York City's *la Pequeña Colombia*, ("Little Colombia")— to promote mutual aid and citizenship assistance for Colombian and other Latin American immigrants. LAIC's founding director, Saramaria Archila, had been a Colombian human rights attorney; she had fled her country in response to threats on her life by the right-wing paramilitary. Upon arrival in New York, speaking no English and with professional credentials that were not recognized in the United States, she found herself cleaning houses, like so many other Latina immigrants, until she helped found and then became a paid staff member of LAIC.

In 2001, LAIC hired Saramaria's niece, Ana Maria Archila, to open a new office in Port Richmond, Staten Island. Archila had emigrated from Colombia in 1997 at age 17, and joined the LAIC staff after she graduated from college. In Port Richmond, she organized citizenship and adult literacy classes; later she succeeded her aunt as LAIC's director when Saramaria died of cancer. In 2006, the year before the merger, LAIC had a $702,295 budget and a dozen full-time staff.[7]

MRNY has won significant victories involving immigrants, poor people, and low-wage workers during a time when many other organizations have experienced setbacks and defeats. One major reason for their success is the favorable political environment of New York City, which has higher union density than any other major U.S. city,[8] an enduring social democratic tradition rooted in its labor history,[9] and a relatively immigrant-friendly political culture. These conditions make New York fertile ground for the kind of immigrant-rights and worker-rights organizing to which MRNY is dedicated. Of course, there are many similar organizations and campaigns in New York City that enjoy the same conditions, yet none can claim as strong a record of accomplishment as MRNY, which has amassed a larger staff and budget than any comparable organization in the city.

MRNY has adopted a highly collaborative organizational model that reflects exactly the kind of strategic capacity Marshall Ganz described at the United Farm Workers, with "leaders who take part in regular, open, and authoritative deliberation and are motivated by commitment to choices they participated in making and on which they have the autonomy to act."[10]

MRNY also has a highly deliberative and participatory organizational style—referred to internally as a "high-touch" process. This is similar to Francesca Polletta's analysis of participatory democracy and prefigurative politics.[11] Polletta and MRNY emphasize the importance of *process* in strengthening internal solidarity and enhancing the political impact of social movements. Efforts to win and enforce progressive change, whether through the courts, the ballot box, negotiated union contracts, or legislative bodies, can only succeed in the long term if large numbers of ordinary people are participating at levels high enough to enable them to hold institutions accountable.

Part of the organization's capacity stems from its multi-issue character. MRNY's size has enabled it to operate effectively on a range of issues, including but not limited to workplace justice. As Deborah Axt and MRNY founder Andrew Friedman have noted, "Make the Road" differed from many worker centers in the breadth of issues it addressed that were not directly related to worker or workplace organizing, and in its wider use of in-house legal, education, and other services."[12] A broad issue spread coupled with open and democratic organizational structures helps increase motivation among MRNY leaders and members alike, because different individuals will feel passionately about different issues.

I argue that MRNY is not an advocacy group. By advocacy, as I defined it in Chapter Two, I mean groups like the Center for Constitutional Rights, the American Civil Liberties Union, or Greenpeace—groups that merely campaign *on behalf of* some broad societal goal and/or *on behalf of* a constituency or constituencies. By contrast, Make the Road's members are active players in campaigns and have decision-making in such key areas as hiring and firing staff, approving budgets, and deciding on the direction and priorities of the organization. They also understand that mass collective action is a key source of leverage. Another sign that Make the Road goes beyond a pure advocacy approach is that they are not simply trying to win specific legislation or material benefits, but also trying to make long-term, structural changes in the power structure of the wider society, shifting the balance of power toward the organization's base constituency and away from the forces that oppress them. I will provide of examples how this works later in the chapter.

¡Despierta Bushwick! ("Wake Up, Bushwick!")

Make the Road's initial workplace justice efforts were limited to a direct-action approach in on-the-job grievance handling, though the grievances were limited to wage and hour violations, taking advantage of the Fair Labor Standards Act (FSLA). When an employer refuses to pay a member, or denies overtime, pays less than minimum wage, or shorts the worker's hours, the worker is teamed up with other MRNY members who go *en masse* to the worksite and demand the money with a shame-based solidarity protest. If the employer ignores this direct confrontation and refuses to pay, Make the Road's attorneys go after the employer legally. This program has long been the most important recruitment tool for Make the Road's worker justice campaign. Deborah Axt explains that that this program has deep value beyond recruitment: "These individual and small-scale fights matter a great deal, because the members can get involved and exercise, test, and improve upon their leadership immediately. It's like having dozens of mini campaigns going on all at once all the time."

By 2004, Make the Road had decided to try something new in their worker justice campaigns: organizing unions. It was a bold move, with a high risk of failure, because the precariat workers that dominate the lowest wage sector have proven particularly difficult to unionize. Union election victories are hard to come by in any sector, given the incentive for employers to systematically violate the few remaining worker protections under U.S. law. But given the sheer numbers of individuals experiencing wage theft, Make the Road wanted to scale up. If the workers could form unions, it would give them access to ongoing assistance and potentially raise their wages and living standards above the poverty line. Make the Road sought a union partner—Enter the Retail, Wholesale and Department Store Workers Union, RWDSU.

The RWDSU, under Stuart Applebaum's leadership, joined up with Make the Road to attempt the nearly impossible—a win in marginal retail in the shadows of a big city in the Bush presidency. The ¡Despierta Bushwick! ("Wake Up, Bushwick!") campaign was born. According to Ed Ott, a distinguished lecturer at CUNY's labor school and a former longtime and highly respected executive director at the NYC Central Labor Council:

> "From almost day one, Make the Road caught the attention of NYC's unions because the group's leaders understood that a union contract could be a tremendous tool for their members. This union-friendly approach and their demonstrated ability to turn out large numbers of their members for events in NYC set them apart from every other group in New York."[13] In fact, borrowing union power has been the key to the group's success.

The first tactical move for Make the Road was to map a geographic boundary of two blocks in either direction off Knickerbocker Avenue— an area where the organization had strong roots. Over the course of six months they knocked on more than 6,000 doors, talking with residents about the conditions faced by workers along the avenue. Many of these residents had firsthand experience with the stores, as store employees themselves or as friends or family of store employees. At the end of each conversation, the canvassers asked the resident to sign a pledge card stating that they would boycott any store that didn't respect its workers. The canvassers also gathered information from each resident about which stores they patronized on Knickerbocker, as one way to gauge the potential impact of consumer pressure.

While Make the Road talked with the folks off Knickerbocker Avenue, the RWDSU organizers were talking to the workers. The collaborative team began to pitch in with the attorney general's office to file unpaid-wage claims. The idea was to ratchet up the amount of back-pay claims a resistant employer might face, then offer a no-cost alternative: The workers would drop the claims in exchange for the employer's agreement to not fight the unionization effort. At the time, the attorney general was Eliot Spitzer, who proved sympathetic to the union drive.

In August of 2005, with back-to-school shopping about to begin, Make the Road sent a letter to two of the chains on Knickerbocker that typified the strip—FootCo and Shoe Mania. The letter notified the store owners that unless they were prepared to sign a binding agreement to cease their unjust practices and permit their employees to make a decision to unionize, free of intimidation or harassment, MRNY would call for a boycott at a press conference. Shoe Mania shut down its local operation, almost certainly a response to the union threat. But FootCo agreed immediately, and by the campaign's end, the workers had formed a union with the RWDSU and negotiated a collective bargaining agreement, covering 110 workers across ten stores, that included health insurance, paid sick and vacation time for all workers, and a $3.00-an-hour raise. The FootCo contract would be renegotiated successfully until the company succumbed, along with thousands of other small retail stores, to the 2008 economic crisis.

Beyond FootCo, there were several other results from ¡Despierta Bushwick! MRNY built deep relationships with key staff at city and state agencies that would enable them to engage in what they call strategic sweeps: Make the Road and one of their union partners—typically RWDSU—gather information from workers in a specific industry and a targeted area and provide it to enforcement agencies, which swoop in and cite several employers at once.[14] In May of 2008 and again in June of 2009, MRNY played a crucial role in getting the New York State Attorney General's Office and the New York State Department of Labor to go after grocery stores for systematically stealing the wages of grocery baggers. The result was substantial back-wage payments: C-Town in Queens had to pay baggers more than $300,000 in back wages, Pioneer Grocery in Brooklyn had to pay more than $160,000, and Key Foods in Brooklyn more than $44,000. Prior to the sweeps, these employers had typically made workers sign agreements classing them as independent contractors, working for tips and receiving no wages, and yet treated them just like employees, assigning them other jobs, such as cleaning, and firing them if they wouldn't comply. MRNY's large membership helps the generally underfunded state agencies launch "sting" operations against these unscrupulous employers, and the impact ripples out well beyond the shops that get fined.

But even after a couple of years of strategic sweeps that significantly elevated the scale of their success, MRNY members were becoming increasingly frustrated by the inadequacies of the laws they were enforcing, and decided to attack those deficiencies next. Axt said, "For the many workers in the informal economy and the nonunion [meaning outside the NLRA] economy, we are trying to put as many pieces together as we can that offer protections like a [union] contract."

Wage Theft Legislation

MRNY has been active in campaigns to rectify minimum wage and other workplace violations throughout its history, winning over $25 million in back pay and wrongfully denied government benefits settlements between 2007 and 2010 alone.[15] Frustrated by the slow pace of the legal process and the persistence of wage theft in the low-wage labor market despite the many highly publicized efforts to combat it, in early 2010 MRNY members decided, in committee meetings and eventually in a board meeting, to launch a campaign to strengthen the state law.[16] They helped mount a successful coalition effort to pass the New York State Wage Theft Protection Act (WTPA), which was signed into law in December 2010 and took effect on April 9, 2011.

The new law increased criminal and civil penalties for minimum wage and overtime violations from 25 percent to up to 100 percent of back wages, along with additional penalties of up to $10,000 for employers who retaliate or threaten to retaliate against workers for complaining about wage theft. The law also strengthened employer payroll record-keeping requirements and also required more detailed written notice to employees regarding pay rates and deductions than before, including a new provision that these notices must be in the employee's primary language. While a rule regarding paycheck notices may seem a modest gain, its thrust is important, because it directly enhances the ability of ordinary workers to understand their employers' actions, and also provides a tool for enforcement mechanisms similar to those in union contracts. By forcing employers to document pay rates and deductions in each paycheck in the native language of the employee, the law enables workers themselves, with assistance from the MRNY staff in some cases, to fight back if the employer has cheated them out of the pay to which they are entitled. Thus the law "makes the hammer of reach and enforcement much bigger," as Axt put it in an interview.[17] "Our members are really proud of this victory and are now involved in outreach and education to all sorts of organizations across the city that we are teaching how to use the new tools afforded by the law."

In 2014, the organization successfully fought for yet more improvements to the Wage Theft Prevention Act, including further-enhanced anti-retaliation provisions, increases in the liquidated damages provisions from the $10,000 they won in 2010 to $25,000, and an expansion of the act's language to incorporate a new focus on the construction sector.[18]

The Secure Communities Campaign

On November 22, 2011, Mayor Bloomberg—flanked by members of Make the Road—signed a city council measure ending the city's cooperation with federal Immigration and Customs Enforcement (ICE) authorities under the Secure Communities deportation program, which relies on partnership among federal, state, and local law enforcement agencies. Unlike the WTPA, which was developed and passed in less than a year, this campaign took years of careful work. "When we first decided to launch this campaign, everyone said, 'You are fucking crazy,' " recalled campaign leader and MRNY co–executive director, Javier Valdes, a longtime immigrant rights advocate formerly on the staff of the New York Immigration Coalition.

In early 2009, Peter Markowitz, director of the Immigrant Justice Center at Cardozo Law School and a trusted collaborator of MRNY,

approached the group with a plan to challenge New York City's cooperation with ICE. Because this campaign idea did not originate directly
from the grassroots base, MRNY staff conducted a membership survey
to see if the issue mattered enough to members to warrant a shift in
organizational priorities.

In response, members described cases of family and friends being
deported after arrests for minor infractions, and in some instances even
when they were found innocent. At the time, Rikers Island prison officials were holding immigrants suspected of being undocumented for
up to 48 hours *after* their scheduled release and turning them over to
ICE officials to be "interviewed." Between 2004 and 2008, more than
13,000 undocumented immigrants had been shipped from Rikers to
detention facilities outside of New York. According to Valdes, Rikers
officials were deceiving immigrants into thinking they were going to
meet with an attorney about their case, rather than with an ICE official.[19] The interviews would begin with innocuous questions that were
intentionally misleading, to encourage detainees to reveal how they
had gotten to the United States. As the survey documented, MRNY
members saw this as an urgent issue, and the board approved the
campaign.

Along with the New Sanctuary Coalition and the Northern
Manhattan Coalition for Immigrant Rights, MRNY demanded that
Rikers Island officials be required to explain to detainees in very explicit
terms that these "interviews" were *not* with friendly attorneys. In June
2009, the campaign scored its first victory when the city's Department
of Corrections officials agreed to provide a written form in multiple lan-
guages to every detainee at Rikers *before* the interviews, explaining that
the interviewers would be ICE officials and detailing what could result.
Rikers officials were also required to get signed consent forms from a
detainee before any such "interview" could occur.

By February 2010, thirteen more groups had signed on to the campaign.[20] MRNY then successfully drove what had become a large coalition effort, and eventually persuaded newly elected Governor Andrew
Cuomo to announce, in June 2011, that Secure Communities would
no longer be implemented in New York State.[21] Six months later, on
November 22, 2011, in a move that gave new meaning to Thanksgiving
for many New York City immigrants, Mayor Bloomberg signed City

Council Bill 656, which prohibits the Department of Corrections from using city funds to detain immigrants, effectively ending the city's collaboration with ICE.

Concurrent with the three-year-long fight against Secure Communities, MRNY led several other successful campaigns that had a significant impact on public policy. Gains from these included the 2009 Language Access in Pharmacies Act, requiring that 3,000 chain pharmacies in New York City provide translation and interpretation services; the 2010 Multiple Dwellings Registration Act, which strengthened enforcement of tenants' rights; Governor Cuomo's Executive Order #26, signed in fall 2011, extending to all of New York State an earlier MRNY victory requiring city agencies to provide interpretation and translation services; and the 2011 Student Safety Act, making police and in-house school discipline more transparent.

MRNY was active on many other fronts during this period as well. In 2010 the organization negotiated a settlement with the retail chain American Eagle over discrimination against transgender employees. The same year, MRNY's Youth Empowerment Project successfully blocked a city plan to cut funding for subsidized student MetroCards. And MRNY filled forty-two buses with protesters for the May 1, 2010 immigrant rights march in Washington, D.C.—the largest turnout of any single group in the nation.[22]

By 2014, despite real reductions in the number of immigrants being detained, MRNY took further action and succeeded in getting the New York City Council to pass a law banishing the ICE officers from Rikers Island altogether. The law was passed in October 2014 and took effect in February of 2015.[23]

Car Wash Worker Organizing: ¡Despierta Bushwick! Redux

In 2012, the late Jon Kest, former head of ACORN New York, who was then the executive director of ACORN's successor, New York Communities for Change, was looking for a worker-organizing campaign where the NYCC could make a difference. He began talking with Deborah Axt at Make the Road because of the group's long history of deep collaboration with unions, especially the RWDSU. The car wash campaign that came out of these conversations represents a bigger, smarter evolution of what Make the Road and the RWDSU had begun on Knickerbocker Avenue almost ten years earlier. A key strategic improvement was that MRNY and its collaborators were targeting a more stable industry within the desperately low-wage retail sector: Car wash owners have a lot invested in big machinery that they won't easily abandon or move.

By the spring of 2013, the campaign was under way. At the first-ever citywide Car Wash Workers General Assembly, dozens of immigrant car-wash workers used a form of popular theater common in social movements throughout the Latin American countries they'd emigrated from: a play about their plight. In front of an audience of 200, they dramatized the bad treatment and dangerous conditions in New York City's car washes. In the play's final act, the *carwasheros* unfurled six homemade, body-length banners to communicate their demands: (1) Respect; (2) Better pay, paid vacation, and sick days; (3) Health care; (4) Protection from abuse; (5) 100 percent of their tips, on top of the minimum wage; and (6) A union contract.

It's that last demand—"*¡Un sindicato!*"—that brings the folks in the middle of the hall to their feet, loudly stomping and chanting, "*¡Sí, se puede!*" The bulk of the audience is indistinguishable from the actors, made up mostly of other *carwasheros*. But around the outside walls of the room was an impressive lineup of New York City power brokers, including then–city council speaker Christine Quinn; about as many city council members as it would take to have a quorum; the Manhattan borough president; and all sorts of lesser-known candidates running for local office in one of the largest cities in the world. In the campaign's first year, workers at seven different car washes had voted yes to forming a union in National Labor Relations Board elections, which require a majority to win. Workers at three more car washes have formed unions since then.[24] For 1,000 workers in the industry not yet under union contract, $4.5 million in back pay claims were secured through litigation.[25]

After the initial burst of workers' wins, car wash employers began to collaborate with one another in an effort to hobble the unionization drive. Fighting back, the CarWashero campaign succeeded in passing a new citywide law, the Car Wash Accountability Act, in the summer of 2015, with the active support of the city's new, pro-union mayor, Bill de Blasio. The workers hope the new law will succeed in providing enough incentive to soften the employers' resistance. The law protects workers from the industry's rampant wage theft by requiring employers to purchase expensive surety bonds to guarantee that workers' wages get paid. If the individual car wash is not unionized, the bond is $150,000; that rate plunges to just $30,000 if the employees of a car wash have a union contract.[26] In 2016, all of the initial six union contracts will expire, and the organizers are hoping that the momentum of a contract campaign, along with the new law, will reinvigorate the drive to unionize car-wash workers throughout the city.

Strategic Capacity

How does Make the Road get so much accomplished? A large part of the answer hinges on what Ganz calls strategic capacity. MRNY's original five-member Strategic Leadership Team (SLT) included three women and three people of color, one of whom, Ana Maria Archila, is also an immigrant, originally from Colombia. Another member, Javier Valdes, was born in the United States, but when he was just three months old his parents' visas expired, and the family, originally Argentinian, had to move to Venezuela. Valdes returned to the United States at age eleven, when his father, a civil engineer, was hired at Texas A&M—a job that allowed him to obtain permanent resident status. Archila and Valdes both went to college in the United States and both took jobs in progressive organizations soon after graduating. Oona Chatterjee was born in the United States to Indian immigrant parents. She was influenced by family stories about the fight for Indian independence, just as Archila and Valdes were shaped by their parents' experience of fleeing repression in South America. The other two SLT members, Andrew Friedman and Deborah Axt, are white and U.S. born. Friedman had politically progressive parents.[27]

Friedman, Chatterjee, and most recently Archila have moved to a new organization that is attempting to nationalize the success of Make the Road New York. All five of these founding SLT leaders are passionately devoted to their work, exemplifying another aspect of Ganz's strategic capacity: motivation.[28] And they still share office space. Valdes and Axt remain in the top leadership, with other newer team members stepping into today's SLT. The following excerpts from interviews with SLT members illustrate their level of motivation:

FRIEDMAN: *"We lose before we even start if we remain risk-averse. We constantly take risks here!"*

ARCHILA: *"I fell in love with the folks I was teaching, and knew I was hooked."*

CHATTERJEE: *"We want to build power. We want to be consequential in everything we do and move the ball forward."*

AXT: *"We are not so good at slow, methodical approaches. This is both a strength and a weakness—we tend to go headlong into an effort."*

VALDES: *"It's a magical space here. The level of commitment to the cause— I have never experienced it anywhere as much as here. It's not just the leadership, it's everybody. Every member and all the staff know this institution matters."*

The relationships among and between just about everyone on the staff team start and end with respect for one another, vertically and horizontally. For Ganz, this combination is key to the success of organizations fighting for social and economic justice. The frequent use of the word love (Chatterjee, "we love each other here"; Valdes, "we are rooted in love and community here") reflects the deep commitment of the SLT to a highly participatory and equally diverse membership.

The full-time MRNY staff as a whole is also highly motivated, with a group of talented, accomplished organizers who work around the clock with extraordinary dedication. As Table 6.1 (prepared as part of a grant

TABLE 6.1 Make the Road New York Staff, by Gender, Race, and Ethnicity[36]

	Board*	Support Staff	Professional Staff
Women	44%	78%	74%
Men	41%	22%	26%
Latino	60%	100%	61%
White	11%	–	28%
Black	7%	–	5%
Asian	7%	–	2%
Other	–	–	4%

*Vacant seats account for why these don't add up to 100%

proposal submitted to the Ford Foundation) shows, the staff is also extremely diverse in terms of gender, race, and ethnicity.[29]

Participatory Democracy and Make the Road's "High-Touch" Model

Francesca Polletta argues that participatory democracy strengthens social movements and their organizations. Among "people with little experience of routine politics," she argues, "making decisions by consensus and rotating leadership has helped create a pool of activists capable of enforcing the gains made by this movement and launching new rounds of activism. Participatory democracy's potential benefits ... cannot be reduced to 'personal' or 'cultural' changes. They go to the heart of political impact." She adds, "Participatory democracy ... can advance efforts to secure institutional political change ... [and] can be strategic."[30]

MRNY has adopted a detailed and transparent decision-making process. Most decisions are made by consensus, and rotating leadership is standard practice at meetings. MRNY's "Decision-Making Authority" document (available to members in both Spanish and English) specifies in detail how people are chosen for every role and every sub-body in the organization, and specifies the authority embodied in each role and sub-body, much like a union constitution.[31]

MRNY has committees focused on key programmatic areas, including core issues that have long defined the organization's agenda—immigrant rights, civil rights, affordable housing, workplace justice, and environmental justice—and also more ad-hoc committees, devoted to campaigns like those organized to fight Wage Theft and Secure Communities. Each MRNY member is involved in one or more of these programmatic committees, all of which hold weekly meetings concurrently at MRNY's four offices in Port Richmond, Staten Island; Bushwick, Brooklyn; Jackson Heights, Queens; and Brentwood, Long Island. As Javier Valdes explained, "The weekly meetings serve the same purpose as church. It's a ritual ... it's the same time, the same day, every week, in the same office." He added, "Having access to the membership so frequently provides a constant opportunity for growth and political education. The members all run the meetings and . . . spend time every week thinking about the agenda and about how to run an effective meeting."[32]

Members actively participate in the process of hiring new staff, and are included on hiring committees and interview teams. After multiple and sometimes grueling interview rounds, finalists are asked to demonstrate their skills in front of members by either facilitating a meeting or running a workshop. Sabrina Harewood, a 20-year-old Afro-Caribbean member of the LGBT working group, explained, "We want to see the potential staff facilitate a meeting . . . we want to see how they respond to members' questions, if they can teach us anything new, and how they get along with people."

MRNY's "high-touch" decision-making process is also illustrated by the "Trabajadores en Acción" meeting described at the beginning of this chapter. In 2009, as part of a comprehensive strategic planning process, MRNY adopted a new set of leadership development protocols for both volunteer members and staff. Members who want to become leaders meet one-on-one with the organizers responsible for each programmatic area, and carry out a series of assignments (in this case, learning to run a large meeting). This is one of several prerequisites for running for election to the MRNY board of directors, the majority of whom are elected from the membership.

MRNY is predicated on the idea that its success depends on its ability to recruit, develop, mobilize, and retain members. But the deep commitment to democratic practice and leadership development is also a source of tension and what cofounder Andrew Friedman calls democracy fatigue, describing the more than thirteen regular weekly meetings—all of which require tremendous energy and attention. There is, according to Friedman, a dull but persistent discussion of the endless attempt to reduce and shorten meetings. Friedman absented himself from this fatigue by creating the Center for Popular Democracy, a national group without the kind of day-to-day base accountability that Make the Road still maintains. But Javier Valdes (who would later replace Andrew as a co–executive director) and others involved in building MRNY's member participation program insist that any compromise in the highly participatory nature of the organization would weaken MRNY's effectiveness.

Challenges

Make the Road New York has its critics, as became apparent at a December 2011 press conference about the proposed New York State Dream Act, when one group—the New York State Youth Leadership Council (NYSYLC)—accused MRNY of insider politics and deal cutting.[33] MRNY's leaders and some other groups in the coalition countered that the issue in contention (whether to support the bill's limited expansion of state-based financial aid to undocumented youth) had already been resolved in previous meetings. When asked about such tensions in coalition politics, MRNY staff and leaders defend themselves with the claim that they put considerably more into coalitions than they get out of them.

MRNY officially withdrew from the New York Immigration Coalition, a move that led some coalition members to accuse the group of arrogance and of being unwilling to share power with others. Yet at the 2011 December Dream Act press conference, the New York Immigration Coalition itself defended MRNY against the youth group's accusations. MRNY's success does open the organization to the danger of becoming arrogant and isolated, as is the case for any group that quickly pulls ahead of its peers. Indeed, a similar dynamic emerged in recent decades when the rapid growth of the Service Employees International Union (SEIU) outpaced that of many other unions.

The special burden of the most successful organizations across all sectors is the need to maintain their own momentum while exercising the kind of solidarity that lifts the floor of success across the entire progressive social movement spectrum.

External accusations of insider dealings are commonly made when one organization gains considerably more power and therefore more access to the power brokers than its counterparts. However, one critique, written by former MRNY staffer Steve Jenkins, is important and should be noted.[34] Jenkins criticized MRNY for being an *advocacy organization*, a claim I refute and that Jenkins himself later changed:

> I was writing for a world where unions are either ignored or reviled and where the most basic market analysis that a first-year union researcher would undertake was ignored in favor of proclamations about the

power of oppressed workers. And if I criticized MRNY, it was simply because I worked there and thought that was the most honest and effective way to make the point I was making. In actuality, they would have been at the bottom of the list of organizations to go after, as they understand these dynamics and struggle with them every day.[35]

In fact, the issues he raised were excellent and are still worth debating. Jenkins cited MRNY's early worker-rights campaigns as examples of the difficulties that face nonprofit organizations as they wade into workplace efforts. He suggested that unions have greater ability to build effective worker leverage against employers and that the union is therefore a superior organizational form. He was correct to claim that an organization that is not in the workplace can't quite measure up to a very good union. But after ten years of working inside the labor movement at SEIU, he now has a better understanding of how few good unions there are today. In his article, Jenkins ignored the fact that many unions engage in campaigns—like the one that led to the shutdown of Shoe Mania—called hot shop organizing, which means organizing isolated workplaces in response to immediate worker discontent, rather than as part of an industry-wide or strategic geographic organizing strategy. Targeting and strategy matter, whether for unions or social movement organizations.

One of his key claims was that reliance on foundation funding—characteristic of MRNY as well as other worker centers and community-based organizations with limited dues income—creates dependency on philanthropic elites who set strategic and tactical restrictions on the types of activities the organization can undertake. True enough. But Jenkins contrasts this with the case of labor unions, which are funded almost exclusively by members' dues and thus enjoy more autonomy. Also true. However, he all but ignores the fact that unions' strategic and tactical repertoires *can also be highly constrained* by such mechanisms as the no-strike clauses in collective-bargaining agreements, which are present in most contracts.

In addition, unions like Washington's Local 775, profiled in earlier chapters, and many New York City unions have chosen to develop deep institutional ties to political and economic power-holders that limit their own effectiveness and constrain rank-and-file workers. The SEIU, where Jenkins now works, frequently limits the options available to its members by signing growth accords or cutting contract deals with employers that require the union to stand down on legislation, organizing, bargaining, and other forms of activism. Once again the question is, What are the motivations or ideologies of the key players? The issue is less the institutional form and more the central question of where the agency for change lies. Aversion to risk and a lack of faith in the intelligence of ordinary people is the central problem here, for unions and other types of worker organizations.

The high participation that characterizes MRNY's high-touch model separates it from more typical social-movement organizations, in which "membership" is nothing more than *subscribership*. MRNY's ability to mobilize its members in civic actions is palpable at legislative hearings; on street corners and in marches; in its many press conferences; and in the forty-two buses they sent to Washington, D.C., to demand immigration reform.

Underlying MRNY's work is a commitment to its high-participation, high-touch organization-building model. Its wide array of weekly and biweekly meetings create meaningful points of entry and leadership development for its thousands of members. Committee meetings share commonalities: Members cook and serve dinner at the office near each meeting's end while debriefing, discussing recent actions, and planning for upcoming ones.

But MRNY has never had to confront the level of opposition that the workers faced in rural North Carolina in the Smithfield fight. The specter of 2,000 Latinos all being run out of their jobs and their town by Immigration and Customs Enforcement couldn't be further from the relative ease with which MRNY was able to get ICE itself banned from New York City and New York State. For all the incredible value of MRNY, the high-touch model is an activist approach that wouldn't stand up to the kind of employer opposition faced by workers in really tough campaigns. MRNY has built a terrific organization, sheltered in the most pro-union, pro-immigrant city in the nation, and it has been able to get more done than any other New York group. But having built an activist model embedded in a self-selecting organization means MRNY's members are superb *mobilizers*.

MRNY has achieved a lot, but it has not gone beyond being a mobilizing model. Like most community 'organizing' groups, with the exception of the isolationist-inclined Industrial Areas Foundation (IAF), it has yet to develop a theory of organic-leader identification, and it has yet to systematically chart its members' relationships in order to more effectively understand all of their many potential points of ordinary-people power. MRNY's approach is on its way to being tested outside New York, as Make the Road spreads into three neighboring states, Pennsylvania, Connecticut, and New Jersey. But these states are not the rural Deep South.

A spin-off group, the Center for Popular Democracy (CPD)—helmed by three of MRNY's early founders—promises to take the model nationwide. However, all of the early successes they list were in union-strong states. It's highly encouraging to see MRNY and now the CPD partnering with what they call progressive unions; less so to see MRNY growing as dependent on these unions as it is on private foundations, so that it may soon be unable to critically evaluate the unions' strategy. The more time MRNY spends with unions like SEIU, the less committed they seem to be to their own model, historically a largely member-led organization. In the past few years, unions like SEIU have made large donations to a more recently established sister organization, Make the Road Action Fund, incorporated as a 501(c)(4), a tax status that allows the group to engage in politics, which is a good development, but with negative aspects. One is that the 501(c)(4) board isn't democratically run, and the grassroots board does not control these growing funds, which threaten to outweigh the democratic nature of the 501(c)(3) operation. This situation recalls that of the National Toxics Campaign twenty-five years ago, an initially member-driven organization that imploded over issues of accountability and the C3 and C4 boards.

CPD could also wind up like Saul Alinsky when he first set out from Chicago in the mid-1940s. Alinsky found it extremely difficult to try to build power without the Packing House Workers Organizing Committee. Which emphatically begs a question central to this book: What happens if unions go away?

7

Conclusion: Pretend Power vs. Actual Power

Moreover, at most times and in most places, and especially in the United States, the poor are led to believe that their destitution is deserved, and that the riches and power that others command are also deserved.

Frances Fox Piven and Richard Cloward, *Poor People's Movements*[1]

THE BIGGEST SUCCESS OF THE neoliberal project has been a doubling down of the self-blame articulated above by Piven and Cloward. Self-blame demobilizes people, and it is a strategy.

Trade agreements pitting decently compensated manufacturing workers against slave-labor conditions in highly repressed countries were key to decimating, not just demobilizing, labor in the private sector. Now the same corporate class that marshalled the message that U.S. manufacturing workers were "paid too much" is sounding a drumbeat again demonizing today's most heavily unionized workforce: public service workers—mostly women, often women of color—pitting them against the 94% of so-called private sector workers who no longer have unions thanks to the sustained multi-decade effort to move manufacturing out of once unionized regions. The corporate class has added a new riff: the fiction that "government" workers are overpaid at "our" expense—not a faceless corporation's, not the Koch brothers' or Exxon-Mobil's massive public taxpayer subsidies—because "we" taxpayers are the government workers' *real* employers.

Mistrust of government has become so overwhelming that most Americans hold successful CEOs in higher regard than they do civic or political leaders. Americans have come to trust business leaders far more than politicians, corporations more than government, and the individual more than the collective.[2] This has set the stage for the corporate class' successful messaging to a raise-denied working class that tax cuts (which hurt the working class by eroding funding for a social safety net) are the working classes' best hope for a raise. When you view this as a *fifty-year highly successful strategy*, it's not so hard to understand why people might be confused about whom to blame for the lack of decent jobs today. In 2012, Michigan voters resoundingly voted *against* ensuring the right to collective bargaining in their state constitution. Mere weeks later, smelling blood and sensing opportunity after seeing the working class in the United Auto Workers' home state voting unions down, Governor Rick Snyder quickly moved to turn Michigan into a right-to-work state.

Despite spending $23 million on the ballot-initiative campaign,[3] unions lost: No amount of spending could erase five decades of newly hired employees blaming their union—not their employer, not corporations—for their lesser status and share of compensation under the union contract. This was the result of strategic decisions decades earlier by leaders in the UAW to accept two-tier contracts rather than to fight like hell against them, as their counterpart to the north, the Canadian Auto Workers had done. New employees' anger at being on the lower tier and less well compensated than their colleagues may also help to explain why 38 percent of union households in neighboring Wisconsin voted to retain their anti-union governor, Scott Walker, when labor attempted a recall campaign.

With Wisconsin and Michigan unions flat on their backs, Illinois Governor Bruce Rauner, a hedge-fund billionaire with a strong political resemblance to Walker, is driving frames like "tax cuts are your best way to a raise" and "collective bargaining made you individually more poor." These frames play *into*—not against—individualism, the dominant narrative in the United States. They are part of the demobilizing strategy—a narrative that U.S. capital, now global, is exporting as fast and hard as it can. When movement strategists think that frames alone will work for progressive causes, they don't quite get that most progressive messaging and framing run *counter to* the dominant narrative. Frames work for the corporate right, as does smoke-and-mirror, and grasstops mobilizing, because the right is *running with—not against*—America's deeply ingrained individualist creed.

Examining the biggest successes covered in this book, you could make a strong case that before the working class can shake the stranglehold of self-blame—the sense that they are individually inadequate, and so doomed to an inadequate compensation for their labor and a generally inadequate life—they have to *experience* collective struggle. These findings reinforce Rick Fantasia's excellent argument in *Cultures of Solidarity*, published almost twenty years ago. No number of pollster-perfected frames will undo the 100 years of social conditioning that have taught Americans to accept their economic and political roles, and to think "collectivism bad" and "individualism good," because the world's most sophisticated marketers—Madison Avenue and its clients—can and do outframe and outspend liberal messaging.

Yet there is a mountain of evidence that people in this country possess a deep sense of human solidarity. We see it with every disaster, in critical situations such as the aftermaths of September 11 and Hurricane Sandy. People display soul-affirming levels of instant and intense solidarity and sympathy, and the images preserved of people helping one another in these dire situations can make the toughest cynic cry. But the solidarity that follows disasters, natural and otherwise, is created in a moment of fierce emotional heat that flares up and quickly smolders. Real organizing, the kind done by the Chicago teachers, the nursing-home workers in Connecticut, and the meat-production workers of North Carolina, creates a critical situation, too: the employer's war against its workers. The craft of organizing helps people connect the dots between the critical, solidarity-affirming moment and the larger system it challenges, giving the workers in crisis a new way of seeing themselves and a newly formed sense of the society's political economy. The process of deep organizing constructs a kind of solidarity that persists long after the employer's war and when done well, workers also carry their new understanding of how things work with them into the voting booth.

The cases in this book that generated the greatest power, enough to overcome very powerful institutions and players, were those in which large numbers of the workers themselves decided to walk off the job.

Based on those cases, one can argue that the strategic front for the most successful movement effort is *still* the workplace, but not *only* the workplace. When workers walked out of the Smithfield Foods factory in wildcat strikes, they created such a crisis for their employer that even in a region as hostile to labor as eastern North Carolina, the *community* began to take note that something was seriously wrong in that facility. The community mattered a great deal in the win, once the workers helped educate them about the reasons for their actions—the missing fingers and lost limbs, the hogs being treated better than the humans who slaughtered them. Yes, the national consumer campaign helped, but without the agency of the workers and their community, there would have been no Smithfield win.

When Chicago's teachers walked off the job in a strike that riveted the nation, they did so after *several years* of good work with the broader community and *months* of *intentional discussions* with the parents in Chicago. Their community *enabled their success* by backing them against a vicious and powerful opponent who immediately framed the fight as "teachers abandoning their students and their community." And that frame failed the mayor precisely because the relationships between teacher and parent, and between teachers' union and community had already been forged.

The case of the nursing-home workers in Connecticut is even more striking. It takes a gut-wrenching decision for medical workers to walk off the job: They must walk away not only from their livelihood but also from the patients they care for and care about. In Connecticut, they strike only after speaking with the patients' families and preparing them to step in and supplement the inadequate care that temporary staff provides during a majority strike. They realize that even well-intentioned and well-trained temporary staff won't have their own knowledge of the individual, special needs of their patients. The employer may not be, and often is not concerned about that, but the workers and the families do care. Health-care workers can earn the support of the community before a strike by supporting these families—who are often like their own extended families—explaining to them step by step how to care for their loved ones, so that the workers can strike to demand better conditions for their patients and themselves.

There is still a manufacturing workforce in the United States that desperately needs unionization. Although employers' exit threats make it objectively harder, it is not impossible, as we saw in Chapter Five. The U.S. Deep South is to Europe—and, increasingly, to China—what Mexico is to the U.S.: a cheaper place than home to run a factory. The Smithfield workers' story of success demonstrates a path to victory, if only unions would take the community and its traditions more seriously. When the UAW in 2014 tried to form a union in a Volkswagen plant one state away from where the Smithfield workers had their victory, they paid no real attention to the workers or their community. The corporate class did, spending months holding community dinners and forums, putting up billboards, working the sewing circles of the wives of the mostly male workers—all tactics aimed at reaching the workers from *outside* the factory. It is hardly a surprise that the company won that round. (*Note to unions*: Consider Reverend Johnson's words, from the Smithfield chapter: "So labor isn't an 'other,' some 'Northern-based' thing, some 'anti-Southern' thing; it's actually people in our own community.")

Many labor strategists, particularly men, can't see past the need to reorganize the manufacturing sector—and Smithfield demonstrates that it is of course possible. They implore labor to focus more on the logistics sectors, which makes perfect sense and should be high on the movement's to-do list. But given the domination of the service economy today, we need a unifying strategic plan for and within the service economy.

The brilliant organizers of the CIO understood that some sectors of the industrial economy, such as steel and coal, were key; they mattered more than others. Within the service economy, education and health care are *the* strategic sectors. First, because for at least the next couple of decades, there can be no exit threat: Schools, like nursing homes, hospitals, clinics, and other components of the always-changing health-care delivery system, can't be moved offshore or relocated from a city to its suburbs or from the North or Midwest to the South. That is why the corporate right campaigns tirelessly to change the legal structures of the Rust Belt—and the nation—through the cases it brings before the Supreme Court. Immune (for now) to the exit threat, education and health care are also particularly strategic fields for organizing and movement building because of their geographic and social placement in the community: They aren't walled-off industrial parks, and the nature of the services they provide creates an intimate relationship between the workers and their community. There is an urgent need for precisely this kind of solidarity building.

While some see this relationship as a complication, it's actually an incredible strategic advantage. First, as long as the workers—and especially their leaders—grasp the context of this relationship and do what the Chicago teachers did (in stark contrast to the borderline anti-community efforts of most teachers' unions and their national union officers), it is clear they can win over the broader community not only to the importance of the craft of teaching but also, even more fundamentally, to the importance of unions in society.

The success of the national war on teachers has been pretty thorough going. The average self-described good liberal will generally say he or she supports unions—but not a teachers' union. But in Chicago, the teachers showed that a workplace struggle led as a community struggle can be transformational for the whole of the working class. Their strike changed Chicago—not just the teachers, not just the parents, not just the students—because the city's working class assumed agency in an all-out fight for the right to have public schools in their neighborhoods, taught by teachers interested in staying with their kids. The working class also changed its view of teachers, schools, racism, neoliberalism, and the city's slick mayor. That doesn't happen through a messaging campaign or a mobilizing model.

Educators and health-care workers can hone that worker-community relationship by taking the conversation directly to the families they live among and work for, showing them how their needs as workers and the quality of their work life relate directly to student performance and patient outcomes. Education and health-care workers, to a much greater extent than factory workers, are consumers of their own exact form of labor: They have kids and sick family members, and they get how hard they work.

When unions get this right—when they understand the basis of the relationship between the workers and their own community—they can defeat not only a bad employer but also America's centuries-old anticollective messaging; they can change not only their workplace but also society. Howard Kimeldorf pointed out that the social base of a workforce is key to the kind of union it forms. The social base of educators and health-care workers trends fundamentally toward solidarity and collective behavior because the workers are mission-driven: Their motivation for success is high, and they perform their work in teams and in the context of success in outcomes with patients and students—their community. The workers get this. It's too bad their leaders don't, yet.

Because of today's power structure, victories for education and health-care workers will be greatest when all the workers struggle together as one force—in one union—up against their employer in a united front. Craft unions wreak havoc on class solidarity. Why? For the same reason that was true in the 1930s and 1940s. Schools, colleges, nursing homes, hospitals, and clinics are today's factories, measured by the sheer numbers of workers who regularly work *cooperatively* inside them. For the best possible outcomes, health-care workers and educators need to maximize their power inside and outside the workplace, simultaneously, through one unified, united strategy.[4]

Many new teachers being hired in Chicago today are from programs like Teach for America, or are teachers fresh out of graduate school. They see teaching as something they will do for a few years before moving on. They are a whiter group than the city's teachers have been, and are younger and more mobile. They often don't live in their school's community, a big difference from the *social base* of recruitment thirty years ago. A similar difference can be seen between registered nurses and everyone else in the health-care setting. Although the socioeconomic base of the non-nurse health-care workers (and non-teacher education workers) makes them easier to replace, and certainly less valued by employers in spite of their often heroic labor, it also positions them more strongly in the community, in the churches, in the neighborhoods, and in local politics. Because it takes an inside-outside power strategy, driven by the workers themselves, to strike in these sectors and to win a big labor fight, these "more skilled" and "less skilled" workers can't strike at different times and can't be at the bargaining table at different times: They need each other, and must *forge solidarity by struggling together.*

Teachers and nurses are up against financial power brokers in venture capital firms who have invested in a long-term effort to monetize these two fields. Wall Street and bankers—seeing profits where others see patients and students—have chosen automation and privatization as their route to making fortunes off sick people and kids. To succeed, they must first break the unions. Robotizing the jobs of teachers and educators, converting education to test prep and test delivery, is a sure way to get those professionals' salaries down to janitorial level. Changing laws so that any individual tasks that registered nurses or licensed practical nurses do can also be done by certified nurses' aides, and many isolated tasks that certified nurses' aides currently do can be done by anyone (or thing, that is, a robot) is yet another way to cheapen the cost of staff and increase profits. The fight to save education and health care is a fight against the logic of neoliberalism, and it's deeply personal to every worker in each field.

The core argument of this book is that for movements to build maximum power—the power required in the hardest campaigns—there is no substitute for a real, bottom-up organizing model. This argument involves a set of three associated questions aimed at understanding the three common elements of the most successful strategies in this book. Power is variable, so how do you assess the power the workers need to win their fight? What strategy will win it? Will the power built be enough to execute the strategy? In effect, can the approach chosen generate the power required to win?

Because production-crippling *majority* strikes were the most successfully deployed strategy in all three cases—Chicago's teachers after 2010, Connecticut's nursing-home employees, and North Carolina's meat-production workers—I argue that for workers to win substantial gains, the strike weapon is essential. More important, this book suggests what steps are necessary for workers to deploy the strike today on a mass scale.

There are two clear and distinct models inside and outside unions in the New Labor era, *only one of which can enable majority strikes*. I name these distinct models the mobilizing model and the organizing model, and they produce different levels of success. The mobilizing model places primary agency on *staff* and is only capable of winning under certain restrictive conditions: those that do not require high levels of power. An organizing model places the primary agency for success on an *ever-expanding base of ordinary people*, and it can win in much more difficult circumstances, those requiring high levels of power. In each model, staff plays a very significant but radically different role. The key difference is where and with whom the agency for change lies.

Paying close attention to today's conditions and looking at which sectors in the U.S. economy are expanding, or at least stable, with little or no threat of exit, and being mindful of the workforce in these sectors, I conclude not only that success is contingent on the organizing model as it has been deployed by a handful of successful unions inside the workplace, but also, for even these unions to keep winning, the model must be expanded into the community *via the workers* themselves. For labor's community actions to be as successful as the best workplace unions, agency must rest with workers, not staff. Today's good organizing unions face a choice: see the community their members and unorganized coworkers live in as their key additional power strategy, or surrender that element to expensive consultants who promise a strategy of perfect messaging, high-quality consumer data, and slick (but shallow) community-labor alliances. That kind of so-called community plan has failed and will fail—again and again.

This is strong evidence that an expanded vision of the organizing model, one that bridges the workplace and the community through the workers, is more capable of winning the hardest fights than the carrot-and-stick corporate campaign model that labor has chosen over the past twenty years. In 1995, despite the promise of bold new organizing, the New Labor leaders ushered in an era of electionless unions, workerless unionization growth deals, and contracts settled by national agreements between union and corporate lawyers rather than by committees consisting of actual workers. They converted a tactic, mobilizing, into a model.

Ironically, Alinsky's brilliant understanding of power and tactics has morphed into New Labor's grossly disproportionate emphasis on the corporate campaign—good rope twisted into a noose. It's not that unions and other organizing groups don't need smart research; of course they do. But smart research should augment, not replace, workers as the primary source of leverage against employers. Smart union and social movements' research departments could shift from staff-only corporate-focused research to worker and staff–led geographic power-structure analysis that involves workers themselves in the research process. With workers as research partners, the strategy of understanding who holds power—how and why, and how to change the balance—can be arrived at for far less money and without recourse to highly paid consultants.

And in the process, the workers can learn about power in their own community and make informed decisions whether in a workplace fight or in the voting booth.

During interviews and research conducted for this book, I heard union staff describe the latest scheme to avoid engaging workers in their own liberation: Following the Obama campaign's data-driven successes in 2008 and 2012, the consultant-industrial complex that straddles national unions and the national Democratic Party has been urging unions to spend tens of millions of dollars purchasing consumer databases—data gathered and aggregated by search engines like Google—and develop predictive models for which workers might be inclined to vote yes for a union. That is incredibly expensive, and like the information gathered from polling and pollsters, the "data" is derived *outside the context of an employer fight*, rendering it as useless as the promise of "framing" has been for the past two decades. Data, like messaging, can be useful, but not when the people driving the data and driving the polling are also driving transactional, one-time get-out-the-vote, efforts. Transformational experiences come through high-risk collective action, not through data-crunching or air attacks on the corporate boardroom.

Some of the misunderstanding of the promise of the corporate leverage and top-down research, with its minimal worker involvement, stems from a misunderstanding of which kind of sectors and what types of workers are involved, and what the relative concession costs will mean to the employer. A handful of so-called authentic messengers and a minority of workers engaged might work for a Justice for Janitors campaign, where concession costs are a *tiny* fraction of those involved in a hospital workers' campaign, or of the pension plans still enjoyed by 28,000 teachers in Chicago. High concession costs require high power. High power is what progressives need to beat the Koch brothers and the power elite—to reclaim the country from the corporate right.

The greatest damage to our movements today has been the shift in the agent of change from rank-and-file workers and ordinary people to cape-wearing, sword-wielding, swashbuckling staff. To deny that having experienced staff can be the difference between workers winning and losing is ridiculous and counterproductive. Way more counterproductive has been the wholesale elimination of the crucial role of the rank-and-file workers (at work and at home). Having experienced staff matters, but the role of the staff should be coach, mentor, history teacher to the organic leaders. Without reorienting the focus of everything staff does back to identifying and enabling the central role of organic leaders among the workers, today's movements can't achieve scale. Scale comes from seriously developing the skills of the *organic leaders* among the masses of ordinary people.

Saul Alinsky unfortunately obscured the issue of agency by declaring that there are *organizers* and there are *leaders*: The organizer is a behind-the-scenes individual who is not a leader, who does not have anything to do with decision-making, and who must come from *outside* the community; the leaders must come from the base constituency, and they make all the decisions. Yet near the beginning of his chapter "The Education of the Organizer," Alinsky writes, "Since organizations are created, in large part, by the organizer, we must find out what creates the organizer." He then reveals his real point:

> Those out of their local communities who were trained on the job achieved certain levels and were at the end of their line. If one thinks of an organizer as a highly imaginative and creative architect and engineer, then the best we have been able to train on the job were skilled plumbers, electricians, and carpenters, all essential to the building and maintenance of their community structure but incapable of going elsewhere to design and execute a new structure in a new community.[5]

By "on the job," he means grassroots leaders. Outsiders are "imaginative and creative architects," and community members are "plumbers and electricians." This inviolable Alinskyist principle relates directly to a core concept of the New Labor era: the distinction between organizer and leader, and the corollary between external organizing and servicing. External organizing is the supreme driver, and existing worker-leaders and the shop floor are relegated to the backseat—or, sometimes, the trunk. The result is an ineffectual contract like that "negotiated" *for* Washington's nursing-home workers, which stripped them of shop-floor rights, of meaningful negotiations, and of the right to strike, and brought them instead a marginal material gain.

New Labor's efforts at developing a more robust political program, considered a hallmark of the post-1995 era, have not made matters better, and for the same reason: The focus has been away from the shop floor. The unions' chief priority has been to massively increase the *money* they raised and coordinated for the Democratic Party. But while labor unions ponied up more and more for election coffers—mostly at the national level—big-business groups working with right-wing forces got busy on two salvos that would obliterate union hopes of competing in the election-spending game. First, they launched a legal strategy in the courts that resulted in the Citizens United and McCutcheon decisions, blowing the doors open on campaign spending. This strategy began in the early 1970s; a case that gets too little attention is *Buckley v. Valeo*, decided in 1976, it laid the groundwork for the other two. Second, they developed their own evangelically anti-union candidates and ran them in local and state races, resulting in the 2010 election cycle progressive rout, which was repeated in 2014—a disaster for workers and their communities. Tellingly, in the wake of the 2010 elections, Wisconsin's new governor, Scott Walker, provoked a showdown with the state's public-sector unions. After stripping these workers of their collective-bargaining rights, Walker faced a union-financed recall campaign—and defeated it. The margin of victory for a recall had existed well within Wisconsin's union households, but fully 38 percent of those households voted to retain Walker. All the union financing in the world will not give the union political power if the union's rank-and-file members don't understand who is causing their problems, or why, before they go into the voting booth. Walker's re-election in 2014, like Rick Snyder's re-election in Michigan after he instituted a right-to-work rule— feels like someone is hitting the replay button over and over again. Data geeks may have mobilized enough first-time voters for victory in the 2008 and 2012 national presidential election cycles, but obviously, each midterm election cycle has produced bigger and bigger disasters. *Mobilizing is not a substitute for organizing.*

The community-organizing sector today is weak, and labor is weak— and weak plus weak does not add up to the strength that can stem the anti-labor tide. Forty years of Alinsky-inspired community organizing have not done it, fifty years of business unionism have not done it, and the past twenty years of a mobilizing model veneered as a robust organizing plan to revitalize unions, relegating workers to one of a dozen points of leverage, have not done it, either. *This is pretend power, and it doesn't fool the employers.*

Today there is almost no organization left among private-sector workers. If the corporate class has its way, this will soon be true among the public sector too. Sprightly strategy and cunning tactics matter, but labor cannot jujitsu its way out of its demise. It is time to acknowledge that growth strategies and theories that rely on giving workers *less* say in the workplace only compound the problems that put New Labor and its promises of reform in power in the first place. New Labor desperately needs to return to bottom-up base-building as its core strategy: organizing, not merely mobilizing.

The low-to-no-exit workplaces with strategic power are heavily made up of women of color. Imagine a new movement filled with tens of thousands of Karen Lewises. Yes, they really are out there. True, Lewis is charismatic—but so are tens of thousands of educators and health-care workers. To be good at their job, which the vast majority aspire to be, they either arrive with or have to develop a strong sense of confidence. Making real decisions that have significant impact on kids and patients is central to their work. They must possess strong powers of persuasion to lead students and patients through challenging, sometimes frightening, moments; they must know how to explain a plan of action for a successful outcome. They must build intense relationships with families and the community. As Karen Lewis developed her power through a massive struggle and strike, so can millions more. The Whole Worker model offers a way to overcome the silos analyzed by Ira Katznelson in *City Trenches*, because it *structures* class into the community via rank-and-file union members. This is a considerably different approach from today's labor-community coalitions, or what is typically considered social unionism, which reinforces rather than resolves the Katznelson divide.

Unions are under pressure from extraordinary external forces. But unions are also dying from the inside out. Although many of the external factors in play would be difficult for unions to change, returning to a genuine bottom-up organizing model, one that encourages and equips workers to resist the multifaceted assault on their interests inside and outside the workplace, is within the decision-making control of today's unions.

There are no shortcuts.

NOTES

Chapter 1

1. Joseph E. Luders, *The Civil Rights Movement and the Logic of Social Change*, New York, NY: Cambridge University Press, 2010. The full footnote from which this sentence is taken is: "I suggest that economic actors differ in their exposure to the disruption costs that movements generate in launching protest marches, sit-ins, boycotts, picketing and so on. Some of these insights have been investigated by labor historians and economists seeking to explicate strike outcomes. Curiously, the labor movement is conventionally ignored by scholars of social movements."

2. C. Wright Mills, *Power Elite*, New York, NY: Oxford University Press, 1956.

3. Frances Fox Piven and Richard Cloward, *Poor People's Movements: Why They Succeed and How They Fail*, New York, NY: Vintage Books Edition, 1979.

4. Bertrand Russell, *Power*, New York: Norton, 1969.

5. Coral Davenport, "Nations Approve Landmark Climate Accord in Paris," *The New York Times*, Dec. 12, 2015.

6. See Dennis Wrong's book *Power* for a good discussion of power theory and to better understand the forms of power various players exercise.

7. Marshall Ganz, *Why David Sometimes Wins: Leadership, Organization, and Strategy in the California Farm Worker Movement*, New York: Oxford University Press, 2009.

8. David Bacon, *The Right to Stay Home: How US Policy Drives Mexican Migration*, Boston: Beacon Press, 2013.

9. Michelle Alexander, *The New Jim Crow in the Age of Colorblindness*, New York: The New Press, 2012.

10. Theda Skocpol, *Diminished Democracy: From Membership to Management in American Civic Life* (The Julian J. Rothbaum Distinguished Lecture Series) (Kindle Locations 1645–1648). Norman: University of Oklahoma Press. Kindle Edition, 2003.

11. Hahrie Han, *How Organizations Develop Activists: Civic Associations and Leadership in the 21st Century*, New York: Oxford University Press, 2014.

12. Five million unorganized hospital workers, 12 million unorganized factory workers; it is a very long list by sector. See Barry T. Hirsch and David A. Macpherson, "Union Membership and Coverage Database from the Current Population Survey" Industrial and Labor Relations Review, Vol. 56, No. 2, January 2003, 349–54.

13. John D. McCarthy and Mayer N. Zald, "Resource Mobilization and Social Movements: A Partial Theory," *American Journal of Sociology*, Vol. 82, No. 6, May 1977, 1212–1241.

14. Theda Skocpol, ibid, Kindle Locations 1762–1763.

15. Doug McAdam, *Political Process and the Development of the Black Insurgency, 1930–1970*, Chicago: University of Chicago Press, 1982.

16. Heidi J. Swartz, *Organizing Urban America: Secular and Faith-Based Progressive Movements*, Minneapolis: University of Minnesota Press, 2008; and, Mark Warren, *Dry Bones Rattling: Community Building to Revitalize American Democracy*, Princeton: Princeton University Press, 2001.

17. Bronfenbrenner, K., Friedman, S., Hurd, R. W., Oswald, R. A., & Seeber, R. L. (1998). Introduction [Electronic version]. In K. Bronfenbrenner, S. Friedman, R. W. Hurd, R. A. Oswald, & R. L Seeber (Eds.), *Organizing to win: New research on union strategies* (pp. 1-15). Ithaca, NY: ILR Press. http://digitalcommons.ilr.cornell.edu/articles/188/.

18. Swartz and Warren, ibid.

19. Steven Henry Lopez, *Reorganizing the Rust Belt: An Inside Story of the American Labor Movement*, University of California Press, Berkeley and Los Angeles, 2004.

20. Dan Clawson and Mary Ann Clawson, "What Has Happened to the U.S. Labor Movement? Union Decline and Renewal," *Annual Review of Sociology*, Vol. 25, 1999, 95–119.

21. Charles M. Payne, *I've Got the Light of Freedom*, Berkeley: University of California Press, 1995, xviii.

22. Bureau of Labor Statistics, January 1996 and January 2014.

23. Which unions constitute New Labor? I combine a few: CTW is short for the Change to Win Federation. Technically, the UBC and the UFW were also on the CTW list initially. Another commonly used list was developed by Kate Bronfenbrenner and Roger Hickey in Ruth Milkman and Kim Voss's *Organizing and Organizers in the New Union Movement* (Cornell ILR, 2004), accessed here through the digital commons. I also factored in the list of which unions in 1995 initially voted *not* to back Kirkland in the AFL-CIO election, and then the slightly different list of which unions ultimately backed Sweeney. In the end, I combine

them to arrive at a rough list of the most common unions that might be called New Labor.

	CTW	Bronfenbrenner-Hickey
SEIU	X	X
UNITE HERE	X	X
AFSCME		X
UAW		X
CWA		X
UFCW	X	
LIUNA	X	
IBT	X	

24. Lopez, *Reorganizing the Rust Belt*.
25. Julius G. Getman, *Restoring the Power of Unions*, New Haven: Yale University Press, 2010; Richard Hurd, "The Failure of Organizing, the New Unity Partnership, and the Future of the Labor Movement," *Working USA*, Vol. 8, September 2004, 5–25.
26. Many of these accords include language that constrains future action by workers and their community. For example, in a particularly well publicized agreement between SEIU and nursing home operators in California, the union leaders agreed to surrender the future union members' right to arbitration or strike, and the union also agreed to block workers from testifying or speaking about poor conditions inside California nursing homes.
27. William Z. Foster, *Organizing Methods in the Steel Industry*, New York: Workers Library Publishers, 1936.
28. Dan Clawson, *The Next Upsurge: Labor and the New Social Movements*, Ithaca and London: ILR Press and Cornell University Press, 2003.
29. What some people call ideology others call beliefs or world view, and Marshall Ganz uses the words motivation and purpose.
30. Gerring, John, Social Science Methodology: A Critical Frame, (New York: Cambridge University Press) 2001, see especially Chapter Nine, Methods.
31. Ira Katznelson, *City Trenches*, Chicago: University of Chicago Press, 1981, 6.

Chapter 2

1. Charles Payne, *I've Got the Light of Freedom: The Organizing Tradition and the Mississippi Freedom Struggle*, Berkeley: University of California Press, 1995, 5.
2. Joseph E. Luders, *The Civil Rights Movement and the Logic of Social Change*, New York, NY: Cambridge University Press, 2010.

3. Nelson Lichtenstein, *State of the Union: A Century of U.S. Labor*, Princeton: Princeton University Press, 2002.

4. Ibid.

5. Ibid.

6. Jack O'Dell, author interview, January 2011. O'Dell was a legendary organizer and leader. He was a Communist until the 1950s. He was a leader in the National Maritime Workers Union and later a full-time staff member in the Southern Christian Leadership Conference, where he advised Rev. Dr. Martin Luther King on strategy, until the Kennedy brothers asked King to remove him in 1963. Sources: The King Library, Stanford University, website search 9-9-15, http://kingencyclopedia.stanford.edu/encyclopedia/encyclopedia/enc_odell_hunter_pitts_jack_1923.1.html, and Jack O'Dell and Nikhil Singh, *Climbing Jacob's Ladder: The Black Freedom Movement's Writings of Jack O'Dell*, Berkeley: University of California Press, 2012.

7. Ibid.

8. Judith Stepan-Norris and Maurice Zeitlin, *Left Out: Reds and America's Industrial Unions,* Cambridge: Cambridge University Press, 2002.

9. Saul Alinsky, *John L. Lewis: An Unauthorized Biography*, G.P. Putnam & Sons, 1949.

10. Ibid, 153.

11. Ibid, 152–153.

12. Ibid, 256.

13. William Z. Foster, *Organizing Methods in the Steel Industry*, New York: Workers Library Publishers, 1936.

14. Ibid.

15. Ibid.

16. Kristin Warner, author interview, May 2013.

17. In nursing-home strikes, as in hospital strikes, crippling production by 90 percent or more of the regular workforce walking off the job; the employer choosing to hire an expensive, second full set of contract staff; management working regular staff shifts, often around the clock; state inspectors in the facility monitoring the situation, and families often on hand 24 hours a day to care for loved ones, because they mistrust the temporary, union-breaking specialist firms.

18. Lichtenstein, ibid; Aaron Brenner, Robert Brenner, and Cal Winslow, *Rebel Rank and File: Labor Militancy and the Revolt from Below During the Long 1970s*, London and New York: Verso, 2010.

19. Alinsky, ibid, 153.

20. Marshall Ganz, *Why David Sometimes Wins: Leadership, Organization, and Strategy in the California Farmworker Movement*, New York: Oxford University Press, 2009.

21. Brenner et al., ibid, 113; Lichtenstein, ibid, 144.

22. Skocpol, ibid.

23. The discussion in this book has been based on Alinsky's own texts, what he himself said and wrote, in a line-by-line content analysis comparing his first book, *Reveille for Radicals*, with *Rules for Radicals*, arguably the defining Alinsky text; and on his very last public words, an extensive interview conducted by *Playboy* magazine three months before he died, suddenly, of a heart attack. The vast majority of organizers or self-identified radicals who want to study Alinsky read Alinsky; they don't go to work for the Industrial Areas Foundation (IAF), the group Alinsky founded.

24. Eric Norden, "An Interview With Saul Alinsky," *Playboy*, vol.19, no.3, March 1972.

25. Norden, ibid, 17 (when printed out as a standalone article).

26. Hillary Clinton, "There is Only the Fight, An Analysis of the Alinsky Model," a thesis submitted in fulfillment of the Special Honors Program at Wellesley College, 1969.

27. Andie Coller and Daniel Libit, "Conservatives use Liberal Playbook," *Politico*, Sept. 18, 2009, http://www.politico.com/news/stories/0909/27285.html: "And the 1971 agitator's handbook *Rules for Radicals*—written by Saul Alinsky, the Chicago community organizer who was the subject of Hillary Clinton's senior thesis and whose teachings helped shape Barack Obama's work on Chicago's South Side—has been among Amazon's top 100 sellers for the past month, put there in part by people who 'also bought' books by Michelle Malkin, Glenn Beck, and South Carolina Republican Sen. Jim DeMint. Yes, the same folks who brought you Obama the socialist have been appropriating the words and ways of leftists past—and generally letting their freak flags fly."

28. Engel, ibid, 59.

29. Taken from Dollar Times Inflation Calculator, calculated with online tool 8-22-2015.

30. Ibid, 637.

31. Norden, ibid, 18.

32. Sanford D. Horwitt, *Let Them Call Me Rebel: Saul Alinsky, His Life and Legacy*, New York: Vintage Books, 1992.

33. Horwitt, ibid.

34. Eric Norden, ibid, 17 (when printed out as a standalone article).

35. Saul Alinsky, *John L. Lewis: An Unauthorized Biography*.

36. Ibid, ix.

37. Saul Alinsky, "Community Analysis and Organization," *American Journal of Sociology*, Vol. 46, No. 6 (May 1941), 797–808.

38. Horwitt, ibid, 174.

39. Seth Borgos, author interview, August 9, 2015.

40. See Gary Delgado's *Beyond the Politics of Place* (1997) and Rinku Sen's *Stir it Up: Lessons in Community Organizing and Advocacy*, 2003.

41. Mark R. Warren and Karen L. Mapp, *A Match on Dry Grass: Community Organizing as a Catalyst for School Reform*, New York: Oxford University Press, 2011.

42. See Delgado, 1990; Sen, 2003; and Cryan, 2008.

43. Jerry Brown, author interview, May 2013.

44. Saul Alinsky, *Reveille for Radicals*, Chicago: Chicago University Press, 1946, 158.

45. Mary Ann Clawson, "Redistributionist Movements of the 1970s: The Politics of Gender and Race in Labor, Community Organizing, and Citizen Action," paper presentation, annual meeting, American Sociological Association, 2013.

46. Howard Kimeldorf, *Reds or Rackets: The Making of Radical and Conservative Unions on the Waterfront*, Berkeley: University of California Press, 1985.

47. Wendy Fields-Jacobs and Ted Fang, for example.

48. [Author(s) not listed] "Planning to Win, Taking a Comprehensive Approach to Labor's Corporate Campaign," *Labor Research Review*, Cornell ILR, Cornell Digital Commons, 1993.

49. http://www.corporatecampaign.org/media_working_papers_1982.php (retrieved Aug. 17, 2014).

50. Getman, ibid, 79.

51. Marshall Ganz, author interview, February 2015.

52. Bardacke, ibid, entire chapter on Alinsky.

53. Doug McAdam, "'Initiator' and 'Spin-off' Movements: Diffusion Processes in Protest Cycles in Mark Traugott," *Repertoires and Cycles of Collective Action*, Durham: Duke University Press, 1995.

54. Peter Olney, author interview, March 20, 2014. (Olney is now retired as organizing director, International Longshore Workers Union.)

55. Teresa Conrow and Andy Banks, PowerPoint presentation, "Introduction to Strategic Corporate Research," National Labor College, December 1, 2008. These authors and the many like them are surely *not* to blame for the national union leaders' decisions to accept the corporate-campaign strategy while downgrading worker organizing.

56. Searches on union job websites and internal documents.

57. Jennifer Jihye Chun, *Organizing at the Margins: The Symbolic Politics of Labor in South Korea and the United States*, Ithaca, NY: Cornell University Press, 2009.

58. Robert Muehlenkamp, "Organizing Never Stops," *Labor Research Review*, Cornell University ILR, Vol. 1, No. 1, Article 5, 1991.

59. Foster, ibid, emphasis added.

60. Luders, ibid.

61. Technically, it is footnote 6 in Chapter Three.

62. Jane McAlevey with Bob Ostertag, *Raising Expectations (and Raising Hell)*, New York: Verso, 2012.

63. Luders, ibid.

64. Or what the state might force employers to pay because of enforcement mechanisms discussed in the chapter on Make the Road New York; see also Janice Fine, "A marriage made in heaven? Mismatches and misunderstandings between worker centres and unions," British Journal of Industrial Relations 45, no. 2 (2007): 335–360.

65. Rosenfeld, Jake, *What Unions No Longer Do*, Cambridge: Harvard University Press, 2014. Rosenfeld's otherwise good book makes several points with which I don't agree, namely those in his discussion of the public sector. He misses what motivates many people to go to work for the public sector: a deep belief in government service. Many workers take pride in serving their communities in the way soldiers take pride in serving their nation. Workers know they don't get *wage* gain from working for the government—that equivalent work in the private sector is much better paid. Workers understand their lower wage will be made up for by the public sector's significantly better benefits. He incorrectly analyzes the "retirement plans" of each sector, calculating that benefits to workers in each sector are close to equal, or "not much different." Yet the vast majority of plans offered in the private sector don't pay nearly enough to allow people to retire, and he doesn't evaluate the content of the plans—only notes whether they are offered.

Chapter 3

1. Jerry Brown, author interview, May 2013.
2. Paul Brown, "Outsourcing the Picket Line," *The New York Times*, March 11, 2006.
3. Private election accords such as Local 775's conduct unionization fall outside the National Labor Relations Board framework, and therefore outside government-reported or publicly available data. Information here is based on an email from the local union and on conversations with former staff of the local.
4. Leon Fink and Jennifer Luff, "An Interview with President Emeritus Andy Stern," *Labor*, 2011, Volume 8, No. 2, 7–36.
5. Fink and Luff, ibid.
6. Richard W. Hurd, "The Failure of Organizing, the New Unity Partnership and the Future of the Labor Movement" [Electronic version]. Retrieved [14 Aug 2015] from Cornell University, ILR school site: http://digitalcommons.ilr.cornell.edu/articles/297/.
7. LM2 Federal Financial Reports, 2000–2012.
8. Richard Hurd, ibid.
9. Theda Skocpol, ibid. (Kindle Locations 1713–1717).
10. Seth Borgos, author interview, August 9, 2015.
11. Harold Meyerson, "The Seeds of a New Labor Movement," *The American Prospect*, Fall 2014.
12. Steven Greenhouse, "In Biggest Drive Since 1937, Union Gains a Victory," *The New York Times*, February 26, 1999.
13. Greenhouse, ibid.
14. Taken from Ballotpedia, an interactive almanac of U.S. politics, retrieved Nov. 28, 2014: http://ballotpedia.org/Washington_In-Home_Care_Services,_Initiative_775_%282001%29.

15. I was directly involved in the tail end of these machinations as National Deputy Director for Strategic Campaigns for the Healthcare Division of SEIU. Specifically, I was sent to address what was considered a rough transition of the non-nurses into the nurses' union in Seattle. I was privy to many background briefings, memos, etc.

16. Lopez, ibid.

17. Internal memos and PowerPoint presentations in author's possession.

18. Sal Rosselli's refusal to go along with this deal is widely considered a key reason why his union, United Healthcare Workers West (UHW), subsequently found itself in the national union's trusteeship.

19. Ralph Thomas, "Union, Nursing Home Alliance Team Up," *The Seattle Times*, March 20, 2007; and portions of the agreement in author's possession.

20. Ibid.

21. Paul Kumar, author interview, August 2014.

22. Extracted from Local #775's collective bargaining agreement with Avamere Georgian House of Lakewood, August 9, 2013 through August 31, 2015. Available on the union's website; retrieved August 17, 2014.

23. Zach Schonfeld, "Seattle Adopts $15-an-Hour Minimum Wage," *Newsweek*, June 13, 2014.

24. Rick Fantasia, *Cultures of Solidarity*, Berkeley: University of California Press, 1988.

25. Lopez, ibid.

26. Leon Fink and Brian Greenburg, *Upheaval in the Quiet Zone: A History of Hospital Workers Union, Local 1199*, Urbana: University of Illinois Press, 1989.

27. Federal Mediation and Conciliation Services, FMCS, Work Stoppages Data, 2000 to 2013.

28. Contracts in author's possession.

29. Jerry Brown, author interview, May 2013.

30. Rob Baril, author interview, December 2014.

31. David Pickus, author interview, September 2014.

32. Rob Baril, author interview, July 2014.

33. The importance of semantics is also central to George Herbert Mead's discussion of the development of self-identity.

34. The handwriting is that of the scribe David Pudlin, an organizer at 1199NE who would later be elected to the Connecticut legislature. The ideas came from many organizers during a 1985 brainstorming session in a conference in Columbus, Ohio.

35. Ernie Mintor, 1199 member, unpublished organizing manual, in author's possession; David Pickus's 1199NE training document "The Four Stages to the Boss Campaign."

36. Minimum wage in Connecticut was $8.70 per hour in October 2014 and $9.15 in January 2015; minimum wage in Washington was $9.32 per hour in October 2014 and $9.47 in January 2015.

37. Thomas, "Union, Nursing Home Alliance Team Up."

38. Jonathan Rosenblum, author interview, March 2015.

39. Jerry Brown, author interview, May 2013.

40. David Pickus, author interview, September 2014.

Chapter 4

1. Jonah Edelman, recorded in a talk at the Summer 2011 Aspen Institute of Ideas elite gathering. The entire 52-minute video was uploaded onto a website on YouTube, and some teachers edited it down to a shorter 14-minute clip of the highlights of Edelman's remarks. The clip went viral among teachers, and shorter clips were also shown on Chicago television stations. Edelman was forced to apologize to Illinois Speaker of the House Michael Madigan, who was made to look almost as foolish as Edelman. https://www.youtube.com/watch?v=kog8g9sTDS0.

2. Diane Ravitch, *The Reign of Error: The Hoax of the Privatization Movement and the Danger to America's Public Schools*, New York: Vintage Books Edition, August 2014; Dana Goldstein, *The Teacher Wars: A History of America's Most Embattled Profession*, New York: Doubleday, 2014.

3. Micah Uetricht, *Strike for America: Chicago Teachers Against Austerity*, Brooklyn: Verso Press, 2014.

4. Natasha Korechi, "Exclusive Poll: Karen Lewis Could Give Rahm Run for His Money," *Chicago Sun-Times*, August 8, 2014; Rick Pearson and Bill Ruthhart, "Support for Mayor Emanuel Falling Fast," *Chicago Tribune*, August 14, 2014.

5. Jeremy Brecher, *Strike*, Oakland: PM Press, 2014.

6. Tom Alter, "It Felt Like a Community: Social Movement Unionism and the Chicago Teachers Strike of 2012," *Labor Studies in Working Class History of the Americas*, Vol. 10, Issue 3, 2013.

7. One challenge for reform advocates trying to change the retrograde politics of the New York City teachers' union is that under their constitution, retirees vote for the current leadership. This means that legions of teachers who worked in New York City in a very different time, under different circumstances, and who remain loyal to their deceased leader, Shanker, continue to vote against progressive-change candidates.

8. Sara R. Smith, "Organizing for Social Justice: Rank-and-File Teachers' Activism and Social Unionism in California, 1948–1978," unpublished doctoral book, University of California at Santa Cruz, June 2014, 12–14.

9. Lee Sustar, "Will Chicago's Teachers Keep Moving Forward?" *Socialist Register*, May 7, 2013.

10. Technically, teachers and support staff walked the picket line for nineteen days, just as in 2012 they technically walked it for seven—not nine—days. Some people use the workweek in describing the teachers' strikes, but I include the weekends for one primary reason: The teachers themselves are in a state of duress while in high-risk status all weekend, just as are the parents and the employer. I find it silly to officially count only the workweek days, given the unbelievable weekend pressure on the workers to leave the picket line by Monday.

11. George Schmidt, editor of *Substance News* (an alternative teachers' union paper) and former candidate for union president, author interview, September 2014.

12. Leviis Haney, "The 1995 Chicago School Reform Amendatory Act and the CPS CEO: A Historical Examination of the Administration of Chicago Public School's CEOs Paul Vallas and Arne Duncan," 2011, http://ecommons.luc.edu/cgi/view-content.cgi?article=1061&context=luc_diss.

13. This was very different from the 1960s community control movement in New York City, because the 1988 Chicago School Reform law did *not* foment the race war that took place between the teachers' union and the community, a race war begun by the union, not the parents. New York City has yet to recover from this ugly moment in the teachers' union history.

14. Sue Garza and George Schmidt, author interviews, September 2014.

15. Robert Michels, *Political Parties: A Sociological Study of the Oligarchic Tendencies of Modern Democracies*, New York, NY: The Free Press, softcover edition, 1968.

16. George Schmidt, author interview, February 2015.

17. Illinois State General Assembly, Chicago School Reform Amendatory Act, Public Act 89-0015, 1995.

18. Although the idea was set up in the Amendatory Act, it would take one more year and some specific enabling legislation before the first charter schools opened in Illinois.

19. Illinois State General Assembly, ibid.

20. George Schmidt, author interview, October 2014.

21. http://www2.ed.gov/news/staff/bios/duncan.html.

22. *CPS Stats & Facts*, produced annually by the Chicago public schools.

23. Tracy Dell Angela, "South Side Faces School Shake Up," *Chicago Tribune*, July 14, 2004.

24. The schools could also be "independent contract" schools or small schools, which, like charters, were placed outside the union's purview.

25. Maureen Kelleher, "Rocky Start for Renaissance 2010," *Catalyst Chicago*, October 1, 2004.

26. Angela Stich, "School Spirit," NewCity Chicago blog, November 22, 2004.

27. Amisha Patel of the Grassroots Collaborative and Madeline Talbot, longtime leader of the Chicago branch of ACORN, author interviews, September and October, 2014.

28. Alexander Bradbury, Mark Brenner, Jenny Brown, Jane Slaughter, and Samantha Winslow, *How to Jump-Start Your Union: Lessons from the Chicago Teachers*, Detroit: Labor Notes, 2014.

29. Naomi Klein, *The Shock Doctrine*, New York: Picador, a division of Henry Holt Books, 2007.

30. GEM's initial community partners included KOCO, the Pilsen Alliance, Blocks Together, Parents United for Responsible Education (PURE), Designs for Change, Teachers for Social Justice, and a mix of random Local Schools Council (LSC) activists. Bradbury, et al., *How to Jump-Start your Union*.

31. Kristine Mayle, author interview, September 2014.

32. Jackson Potter, author interview, October 2014.

33. Uetricht, ibid.

34. Sarah DeClerk, staff member of the Canadian Union of Public Employees, author interview, May 2014 (CUPE, which represents noneducation staff in the B.C. schools, was the only union in British Columbia to support the B.C. teachers); Kevin Millsep, Vancouver school board member during the teachers' strike, author interview, May 2014.

35. CTU Union website biography.

36. Author interviews with George Schmidt, October 2014 and January 2015.

37. CTU Union website biography, retrieved February 12, 2014.

38. Jesse Sharkey, author interview, September 2014.

39. Jackson Potter, author interview, October 2014; see also Uetricht, ibid.

40. Madeline Talbot, author interviews, September 2014 and January 2015.

41. Uetricht, ibid. The exact numbers were given in a CORE press release on May 22 at 11 A.M. as follows: "At the time of this corrected release based on 17,797 tabulated votes and verified by CORE's on-site representative on the Canvassing Committee charged with CTU election vote-counting oversight, the preliminary vote count stands at UPC 6,283, CORE 5,970, PACT 3,144, CSDU 1,273 and SEA 1,127."

42. http://www.coreteachers.org/video-save-our-schools-rally-may-25-2010/.

43. http://www.coreteachers.org/karen-lewis-ctu-president-elect-acceptance-speech-2/.

44. In author's possession.

45. Chicago Teachers Union By-Laws and Constitution, Article V, Section 1, Letter E.

46. SEIU local 880 was founded and built by Kelleher, who worked for United Labor Unions, an affiliate of ACORN. Mark Splain, who came from Mass Fair Share, had trained Kelleher in Detroit, when he headed up ULU. Even though Kelleher said they were always considered an ACORN local, Rathke did not support Kelleher's move to organize home child care providers, an innovative drive that resulted in tens of thousands of workers being organized across the country, after unions noticed that such a constituency existed and could be organized. Rathke and many others thought these workers were "even more marginal than homecare workers."

47. Keith Kelleher, author interview, January 2015.

48. Matthew Luskin, author interview, September 2014.

49. Jesse Sharkey, author interview, September 2014.

50. http://www.foxnews.com/politics/2010/09/07/chicago-mayor-daley-seek-election/.

51. Amisha Patel, author interview, October 2014.

52. Ibid.

53. Jonah Edelman, in a YouTube video taken at the Aspen Institute of Ideas in the summer of 2011.

54. Ibid.

55. The mechanism for this takeaway was that in this five-year contract, the union had allowed a loophole, which stated, in part, that if there weren't sufficient funds in the final year, the board could reconsider. The union alleges the money was there, and that the CPS board manufactured the crisis. This charge comes from deep financial work conducted by *Substance News* editor George Schmidt and other CTU leaders and staff, discussed in my several interviews with Schmidt.

56. Madeline Talbot, author interviews, September 2014 and January 2015; Jason Zengerle, "Rahm Emanuel's Nemesis Might Just Take Him On," *The New Republic,* July 14, 2014; Ben Javorsky, "Won't You Be My Friend?" *The Chicago Reader,* September 9, 2013; unattributed, "Rahmbo's Toughest Mission," *The Economist,* June 14, 2014.

57. A video was posted on the CORE blog in December 2011: http://www.coreteachers.org/mic-check-at-the-board-of-ed-2/.

58. Jesse Sharkey, author interview, September 2014.

59. Carol R. Caref and Pavlyn C. Jankov, primary researchers, "The Schools Chicago's Students Deserve." This forty-page report remains on the union's website and is also in the author's possession.

60. Madeline Talbot, author interviews, September 2014 and January 2015.

61. Chicago Teachers Union By-Laws and Constitution, ibid.

62. Bob Peterson and Jody Sokolower, "A Cauldron of Opposition in Duncan's Hometown, Rank and File Teachers Score Huge Victory; An Interview with Karen Lewis and Jackson Potter," *Rethinking Schools,* Fall 2010.

63. Although technically the new bargaining process still included some version of the older gag rule, the new union leadership largely ignored it as the bargaining team engaged members and eventually the media too—but in the latter case, they did so because the management team decided to attempt to "bargain in the press" first.

64. http://clas.wayne.edu/Multimedia/lsc/files/collectivebargaing.pdf; when I was going to contract negotiations, in keeping with my training at 1199NE I never once entertained the thought of signing them: That sends an immediate signal to the bosses across the table that bargaining won't be done according to their rules.

65. Author interviews with George Schmidt, October 2014 and January 2015.

66. According to the theater's website, the venue seats 3,901.

67. http://chicago.cbslocal.com/2012/05/23/mayor-chicago-teachers-deserve-a-pay-raise/.

68. Substance.net, September 2012.

69. Sarah Chamber, author interview, September 2014.

70. Lee Sustar, "Will Chicago's Teachers Keep Moving Forward?" *Socialist Register,* May 7, 2013.

71. Jackson Potter, author interview, August 2015.

Chapter 5

1. Rev. Dr. William Barber, author interview, May 2014.
2. All statistics here were taken from https://www.census.gov/quickfacts (retrieved June 8, 2014).
3. Until September 2014, when customer service agents at American Airlines voted to unionize, the Smithfield win was the largest in decades. For the American story, see Jad Mouawad, "After American Airlines-US Airways Merger, Agents Vote to Unionize," *The New York Times*, September 16, 2014.
4. Bureau of Labor Statistics January 2014 news release of the most recent numbers of the 2013 Current Population Survey.
5. Author's email consultation with economist Dean Baker, who crunched the math for this article (email dated May 27, from Dean Baker).
6. Bob Herbert, "Where the Hogs Come First," *The New York Times*, June 15, 2006.
7. Louis Compa, "Blood, Sweat, and Fear: Workers' Rights in U.S. Meat and Poultry Plants," http://www.hrw.org/reports/2005/01/24/blood-sweat-and-fear, January 25, 2006 (retrieved June 7, 2014).
8. Website searches conducted June 2014, United Food and Commercial Workers Union. The other three unions that merged with the PWOC to form the modern union were the Barbers, Beauticians and Allied Industries International Association; Boot and Shoe Workers Union; and the Retail Clerks International Union.
9. Judith Stepan-Norris and Maurice Zeitlin, *Left Out: Reds and America's Industrial Unions*, Cambridge: Cambridge University Press, 2002.
10. Saul Alinsky, "Community Analysis and Organization," *American Journal of Sociology*, Vol. 46, No. 6 (May 1941), 797–808.
11. Upton Sinclair, *The Jungle: The Uncensored Version*, Amherst, Mass.: Seven Treasures Publications, 2011.
12. The National Labor Relations Board, "Decision and Order, The Smithfield Packing Company, Inc., Tar Heel Division, and the United Food and Commercial Workers Local 204, AFL-CIO, CLC, December 16, 2004." In author's possession.
13. Roz Pellas, author interview, May 2014.
14. Vote tallies from "Key Dates in Fight to Unionize Smithfield Plant," Associated Press Financial Wire, December 5, 2008, via LEXIS.
15. Author Interview, April 2013.
16. This aspect, Smithfield actually encouraging illegal migration over the border, is covered extensively in David Bacon's *The Right to Stay Home: How U.S. Policy Drives Immigration*, Boston: Beacon Press, September 2014. The author profiles and documents migrant Mexican hog farmers who lost their livelihoods when Smithfield relocated workers from Mexico to North Carolina.
17. NLRB decision, ibid.
18. FAST is a semiautonomous department within the AFL-CIO, a vestige of the merger between the CIO and the AFL in the 1950s. It was established by the

constitution of the AFL-CIO, and represented the ten unions in food-related industries. Its two top directors, Jeff Fiedler and Gene Bruskin, were elected constitutional officers of the AFL-CIO.

19. Julius Getman, *Restoring the Power of Unions*, New Haven: Yale University Press, 2010.

20. Kate Bronfenbrenner has written extensively about comprehensive campaigns. She describes the difference between a strategic campaign and a comprehensive campaign as one of worker agency. In her analysis, a comprehensive campaign involves workers at all steps, whereas in a strategic campaign, the air war and the ground war are waged separately.

21. Gene Bruskin, author interview, June 2014.

22. He stayed at FAST, was in charge of its payroll, and on loan to UFCW directly. UFCW paid FAST the salary that FAST paid Bruskin. Technically, FAST at that time had become Research Associates of America, because of the Change to Win breakaway from the AFL-CIO, which ruptured both money flows. The AFL-CIO refused to allow breakaway unions to work with FAST, since it was an AFL-CIO constitutional body.

23. Bruskin, ibid.

24. Keith Ludlum, author interview, May 2014.

25. United States Court of Appeals, District of Columbia Circuit, Case No 05-1004; argued March 9, 2006; decided May 5, 2006. In author's possession.

26. Sherri Buffkin, former manager, Smithfield Packing Company, Tar Heel, North Carolina; U.S. Senate Health, Education, Labor, and Pensions Committee hearing, June 20, 2002.

27. Charlie LeDuff, "At a Slaughterhouse, Some Things Never Die," *The New York Times*, June 16, 2000.

28. Jerry Kammer, "Immigration Raids at Smithfield: How an ICE Enforcement Action Boosted Union Organizing and the Hiring of Americans," The Center for Immigration Studies, Washington, D.C., July 2009; http://cis.org/Smith fieldImmigrationRaid-Unionization.

29. Author interviews with workers and organizers, all of whom confirmed these percentages, May 2014.

30. John Ramsey and Sarah A. Reid, "Race and the Union," *Fayetteville Observer*, December 2, 2008; Kristin Collins, *"Raids Aided Union in Tar Heel Plant,"* Raleigh *News and Observer*, January 1, 2009.

31. Kate Bronfenbrenner on the PBS *NewsHour*, February 26, 2014. Transcription available at http://www.pbs.org/newshour/bb/unions-offer-american-workers-today/.

32. LeDuff, ibid.

33. From the NLRB's investigation into Ludlum's firing: "Respondent's former employee Keith Ludlum testified that on January 26, 1994, he was in the locker room on break getting employee Steve Ray to fill out a union authorization card; that Ray asked him if he could get fired or harassed for filling out the card and

he told Ray that he was protected by National Labor laws; that Supervisor Tony Murchinson walked into the locker room while Ray was filling out the card; that Murchinson said to Ray, '[H]ey I wouldn't do that. You will get fired'; that he [Ludlum] told Murchinson that he just violated the Labor laws and it was illegal for him to say what he just said; that Murchinson told him that he could not do it on company time and he told Murchinson that he and the employee were on break; that Murchinson told him that he could not do it on company property and he told Murchinson that he could as long as they were on break; and that Ray then tried to give him the card back."

Later, in the same NLRB investigation report:

"Respondent's former employee Keith Ludlum testified that on February 2, 1994, while he was handbilling employees with union representatives at the front of the plant, he saw Danny Priest, who is in charge of security at the plant, and Kevin Peak; that they were parked on the grass about 15 to 20 feet away from the handbillers; and that whenever someone in a vehicle accepted a handbill he saw Peak looking at the back of the car, saying something and Priest appeared to be writing something. On cross-examination Ludlum testified that Priest and Peak stayed there for about 30 to 45 minutes; that he could not see what Priest was writing on; that he saw a pen in Priest's hand; and that he had seen them parked out there before."

34. One indication, of many, that the company did not intend to honor its promise to follow the 1997 order was that it refused to put illegally fired workers back in the plant. That the union missed these clues underscores its incompetence at the time.
35. NLRB report, ibid.
36. Ollie Hunt, author interview, May 2014.
37. Ironically, the length of time it took workers to get to work, and to where the employer stationed the time clock, would become an issue in the first contract negotiations. The Livestock workers won the right to a parking lot in the back, and saved over one hour each day of walking the plant in unpaid status. These same workers now have the legal right to walk through their own factory anytime, often in paid status, to conduct union building efforts post–contract settlement.
38. LeDuff, ibid.
39. Kate Bronfenbrenner, "No Holds Barred: The Intensification of Employer Opposition to Organizing," Briefing Paper No. 235 (electronic version), Washington D.C. Economic Policy Institute, May 20, 2009.
40. Gene Bruskin, author interview, May 2014.
41. Terry Slaughter, author interview, May 2014.
42. Steven Greenhouse, "Hundreds, All Non Union, Walk Out at Pork Plant," *The New York Times*, November 17, 2006; Al Greenwood, "Smithfield Workers Return," *Fayetteville Observer*, November 19, 2006.
43. Greenhouse, ibid.

44. The following year, with the threat of actions once again and the percentage of African-American workers having grown, Smithfield Foods granted workers in *all* nonunion Smithfield Foods plants a paid Martin Luther King holiday.

45. Kevin Maurer, "Latinos Walk off the Job," *Fayetteville Observer*, January 28, 2007.

46. Rev. Nelson Johnson, author interview, May 2014.

47. Johnson, ibid.

48. Baldemar Velasquez founded a 501(c)(3) nonprofit mutual aid and community organization called the Farm Labor Organizing Committee. The FLOC represented the only real organizing among Latinos in North Carolina, starting mostly as a migrant workers' organization, because when it was founded, almost none of the workers were immigrants. Rather, they were migrants, moving in for the harvest season and back out again.

49. Sarita Gupta, author interview, May 2014.

50. http://www.htadgroup.com/legacy/Our_Journey/index.html#/20/.

51. http://www.indyweek.com/indyweek/tar-heel-pinkertons/Content?oid=1195248.

52. Bob Geary, author interview, May 2014.

53. http://www.ufcw.org/about/.

54. Sarita Gupta, author interview, May 2014.

55. "Jobs with Justice Support for the Justice@Smithfield Campaign, a Case Study," an undated internal six-page report evaluating Jobs with Justice's role and effectiveness in the campaign. Paula Deen information is from page 5 of this report. In author's possession.

56. Kevin Pang, "Deen Appearance Has Lots to Chew On," *Chicago Tribune*, November 19, 2007.

57. Memorandum in Support of Defendants Motion to Dismiss Under Rule 12 (b)(6), Fed. R. Civ. P., Civil Action #3:07CV641, Smithfield Foods Inc., and Smithfield Packing (Plaintiffs) v. United Food and Commercial Workers (UFCW). In author's possession.

58. Steven Greenhouse, "Crackdown Upends Slaughterhouse's Work Force," *The New York Times*, October 12, 2007.

59. Kristin Collins, "Smithfield Suit Targets Union," *The Charlotte Observer*, November 28, 2007.

60. Bruskin, June 2014, ibid, G. Robert Blakey, consultant to the congressional committees that devised RICO, and, at the time, a professor of law at Notre Dame.

61. In many ways, this fishing expedition by Berman can be seen as his examination of exactly how community groups and allies were supporting unions, and how the corporate campaigns were being run.

62. http://www.shopfloor.org/wp-content/uploads/smithfieldopinion5302.pdf (retrieved June 9, 2014).

63. Several top staff at UFCW and Change to Win had all recently left SEIU.

64. The Interfaith Campaign for Worker Justice in Chicago helped with this action, too.

65. Laura Barron-Lopez, "Union Threatens Retribution for House Dems Opposed to Keystone," *The Hill*, April 11, 2014.

66. Gene Bruskin, author interview, February 2014.

67. Steven Greenhouse, "After 15 Years, North Carolina Plant Unionizes," *The New York Times*, December 13, 2008.

68. Patrick O'Neil, author interview, May, 2014.

69. Keith Ludlum, author interview, May 2014.

70. Rev. Dr. William Barber, author interview, May 2014.

71. Sarita Gupta, author interview, May 2014.

Chapter 6

1. Juan Bosch was the first democratically elected president of the Dominican Republic. Exiled both before and after his brief presidency—which lasted only seven months, in 1963—he was known for his plain words.

2. The organization's name mirrors a phrase in a 1912 poem by Antonio Machado, "Proverbios y Cantares": *We make the road by walking*. It is also used in the title of an article by Jennifer Gordon, "We Make the Road by Walking: Immigrant Workers and the Struggle for Social Change," *Harvard Civil Rights-Civil Law Review*, 1995; and in the book *We Make the Road by Walking: Conversations on Education and Social Change edited by John Gaventa and John Peters*, Temple University Press, reprinted 1990, which includes the reflections of Myles Horton, a radical educator and the founder of the Highlander Research and Education Center, in conversation with Brazilian educator Paulo Freire.

3. Youth members are not charged dues until they turn twenty-one. Adult members who cannot afford to pay $120 up front can borrow that sum from a local credit union, and pay it back in installments over the course of the following year.

4. Deborah Axt, author interview, April 19, 2015.

5. Interview on Eldridge & Company, April 27, 2007: http://www.youtube.com/watch?v=07l4vy3yEc8 (retrieved April 12, 2011).

6. http://www.maketheroad.org/AnnualReport_06.pdf.

7. IRS form 990 for the tax year 2006.

8. Laura Braslow and Ruth Milkman, "The State of the Unions 2011: A Profile of Organized Labor in New York City, New York State and the United States," Murphy Institute for Worker Education and Labor Studies, Center for Urban Research, September 2011.

9. Joshua Freeman, *Working-Class New York: Life and Labor Since World War II*, New York: The New Press, 2000.

10. Ganz, 2000, ibid, 1017.

11. Francesca Polletta, *Freedom is an Endless Meeting: Democracy in American Social Movements*, Chicago: University of Chicago Press, 2002.

12. Deborah Axt and Andrew Friedman, "In Defense of Dignity," *Harvard Civil Rights-Civil Liberties Law Review*, 45 Harv, C.R.-C.L. L. Rev. 577, Summer 2010.

13. Ed Ott, author interview, June 2011.

14. Janice Fine has written extensively on how groups like MRNY can be effective partners with state and federal agencies in innovative enforcement schemes among low-wage workers.

15. Annual Reports 2007–2010.

16. Multiple author interviews with Deborah Axt and Andrew Friedman, spring 2011.

17. Deborah Axt, author interview, April 19, 2015.

18. Albor Ruiz, "Governor Cuomo Signs New Legislation Making it Easier for Workers and the State Labor Department to Fight Wage Theft," *Daily News*, Jan. 4, 2015.

19. Javier Valdes, author interview, December 2, 2011.

20. The coalition included the American Civil Liberties Union; ACLU of NJ; American Friends Service Committee of NY; American Immigration Lawyers Association of NY; Cardozo Immigration Justice Clinic; Center for Constitutional Rights; Families for Freedom; Immigrant Defense Project; Legal Aid Society; New York University Immigrants' Rights Clinic; New York Immigrants' Rights Coalition; Youth Ministries for Peace and Justice.

21. Kirk Simple, "Cuomo Ends State's Role in Checking Immigrants," *The New York Times*, June 1, 2011.

22. Steve Jenkins, SEIU 32BJ staffer, author interview, April 11, 2011; also public remarks made by SEIU 32BJ president Mike Fishman, at MRNY awards reception, April 16, 2011.

23. Courtney Gross, "City Council Crafting Bill to Remove ICE from Rikers," *NY1*, Oct. 2, 2014.

24. One of the car washes where workers voted yes in the initial wave of elections subsequently closed, so the campaign in fact won elections at ten shops, but secured first union contracts at nine.

25. http://www.maketheroad.org/article.php?ID=4079, downloaded September 15, 2015.

26. A copy of the Act downloaded from the NYC City Council website on Sept. 16, 2015, http://legistar.council.nyc.gov/LegislationDetail.aspx?ID=1680981&GUID=60B3BFFF-64AB-4833-A7B0-E53215C9E242.

27. Friedman's grandparents were part of the early-twentieth-century wave of Jewish immigration from Eastern Europe.

28. Ganz 2000, ibid, 1014.

29. The proposal also states, "Make the Road New York's members, Board of Directors, and staff are all representative of the low-income communities of color within which we work. All of these bodies [listed in the table] are comprised of at least seventy-five percent people of color and fifty percent women. A majority of our staff, as well as our Board of Directors, live in the communities within which we work. Having a constituency comprised of neighborhood residents enables Make the Road New York to address directly the community problems identified by the membership."

30. Polletta, ibid, 2–3, 7.

31. Additional documents available to members include the By-laws, an Employee Manual, Leadership Team Criteria and Responsibilities, Employee Evaluations, Leadership Development Plans, and a Board of Directors Goal Review. All of these are regularly updated. Copies in author's possession.

32. Javier Valdes, author interview, December 2013.

33. December 9, 2011 Dream Act press conference at City Hall. Groups in attendance included the Chinese Progressive Association, DREAM Scholars, Hispanic Federation, Make the Road New York, Minkwon Center for Community Action (see McQuade, this volume), the New York Immigration Coalition, New York State Youth Leadership Council, and the Professional Staff Congress (the union of CUNY staff and faculty).

34. Steve Jenkins, "Organizing, Advocacy and Member Power, A Critical Reflection," *Working USA*, Vol. 6, No. 2, 2002, 56–89.

35. Steve Jenkins, author interview, April 4, 2013.

36. MRNY Proposal to the Ford Foundation, July 2015. Copy in author's possession.

Chapter 7

1. Frances Fox Piven and Richard Cloward, *Poor People's Movements: Why They Succeed, How They Fail*, New York: Vintage Books, 1977, 2, 6.

2. Robert N. Bellah, Richard Madsen, William Sullivan, Ann Swidler, and Steven Tipton, *Habits of the Heart: Individualism and Commitment in Public Life*, Berkeley: University of California Press, 1996.

3. By a large margin, voters rejected a ballot initiative to enshrine the right to bargain collectively in the state constitution. Union leaders pushed the measure with the aim of preventing Michigan's legislature from curbing government employees' bargaining rights. The measure lost, 57.4 percent to 42.6 percent statewide— winning only in Genesee and Wayne counties—despite the $23 million the unions spent to get it passed.

4. For a thorough discussion of this, see my chapter in the 2015 issue of *The Socialist Register*.

5. Saul Alinsky, *Rules for Radicals*, New York, NY: Vintage Books, 1971, 65.

BIBLIOGRAPHY

Saul Alinsky, *John L. Lewis: An Unauthorized Biography*, New York, NY: G.P. Putnam & Sons, 1949

Saul Alinsky, *Reveille for Radicals*, New York, NY: Vintage Books, 1946

Saul Alinsky, *Rules for Radicals*, New York, NY: Vintage Books, 1971

Frank Bardacke, *Trampling Out the Vintage: Cesar Chavez and the Two Souls of the United Farm Workers*, New York, NY: Verso Press, 2012

Colin Barker, Laurence Cox, John Krinsky, and Alf Gunvald Nilsen, *Marxism and Social Movements*, Leiden: Brill, 2013

Robert N. Bellah, Richard Madsen, William Sullivan, Ann Swidler, and Steven Tipton, *Habits of the Heart: Individualism and Commitment in Public Life*, Berkeley: University of California Press, 1996

Jeremy Brecher, *Strike*, Oakland: PM Press, 2014

Kate Bronfenbrenner, *Organizing to Win: New Research on Union Strategies*, Ithaca, NY: Cornell University Press, 1998

Jennifer Jihye Chun, *Organizing at the Margins: The Symbolic Politics of Labor in South Korea and the United States*, Ithaca, NY: Cornell University Press, 2009

Dan Clawson, *The Next Upsurge: Labor and the New Social Movements*, Ithaca, NY: Cornell University Press, 2003

Mary Ann Clawson, paper presentation: "Redistributionist Movements of the 1970's: The Politics of Gender in Labor, Community Organizing and Citizen Action," 2013 annual meeting, American Sociological Association

Phillip Cryan, "Organizing Without Politics: Constitutive Exclusions in Saul Alinsky's 'Rules,'" unpublished paper for Professor Ananya Roy, City and Regional Planning, Cornell University, Ithaca, NY, 2008

Gary Delgado, *New Directions in Community Organizing*, Oakland: Applied Research Center, 1990

Émile Durkheim, *The Division of Labor*, New York, NY: The Free Press, 1997

Rick Fantasia, *Cultures of Solidarity: Consciousness, Action, and Contemporary American Workers*, Berkeley: University of California Press, 1989

Janice Fine, *Worker Centers: Organizing Communities at the Edge of the Dream*, Ithaca, NY: Cornell University Press, 2006

Leon Fink and Brian Greenburg, *Upheaval in the Quiet Zone: A History of Hospital Workers' Union, Local 1199*, Champaign: University of Illinois Press, 1989

Bill Fletcher Jr., and Fernando Gapasin, *Solidarity Divided: The Crisis in Organized Labor and a Path Forward*, Berkeley: University of California Press, 2009

William Z. Foster, *Organizing Methods in the Steel Industry*, New York, NY: Workers Library Publishers, 1936

Joshua Freeman, *Working-Class New York: Life and Labor Since World War II*, New York, NY: The New Press, 2000

Marshall Ganz, "Resources and Resourcefulness: Strategic Capacity in Unionization of California Agriculture, 1959–1966," *American Journal of Sociology*, Vol. 105, No. 4, (2000), 1003–1062.

Marshall Ganz, *Why David Sometimes Wins: Leadership, Organization, and Strategy in the California Farm Worker Movement*, Oxford University Press, 2009

H.H. Gerth and C. Wright Mills, *From Max Weber*, New York, NY: Routledge, 2009

Julius G. Getman, *Restoring the Power of Unions*, New York, NY, and London: Yale University Press, 2010

Dana Goldstein, *The Teacher Wars: A History of America's Most Embattled Profession*, New York: Doubleday, 2014

Jeff Goodwin and James Jasper, *Rethinking Social Movements: Structure, Meaning and Emotion*, Lanham, Md: Rowman & Littlefield, 2004

Jennifer Gordon, *Suburban Sweatshops: The Fight for Immigrant Rights*, Cambridge, MA: Harvard University Press, 2005

Hahrie Han, *How Organizations Develop Activists, Civic Associations and Leadership in the 21st Century*, Oxford University Press, 2014

Sanford D. Horowitz, *Let Them Call Me Rebel*, New York, NY: Vintage Books, 1992

Quinton Huare and Geoffrey Nowell Smith, ed. and transl., *Antonio Gramsci: Selections from Prison Notebooks*, London: Lawrence and Wishart, 1999

Howard Kimeldorf, *Reds or Rackets: The Making of Radical and Conservative Unions on the Waterfront*, Berkeley: University of California Press, 1985

Nelson Lichtenstein, *State of the Union: A Century of American Labor*, Princeton, NJ: Princeton University Press, 2002

Steven Henry Lopez, *Reorganizing the Rust Belt: An Inside Study of the American Labor Movement*, Berkeley: University of California Press, 2004

Joseph E. Luders, *The Civil Rights Movement and the Logic of Social Change*, New York, NY: Cambridge University Press, 2010.

Gregory M. Maney, Jeff Goodwin, Rachel Kutz-Flamenbaum, and Deana Rohlinger, eds., *Strategies for Social Change*, Minneapolis: University of Minnesota Press, 2012

Karl Marx and Friederich Engels, *The Marx-Engels Reader*, Charles Tucker, ed., Princeton, NJ: Princeton University Press, 1972

Doug McAdam, *Political Process and the Development of the Black Insurgency, 1930–1970*, Chicago: University of Chicago Press, 1982

Doug McAdam and Karina Kloos, *Deeply Divided: Racial Politics and Social Movements in Post-War America*, Oxford University Press, 2014

Doug McAdam, "'Initiator' and 'Spin-off' Movements: Diffusion Processes in Protest Cycles," in *Repertoires and Cycles of Collective Action*, Mark Traugott, ed., Durham, N.C.: Duke University Press, 1995

Jane McAlevey with Bob Ostertag, *Raising Expectations (and Raising Hell)*, New York, NY: Verso Press, 2012

George Herbert Mead, *Mind, Self and Society, From the Standpoint of a Social Behaviorist*, Chicago, IL: University of Chicago Press, 1934

Robert Michels, *Political Parties: A Sociological Study of the Oligarchic Tendencies of Modern Democracies*, New York, NY: The Free Press, softcover edition, 1968

C. Wright Mills, *The Marxists*, New York, NY: Penguin Books, 1962

Ruth Milkman, *L.A. Story: Immigrant Workers and the Future of the U.S. Labor Movement*, New York, NY: Russell Sage Foundation, 2006.

Ruth Milkman and Kim Voss, *Rebuilding Labor: Organizing and Organizers in the New Union Movement*, Ithaca, NY: Cornell University Press, 2004

Aldon Morris, *The Origins of the Civil Rights Movement*, New York, NY: The Free Press, 1984

Charles Payne, *I've Got the Light of Freedom: The Organizing Tradition and the Mississippi Freedom Struggle*, Berkeley: University of California Press, 1995

Frances Fox Piven and Richard Cloward, *Poor People's Movements: Why They Succeed, How They Fail*, New York, NY: Vintage Books, 1977

Piven and Cloward, "Rule Making and Rule Breaking," *The Handbook of Political Sociology*, Thomas Janoski, Robert Alford, Alexander Hicks, and Mildred A. Schwartz, eds., New York, NY: Cambridge University Press, 2005

Frances Fox Piven, *Challenging Authority: How Ordinary People Change America*, Lanham: Rowman and Littlefield, 2006)

Francesca Polletta, *Freedom is an Endless Meeting: Democracy in American Social Movements*, Chicago: University of Chicago Press, 2002

Robert Putnam, *Bowling Alone: Collapse and Survival of the American Community*, New York, NY: Simon & Schuster, 2000

Diane Ravitch, *The Reign of Error: The Hoax of the Privatization Movement and the Danger to America's Public Schools*, New York: Vintage Books, August 2014

Adam Reich, *With God on Our Side: The Struggle for Rights in a Catholic Hospital*, Ithaca, NY: Cornell ILR Press, 2012

Jake Rosenfeld, *What Unions No Longer Do*, Princeton, NJ: Princeton University Press, 2014

Rinku Sen, *Stir It Up: Lessons for Community Organizing and Advocacy*, San Francisco: Chardon Press Series, Jossey-Bass/Wiley, 2003

Randy Shaw, *Beyond the Fields: Cesar Chavez, the UFW, and the Struggle for Justice in the 21st Century*, Berkeley, CA: University of California Press, 2008

Judith Stepan-Norris and Maurice Zeitlin, *Left Out: Reds and America's Industrial Unions*, Cambridge, U.K.: Cambridge University Press, 2002

Heidi J. Swartz, *Organizing Urban America: Secular and Faith-Based Progressive Movements*, Minneapolis: University of Minnesota Press, 2008

Amanda Tattersal, *Power in Coalition: Strategies for Strong Unions and Social Change*, Ithaca, NY: Cornell ILR Press, 2010

E.P. Thompson, *The Making of the English Working Class*, New York, NY: Random House, 1966

Alexis de Tocqueville, *Democracy in America*, New York, NY: Penguin, 2003

Micah Uetricht, *Strike for America: Chicago Teachers Against Austerity*, Verso Press, 2014

Mark Warren, *Dry Bones Rattling: Community Building to Revitalize American Democracy*, Princeton, NJ: Princeton University Press, 2001

INDEX

Tables and figures are denoted by an italic *t* or *f* following the page number.